1966

FOUR
VICTORIAN POETS

FOUR
VICTORIAN POETS

A Study of

Clough   Arnold

Rossetti   Morris

With an Introduction on the Course of Poetry
from 1822 to 1852

BY

STOPFORD A. BROOKE

New York
RUSSELL & RUSSELL
1964

FIRST PUBLISHED IN 1908

REISSUED, 1964, BY RUSSELL & RUSSELL, INC.

L. C. CATALOG CARD NO: 64—15024

PRINTED IN THE UNITED STATES OF AMERICA

CONTENTS

iii

FOUR VICTORIAN POETS

INTRODUCTORY

WHEN Byron and Shelley died, the impulse given to poetry by the ideas concerning man, which we now call democratic, was exhausted for a time in English poetry. At the same time the impulse given to poetry by the hatred of them had also been exhausted. There was no passion for or against these ideas left in the nation. And England, thus deprived of animating conceptions concerning man—derived either from the far past or from the present—sank into a dreary commonplace.

Then Keats, who had felt this exhaustion before the death of Bryon and Shelley, finding no ideas in the present, recovered for poetry the ideas of the past. He called on England to live for beauty, and bade her find it in the myths of Greece, and in the stories of romance. In these, he thought—recast so as to manifest the power of love, truth, and beauty—the poet would receive into his heart the impassionating ideas of the past, realise the deep emotion he needed for his work, and give to men the high pleasure which is the use and honour of his art.   He has done that for us, he has secured to English poetry a devotion to beauty.   But in his own time his effort failed.   There was no response. Charmed he never so wisely, England, a deaf adder, stopped her ears.   The poetry of Keats awakened no new poetic life in the England of his time ; it had no children then.

There was one man, however, who might be called a younger brother of Keats, and whom we cannot class among those who merely kept poetry alive in the years which followed the deaths of Shelley, Byron, and Keats. Charles Wells stands on a higher level than the poets of that weak parenthesis which ended with the rise of Browning and Tennyson in the famous years of 1830 to 1833, when romance was re-born both in France and England.   Inferior in genius and in art to Keats, he was his personal friend, and drank of his spirit.   But the deadness of the time seized on him and he only produced a single poem—the drama of *Joseph and his Brethren*.   As Keats revealed afresh the beauty of the Greek and mediæval stories, so Wells unfolded the beauty of a Hebrew tale, recast it for modern thought and feeling, and filled its outlines with modern imaginations.   Nevertheless, and this marks his power and taste, he did not spoil its simplicity.

When we have read the drama, the old story still stands apart with quiet steadfastness.   It is not spoiled by its new clothing.   Yet what we read is Western not

Eastern, not Hebraic but romantic. The events are the same, but the atmosphere is changed. The characters are fully developed, and distinguished each from each in modern fashion. The great situations are worked out with a close analysis, and into a great complexity quite apart from the Hebrew genius. The ornament is lavish, and the scenery, which the Hebrew story does not touch, is invented, both for Palestine and Egypt, with all the care, observation, and pleasure of a poet who had read the nature-poetry of Shelley and Wordsworth and walked hand in hand with Keats, his lover and friend, through the landscape of England.

The book was published a year after the death of Keats, under the pseudonym of H. L. Howard. It fell out of sight for nearly fifty years when Rossetti, in Gilchrist's *Life of Blake*, spoke of it as "poetry of the very first class whose time will surely come." Thirteen years afterwards, in 1876, Mr. Swinburne republished it with a preface, in which he over-topped Rossetti's praise by praise of his own, but neither of these fine artists have succeeded in securing for it the general admiration and reading it deserves.

The story of Joseph, ranging from the pastoral life of a wandering tribe to the life and government of a settled kingdom, passing, as it follows the fortunes of Joseph, through a multitude of events, characters, and types of men, and holding in it the fates of the Jewish people, is one of the great stories of the world, and worth an epic treatment. Charles Wells did not feel the world-wide elements in it, but he felt its varied and profound humanity, and naturally, feeling one side more than another, he chose to make of it a drama, not an epic. Into this subject, enlarged by imaginative invention, he could interweave all he knew and loved of human life. And the poem is indeed remarkable for a distinctive, even a weighty representation, in imaginative forms, of the great forces of the life of mankind ; of the moral passions, high aims, grave issues, and temptations of individual characters. In the beginning the treatment of these matters is rapid, even superficial, but the latter part is dignified workmanship ; as if the writer's life had been solemnised by misfortune into endurance.

The most difficult part of his subject to treat was the temptation of Joseph by Phraxanor, the wife of Potiphar ; and it proves the power of Wells that it is the finest passage in the poem. Art demanded that she should be sensual, yet not trivial or base ; that there should be qualities in her nature which should lift her, in an imperious personality and passion, above the vulgarity of mere immorality. And there is in her, as conceived by the poet, so great an intellectual power in her passion, so frank and bold a will, without one trace of hypocrisy, that she seems, at a far lower dramatic level, to draw towards Shakespeare's Cleopatra, yet without her vanity, her petulance, her flashes of cowardice and courage. She has no repentance, no hesitation ; her wrath is as deep as her

furious love, and both are as intellectual as they are
sensual. His hand rarely weakens as he draws her ;
there is scarcely a line which does not add a fresh
touch to the portraiture. Moreover, she is set off by
the sketch of her attendant, who is a gracious and tender woman, as unlike her mistress as a primrose of the
spring is to the crimson rose of summer. The scene
with Joseph is managed with reticent dexterity, and
the fidelity of Joseph is saved from the awkwardness
of the situation by the nob 1 ideals, both intellectual,
moral, and personal, which Wells, following the story,
has given to the character of this leader of men.

To read the whole drama is to wonder why the poet
wrote so little. Had he been justly praised he might
have done higher work, but total silence greeted his
effort, and he also went into silence. This proves that
he had not that genius which cannot rest without production, on which public indifference has no influence,
and public blame none except fresh impelling. Wells
was not of that great crew. He put so much into this
poem that he exhausted his genius in it. There are
those who, like the fabled aloe, only flower once.
Moreover, it is a characteristic of such persons that
they have not enough of art to stay their hand when
they have said enough. Wells begins and continues
the various parts of his subject with power, but the
power fails into a certain weakness when he closes
them. Thoughts and impressions thin out, not only
in weight but in imagination, and the verse itself,

mostly full and solemn in sound, loses then its strength in a sweetness too delicate to last. In this magniloquent weakness, he is like some of the Elizabethans, whom indeed he studied. He resembled them in audacious picturesqueness, in inventiveness, in opulent creation of varied characters, and in their love of pageantry. The pageant of the glory of Joseph passing through the city is a splendid invention, blazing with colour and light and companied, step by step, with human interest. Finally, the poem places him within the poetic period in which Shelley, Keats, and Byron wrote. He is too good to be classed among the poets who, after the death of Shelley and Byron did no more than keep poetry alive till Tennyson and Browning appeared.

These poets were imitative, sensational, and sentimental, not possessed by any large or animating ideas. They were possessed only by themselves; they lived in their own shadow and wrote only about it. And they naturally became imitators not creators, rivers that were soon lost in the sand, pale reflections of a glory gone.

There was, first, a set that imitated Wordsworth, who sang of the life of the country, pleasant kindly poets like John Clare, whose three volumes a lazy, rustic squire, yet a lover of country sights and sounds, might read with sympathy, and learn how to deal gently with the poor, and wisely with the land.

Again, there was a set of small versifiers who

imitated Byron. They sang with exquisite feebleness
of guilty heroes, they sought to be as world-forsaken,
as desolately cynical as their model, and they caught
his easy music up. Every clerk in a merchant's
house, every fantastic lover, made Byronic songs ; and
the imitation lasted till 1840–50, when Tennyson had
taught the imitators a new method.

But the men who were at this time imitated by those
who had in their breast some true poetic fire were Shelley and Keats. These inspired Thomas L. Beddoes
and George Darley. Beddoes, born in 1803, did " all
his poetic work," says Mr. Gosse, " between 1821, when
he published the *Improvisatore*, and 1826 when he
practically finished *Death's Jest Book*." Beddoes was
himself aware of the exhaustion of the time. The dis-
appearance of Shelley, he declares, " has been followed
by instant darkness, of which whether the vociferous
Darley is to be the comet, or tender, full-faced L. E. L.
the milk and watery morn, I leave to astrologers to de-
termine. But I prophesy nothing but fog, rain, blight
in due succession." The blight fell upon himself. In
a few years his invention and power decayed. He
took to medicine, misanthropy, and closed in madness.
His poems are for the most part fragmentary efforts of
a power which had no power to concentrate itself. It
is not that his song does not flow unbidden from his
lips, as Mr. Gosse thinks, it is that it is too unbidden,
not shaped within into clearness, not fed by thought;
and its spontaneous utterance, desperately striving by

repeated forms of the same idea to express the idea and never lucidly expressing it, was never dominated by the mastery of art crying to him, "Choose the best form and reject the rest." *The Bride's Tragedy* has not stuff enough in it to furnish more than a single act, and it is thinned out into five. There are a few fine passages, but not a single perfect one, and the passion in it is torn to rage. As to *Death's Jest Book*, it is a chaos of crude elements, huddled together, with some noble things ill expressed contained in it, but chiefly made up of those bitter playings of his diseased fancy with death and its revolting forms, which prophesied his insanity, and which, whenever they predominate in poetry of any time, proclaim the death of that poetry. For life, and the will to live eagerly, are the breath and fire of poetry.

His lyrics have been highly praised.   They are based on Shelley, and on the lyrics of the Elizabethan Dramatists which *Lamb's Specimens* had now brought into prominence—a book which touched Darley as well as Beddoes, and was a mighty power in Charles Wells.   But the lyrics of Beddoes have not enough in them either of humanity or of Nature.   The best of them are the lightest, those thrown off in a moment of impulsive fancy.   Of the poems, the one I like best is on the story of Pygmalion, a close imitation, even to the tricks of rhythm, of Keats's *Endymion*.

Charles Darley has been classed among the imitators of Shelley, but not quite justly.   An Irishman, born near Dublin in 1795, his first poem, *The Errours of Ecstasie*, was probably written in Ireland. His *Silvia*, a fairy drama half in prose, published in 1827, is a pretty, graceful thing, full of colours and clinking verse. There is not one weighty thought or word in it. Its treatment of Nature is light and pleasant; the characters are quite boneless. There is, however, a description of the faery host in array for festival which is delightfully fancied, elfish, gay, and glancing. *Nepenthe*, another poem of his, is justly characterised by Mr. Rolleston as an "indescribable rhapsody." He will live by one lyric—"It is not Beauty I demand"— which Palgrave, not knowing who had written it, classed in *The Golden Treasury* among the anonymous writers of the time of Milton from 1616 to 1700. It is worthy of the Elizabethan lyrics, and Darley's imitation of the Elizabethans passed in it from imitation into creation. This visitation of the Elizabethans is the only English thing about him. He was Irish, with the Irish strength and weakness, and in England the Irish strength diminished and the Irish weakness grew. He is an Irish poet writing in an English atmosphere; *that* is at the root of him. It is out of the question to class him as a follower of Shelley, or to place him in the roll of English poets. He might be compared with Thomas Moore, but Moore was far above him. In fancy he approached Moore, but he was more superficial, and he was less national. As to his art, the less said about it the better.

Contemporary with these unoriginal poets in this short exhausted period where the sentimentalists— little rivulets of poetry that assumed to be rivers. They received a gracious welcome from a society which did not desire to be disturbed by ideas, which imagined that the materialism it loved to live in would continue for ever, and which was quite willing to indulge a dainty sympathy for the suffering of the world and the starvation of the English poor, provided no one was bold or ill-mannered enough to ask them to surrender a single pleasure or a single guinea. They liked to read about pain and trouble in the past; they hated to read about it in the present. When suffering was known to be over, and made no claim on them—to read of it gave a pleasant flavour to their luxury and to their degraded peace. Therefore they accepted with a barren gratitude Mrs. Hemans, Letitia Elizabeth Landor, and others who wrote graceful, pathetic, perfumed stories, and pretty lyrics about spring, of love and sorrow, and little deeds of valour, and such religion as their society could accept, religion which promised them in heaven a pleasant extension of their agreeable life on earth.

Mrs. Hemans had a real poetical turn. Her poetry is musical, her love of nature commonplace but truly felt, her copiousness powerless. She had little intellect, and the great matters of humanity did not touch her at all. She was widely read and loved; but all that fame and affection are now gone, so swift is the perishing of the superficial, of that which has no national ideas behind its work. Yet, if we desire to possess an historical example in poetry of this period, we may find in some library on some dusty shelf the volume which contains *The Forest Sanctuary* and some short lyrics by Mrs. Hemans. They mark her pretty capacity, and they embody the sentimental elements of this worn-out poetic period.

Once more, a small set of poets belonging to this time, undertook the defence and propagation of those orthodox views in theology which Shelley had attacked, which Keats ignored, and which Byron had accepted and hated. The best of these was Robert Pollok, who published in 1827 his *Course of Time*, a long poem in ten cantos, describing with many episodes and illustrations the condition of man before the last judgment, and the tremendous event itself. It had a certain harsh and hateful power, but its doctrine was as unspeakable as the Turk. The one inference to be drawn from it is, that it was indeed a mercy that a soul like Shelley's should, in the realm of poetry, have denounced a theology which violated every principle of humanity, and have recalled the hearts of men to love and forgiveness as the ground of religion.

These then were the poetic elements in the air of this parenthesis in the story of our poetry. But England was not to remain a prey to exhaustion, a land without ideas, a nation without national emotions on high matters of human progress, a forest with no

full-voiced birds to sing in its trees. The democratic
ideas, in a new form and fitted to existing circumstances, began to burn again in the poetry, the philosophy, the religion, the social and political realms of
England. Deep-seated, wide-spreading emotion, accompanied by serious thinking, stirred the country and
the towns, even the universities; and the deaf opposition of the baser conservative elements in society only
deepened the excitement. The state of the oppressed
and starving poor, whether in the country or in the
towns, awoke the wrath of Ebenezer Elliott, the Corn
Law Rhymer, and in 1827 his passionate poetic indictment of the shameless wealth and comfort, brought by
the misery of the workers, ran far and wide. He, like
Wordsworth and Crabbe, was the poet of poverty.
But he carried it farther than these men. He began
the crusade against its evils which has continued to
the present day. The return to Nature which Wordsworth sang was good; but Elliott asked, " What have
the poor to return to? The life they live is wholly
unnatural, not according to Nature." Nor has the
voice his poetry began ever failed since, till quite
lately, in English song. A cloud like a man's hand
was rising, full of menacing fire, into the dead grey
sky of England. The democratic ideas were at work
again, and their first instalment was the Emancipation
of the Catholics, the Reform Bill, and the Repeal of
the Corn Laws, events which were the pioneers of a
mighty progress. They stirred England to its depths.

Men could no longer complain that there was no national passion in the country; and this national passion for new ideas fled, like an angel with wings of fire, over the brains and into the souls of the old men who saw visions and the young men who dreamed dreams. Those who were by nature poets received the national emotion, and it stimulated their own. They woke to use both these emotions on their own subjects, and before four years had passed by Tennyson and Browning began the new life of English poetry. Nor was religion unaffected. Just at the same time these poets began, two great religious movements took their rise. Liberal theology began with Maurice; sacerdotal theology with Keble and Newman. One only of these movements had at first a poet, but he had already written in Oxford, in 1827, *The Christian Year*. Both movements were full of passion and thought. Both have not only deeply influenced England, but have also done her great and lasting good; and both illustrate afresh the work of the ideas of the Revolution— the one in its attraction to those ideas; the other in its repulsion from them. Thus England emerged from her vile condition of careless and heavy slumber full of sensual dreams. And with her waking, Poetry awoke. And the light of Thought was in her eyes, and the fire of Love in her heart, and of them was Beauty born.

Elliott and Keble were the precursors of this awakening. Elliott began as a poet of Nature. "Farewell," he cried, "to the town and its horrors; let me live

on the breast of Nature." The passion of Wordsworth was strong in him, though he had read and
loved, but did not justly admire, Keats and Shelley.
But as he grew older, he was drawn aside from contemplation of Nature by the misery of the poor, by the
starvation the Corn Laws, the manufacturers, and the
indifferent landlords imposed on the people. Wordsworth, he thought, had only touched the comfortable
poor. Crabbe gave him more truth, and was nearer to
his heart—"Crabbe, whose dark gold is richer than
it seems"—but Byron had most power over his soul.
Byron's anger, force, love of freedom, even his gloom,
suited one who had to sing the stern and crying
suffering of the people.

Elliott quite understood that Byron would not have
cared about the English labourer. But the revolutionary spirit in Byron, his fierce scorn of the oppressor,
and his dying effort to free Greece, made him a spirit
of power in a mind like Elliott's. Soon, leaving Byron,
he took his individual turn, and concentrated and
consecrated himself as the Poet of the Poor. And well
he did that duty, voicing their silent pain and wrath
with unbroken courage, truth, and fervour. At first
he wrote poems of some length, after the manner of
Robert Bloomfield ; and if we wish to know the state
of rural England in those days, we cannot do better—
and this will illuminate the merely political histories
with the light of reality—than read *The Patriarch of
the Village* and *The Splendid Village.* There, in a lurid

light, but a true one, the rustic England of those times is drawn ; and its miseries were only less than those of the peasants of France before the Revolution. Then, as the struggle against the Corn Laws deepened, Elliott wrote rough, keen, rousing lyrics, close to the very truth of things, the passion of which smote like a dagger, the reality of which could not be more lucidly expressed. What he saw, he wrote. But this denunciation, and all the fierceness of his poetry, were relieved throughout by a gracious love of natural beauty, a joy in the lovely and quiet world which knit him to the past poets, and carried him forward into those who were to come. Moreover, the springs of pity and tenderness were deep in him, and with these, the fountain of a strong and humble faith in God. These saved the poetry, gave it that high and loving note which lifted it above the angers of denunciation, and enabled it to live.

I have often thought that, bad as things are still in town and country, and much as I wish that the poetry of our own day should now enter into the battle—the progress made in social good during the last seventy years of the last century has been so great, and so well founded on steady and well-organized ideas, that it deserves greater praise than has been given to it. To read the *Coronation Ode*, written for the Sheffield Working Men's Association, and to compare it with the profound feeling which ran through the nation at the death of the Queen, is to realise this change. If the people had been suffering even half as bitterly as they were suffering when the Queen was crowned, nothing like that which we have seen when she died could have taken place. I quote this ode of his, even though, as poetry, it is not good. It is not, of course, an attack on the Queen, but a cry against the misery, the oppression, and the past policy of the country. Its sad and terrible note sounds almost incredible in our ears.

CORONATION ODE

Victoria, cypress-crown'd! thou, good in vain!
How the red wreath, with which thy name is bound—
The page which tells the first deeds of thy reign,
Black, and blood-blotted—cheer the Calmuck hound.
Whose growl o'er Brunswick hails thee, cypress-crown'd!

Canada weeps—and yet her *dead* are free!
Throned o'er their blood! who would not be a Queen?
The Queen of *new-made graves*, who would not be?
Of glory's royal flowers the loveliest seen!
So young! yet all that the deplored have been!

Here too, O Queen, thy wo-worn people feel
The load they bear is more than they can bear!
Beneath it twenty million workers reel!
While fifty thousand idlers rob and glare,
And mock the sufferings which they yet may share!

The drama soon will end. Four acts are past:
The curtain rises o'er embracing foes.
But each dark smiler hugs his dagger fast!
While Doom prepares his match, and waits the close!
Queen of the Earthquake; would'st thou win or lose?

Still shall the Car of Juggernaut roll on,
O'er broken hearts and children born in vain,
Banner'd with fire! while " thousand men are one "

Sink down beneath its coward wheels of pain,
That crush out souls, through crunching blood and brain.

Stop!—for to ruin Antoinette was led,
By men, who only when they died awoke!
Base nobles who o'er France vain darkness spread,
And, goading her faint steeds with stroke on stroke,
Loaded the wain—until the axles broke!

Stop!—"for the blasting engine's iron Laws,"
Then saved not thrones from outraged Heav'n's control,
When hunger urg'd up to the cannon's jaws
A sea of men, with only one wild soul!
Hark!—still I hear the echo of its roll!

We can scarcely listen to it without feeling that the main ideas of the Revolution, so long silent in England, were again arising into life. What would England make of them? What would they become in the New Poetry they prophesied and stimulated? The answer poetry gave was no obscure one. The ideas changed their manner; they changed the form of their demands; they were modified by circumstances; but they lived on. They became, not a furious menace from without, but a spirit moving slowly from within, working in quiet ways, infiltrating themselves into almost every sphere of human thought, and moving with dignity, and yet with passion, through the poets from this time till about 1870, when again they began to change their form.

Keble was another precursor of the awakening. That awakening was destined in poetry to be greatly interested in ideas of religion, and one species of these ideas arose in 1827 with the publication of *The*

Christian Year. In this book Keble created a new method and a new aim in religious poetry. The religious poets of the Eighteenth Century were more hymn-writers than poets, but the greater part of Keble's work was quite apart from the inevitable conventionality of the hymn, even when it was written by Cowper. Nor was it fantastic, like that of Herbert, or philosophical like that of Vaughan or More. It was simple, moving on the common meadow-paths of gentle devotion; and its only philosophy was that of the heart of humble men seeking communion with God. At the same time, it bound up with itself a set of large religious ideas. It seized on, and brought into poetry the mighty, emotionalising traditions of the Church from the earliest times; the weight and passion of two thousand years of thought and associated action. It had not force enough to represent the thousandth part of this, but what it did grasp redeemed religious poetry from the narrow limits which confined it to prayer and praise alone. Moreover, it brought religious poetry out of the closed sphere of the inner life into the home, into the trials and temptations of the social life of men and women. The whole range of devotional poetry was expanded. Again, he brought religious feeling into union with the new love of nature for her own sake. The mountains, rivers, woods, and plains, the glories of the morning, evening, and nightly sky, are in his pages, gently, serenely felt. And he used the tender grace, the beauty of the scenery of

Palestine, which then began to be well known, to enhance the poetry which dealt with the gospel history. Many of the poems in *The Christian Year* begin with refined, delicate, and deeply-felt descriptions of nature which are, as symbolism or as teaching, carried on by gracious gradation into the spiritual life. These passages, in their academic peace and delicate feeling, faintly echo Gray, but their loving observation of nature is as true as that of Tennyson. No one has used nature better in the service of the soul. This also was an expansion of the poetry of religion, and it was in harmony with the ideas of the new time.

As to poetry itself, it was possessed of a sweet melody, and the melody was varied into many forms. Its grip on the matters it treated was not always strong; it wavered, and lost its hold only too often; but that is a frequent fault in poets who live in contemplation. I have said that it extended religious poetry into the home and social life of men, but it did this tentatively, and was, naturally enough and chiefly, the poetry of a cloistered soul. But it was, in its own sphere, felicitous, seeking a small perfection, and sufficiently imaginative, though in it the imagination never soared. Above all, it was pervaded by the charm of quiet; of delicate thought and twilight emotion. Historically, it did a great work for the religious movement it was the first to define. Newman added to its poetry some of his own which, though it has taken a high place in the minds of many, seems to be gravely overrated.

These poets opened out the dawn of a new poetic world, and in a few years the sun arose in Tennyson and Browning, moved not only by their own native genius but by the passion of England, now at last awakened into keen life by fresh social, political, artistic, and religious ideas.   On them, and their relation to their time and its movements, I have written at large.   What I wish now to do, before I come to a discussion of the new elements which entered poetry with Clough and Arnold, is, leaving Tennyson and Browning aside, to follow the ideas of the lesser poets who, in this great awakening, sang the imaginative thinking of mature men, and the devious aspirations of the young.

In the ten years which preceded 1842 when Tennyson collected his poems for the first time, when Browning had published *Paracelsus* and *Sordello*, there was, first, one set of poets who rather reverted to Wordsworth than belonged to the new time.   They had nothing to do, however, with the half-dead period on which I have written ; their poetry was of a steady, temperate, highly cultivated quality.   Thought and emotion belonged to it, but it was too philosophic, too much afraid of emotion, and of too curbed an imagination to become of a great or universal influence.   It reacted from the more impassioned work of Shelley, Keats, and Byron, to that of Wordsworth—to Wordsworth, not as the youthful poet, but as the poet of *The Excursion*.   Such poetry as that written wildly and loosely by Beddoes and Darley, such sentimentalism as that which flowed from Mrs. Hemans or L. E. L. were painful to men who had now begun to live among great events, and historical movements of thought.   Again, in this new noise of the world, which grew louder and fiercer from 1830, this type of men took refuge in the silent love of Wordsworth for quiet things, and not least in his spiritual communion with nature, to whose resting-places they fled, in brief holidays, from the storm and stress of affairs.   Moreover, Wordsworth's energetic grasp of the fundamental elements of man's nature, his firm hold on its great and universal truths, appealed not only to middle-aged men, seeking severely for truth in great confusion,—the confusion of a world newly awakened from sleep—but also to young men at the Universities, who were deeply moved by the prospect of a life so full of warring elements, on which they were about to enter.   The poets who voiced this reaction to Wordsworth were only a small school, but they expressed the feeling of a large number of persons at this time.   The most representative of them was Sir Henry Taylor, whose *Philip Van Artevelve* was published in 1834.   This drama, which may fairly be called philosophical, deals with government, popular disturbance, wars and their conduct, in an age crowded with sudden and bold activities; and is full of action, of various types of men, and of thought on public affairs.   And love, treated with some stateliness, even with humour and pathos, legitimate and illegiti-

mate, runs through its seriousness as a secondary not
as a principal part of life.   The interlude, between the
two parts of the drama, is a well-wrought study of a
woman who had loved too much and too often for her
peace; a creature of impulse and fire, with a born ob-
liquity in her nature.   Its lyric form, its natural description of Italy, its revelation of a wildered woman's soul,
and her pathetic self-judgment, is the best poetry in
the book.   In it Taylor let his imagination loose ; in
the drama he curbed it so closely that it lost charm.
He subordinated his poetry to his intellect, and his
other dramas are subject to a similar criticism.

Another school of poets which arose in this excited
time was the school to which was afterwards given the
nickname of *Spasmodic* by persons who were incapable
of writing its poetry.   It had a great vogue.   Bailey's
Festus was praised, and justly, by excellent judges.
Sydney Dobell's *Balder*, and *The Roman*, and the
Poems of Alex. Smith received ovations in their day.
After fully fifteen years, Professor Aytoun's *Firmilian*,
a Spasmodic Tragedy, exaggerating grossly the faults
of the school, killed it.   But *Festus* still continues to
claim our admiration for its high poetic qualities.   It
was published in 1839; and was begun when Bailey
was twenty years old.   He enlarged it till he died.   It
embodied a new theology, neither of Newman nor of
Maurice, but a layman's theology freed from the limits
of authority, of tradition, and of conventional morality.

The unbridled thinking, and unmixed self-consciousness of this time—each man thinking himself a universe—were naturally strongest in the young men, and strongest of all in young poets. That Wordsworthian reversion on which I have dwelt, with its philosophy and quietudes, left the hot-tempered, passionate, aspiring, egotistic young men quite unrepresented. It suited grave men or premature young men, like Stuart Mill, but it stirred rebellion in the impetuous who felt that it left half of life untouched. And the new wine in the land, the emotions of ideas growing into form, and shaping themselves into new circumstances, deepened, as all national movements will, the natural excitement of poetic young men, thirsting for fame and love. Therefore their poems begin, for the most part, with vast soliloquies, many pages long, which describe their soul, its ineffable powers and aims ; and their own passion to reach the top of fame, not only in poetry, but in everything. Again, the hunger for love in many forms, moral and immoral, was raised by these poets into a kind of religion. It was necessary, they thought, for their full development as poets that they should go through, in many different women, varied aspects of love in its joys, its miseries, and its remorse. Nothing could be more unlike the view of love which Wordsworth, Scott, Byron, Shelley, or Keats expressed. With them it was not the whole of life, and it was always naturally treated. These new poets whipped it into a morbid prominence, sometimes into an imaginative sensuality

which pretended to be religious. It was a not unnatural reaction from a school which looked on passion
in love as unworthy of a true philosophy of life, or
from a school which made it into pretty sentiment.
The senses, the appetites are part of human nature.
They also are to be presented in poetry, but there, if
art represents their base extremes, such art has ceased
to be art, and has passed into the science of morbid
conditions.

Another element in this poetry was an over-assertive
individuality. Each of these poets, to his own thinking, contained all nature and all human nature. To
investigate and represent the finity of themselves was
their deepest interest, and ought to be the deepest
interest of the world. Some even seem to think
that they ought to have in their hands all knowledge and all power; the poet, they declare, is the
true governor of the world. Each, at least, believed
himself to be the first of poets. Their egotism is
unlimited, but it is the product of their time. Individualism, as in all periods of quickened life in a nation,
had now become one of the ruling ideas of public and
personal life. It appears, but modified by true genius,
in *Paracelsus* and *Sordello*, and in many poems of
Tennyson. It continued, and very fully, to display
itself in the work of Clough and Arnold; nor did it
lessen much till Morris and Rossetti carried poetry into
another atmosphere, in which the personal soul was
made of less importance. Moreover, it was quite in

harmony with the whole drift of political and social opinion. The glorification of individual freedom to act as it pleased, independent of the interests of the whole—the opposite doctrine to that of collectivism—ruled the internal politics of the State, of trade, and of all social questions from 1832 to 1866, when the first blow was concisely administered to individualism. These poems were the exaggerated exposition in art of this individualism.

Then again, this claim of the poets to absolute freedom of self-development made them claim full freedom for national development and for the overthrow of all oppression. The democratic ideas, scarcely represented by Tennyson or Browning, were ever since 1832 quite awake in England. They grew hotter as the years went on. The reactionary work of the French monarchy, the oppression of North Italy by Austria, the condition of Rome and Naples, the treatment of Poland, the state of the poor and the working men of England, multiplied the power of those ideas. They broke into fierce revolt in 1848; and they were represented by these poets. Sydney Dobell's *Roman*, published in 1849, an indictment of Austria's villainies in Italy, and a claim for a united Italy, with Rome as its centre, ran from edition to edition, and was only one example of poetry filled with sympathy for the struggle for freedom on the Continent. Clough shared in this excitement. Arnold receded from it.

But even more than by fame, love and freedom, these

poets were moved by theology, and into their theology each intruded his own special individuality. The theological excitement had begun in and about 1830 in the Universities, and had now extended over the whole of religious England. Tennyson and Browning shared in it, but with a dignity of genius that separated them from the rest. Clough and Arnold were closely involved in it, and all the minor poets of this time took part in the battle. But these poets, whom I now discuss, represented it in separate, individual, unchartered forms—as it expressed itself in the excited souls of laymen who owned no authority of church or sect, and followed no especial form of creed. They made theology in its relation to life, even more than love, the subject-matter of their poetry. But they were not temperate, concise, or conscious of the limitations of thought, like the greater poets ; they were sensational, endlessly fluent, and claimed to be at home in regions of thought beyond the sight of man. The problems of theology are discussed by them at such portentous length that one can only explain the great vogue of these poems by a universal excitement on the subject in religious society. The best of them was *Festus*. It opens, like Goethe's *Faust*, with God and Satan in colloquy, and Satan is allowed to tempt Festus. It ends with Festus being made King of all humanity and with the immediate destruction of the whole human race. He has, before this, visited with Lucifer Heaven itself and Hell, and all the inhabited planets, and is the friend of several archangels. The scenes are set in Space, in Elsewhere, in Everywhere, in Chaos, and in various parts of the earth, where he develops, with a perfect serenity of conscience, a complete series of different affections for different women. At the end of the poem is the last judgment, and it is worth noting that he was the first of the poets to teach universal redemption. All the human race are saved; evil has only existed for the development of good; and since the work of Satan has been God's instrument to draw forth good, he and all the rebel host are called back by God to take their original places in heaven. *Embrassons nous, mes enfants, disait le bon Dieu, tout s'explique.*

This universalism was only one of the various phases of religious thought which arose in this time of intellectual excitement, and were naturally represented by the poets. Indeed, more and more, theories and questions of religion caught hold of the poetry of England from 1840 to 1860. *In Memoriam* appeared in 1850. The controversy between Newman and his opponents was still hot in Oxford in the forties, and had extended far and wide over England. A liberal theology, into whose tenets I need not enter here, had been well begun, and gathered disciples round it year after year. The authority of the Church was set up against the claim a large class of men made to complete freedom of investigation, criticism, worship, and belief. Others tried to hold the balance between these two extremes, to discover and pave a *via media,* but instead of one *via*

media, different thinkers made many.   And beyond
the main schools of religious thought, there were guer-
rilla schools that fought for their own hand.   Out
of the religious struggle there arose, not only a host of
questions concerning doctrinal theology which excited
the intellect as much as the passions of men, but also
multitudinous questions concerning the problem of
human life—its origin, its end, its conduct, its relation
to God, and His relation to it, whether our will in it
was free or subject to necessity, whether its happenings
mastered us or we them—old questions in new shapes.
Was its evil good or its good evil, was life itself illusion
or reality, what attitude in it was the true attitude of
the soul, and a hundred minor problems clashing together like a swarm of atoms.   As long as men had
faith in the authority of a Church or a Book which
revealed the origin and destiny of man in God's will,
the divine conduct and sacred laws of being, the redemption of the world by the sacrifice and resurrection
of Christ—so long men felt that hope and peace might
be attained in the midst of this turmoil of thought, so
long they believed that into the darkness light could
arise and prevail.   But now, at this very time, the discoveries of science and especially of geological science
threw doubt on the authority of the Book, and historical criticism, coming from Germany, threw doubt on
the Gospel History on which the authority of the
Church reposed.   Wherever men read and thought,
the disturbance which already existed was now deep-

ened, and, as the years went on to the sixties, it deepened
more and more.

Into the midst of this whirlpool of thoughts and
hopes and passions, political, social, ideal, democratic,
but chiefly religious and theological, Clough and
Arnold were cast.   They came up to Oxford between
1836 and 1840, and remained there, absorbing Oxford
and its battlings of thought into their very marrow:
and they represent the tempestuous tossing of their
time, especially in their early poems, far more than
Tennyson or Browning seated above the strife and
moving on larger lines were capable of doing.

ARTHUR HUGH CLOUGH

OF all the poets who played on England as on a harp, Clough was one of the most personal. He was even more personal than Arnold, who could detach himself at times from himself. But Clough was never self-detached in his poetry, even when he tried to be so. He contemplated his soul and its sensitive and bewildered workings incessantly, and saw in them the image of that which was going on in the soul of the younger men in England. Sometimes he is intensely part of the spiritual strife he is conscious of, because he is so conscious of it in himself; sometimes he watches it from without, as a press correspondent might the battle he describes; sometimes, in the course of a single poem, he flits from the inside to the outside position, or from the outside to the inside; but always it is the greater image of his own soul that he watches in the struggle of the whole; always he is intimately close to the trouble or calm, the wondering or the anchoring of the eager, restless, searching, drifting being within, whom he did not wish to be himself. No one is more intimate, more close, more true to this inward life. It is this which makes him so interesting and so much a favourite with those who like him. They see a man in much the same condition as they are, or have been, themselves; they feel that he has been quite true to himself in it, and has done his very best to tell the truth—and to read true things said truly is always a keen, if sometimes a sorrowful pleasure. Moreover, no obscurity, no vagueness, troubles the reader. We are conscious that he has striven with all his might to render the matter in question into the most lucid form he can; and few have put remote and involved matters of the soul into such simple words as Clough.

Again, we see, through all the confused trouble he describes, and in spite of all the wavering and uncertainty, that he has one clear aim—that of getting out of the storm, if possible, into some bright light and quiet air. He does not like the confusion and the questioning, and the trouble, but desires to be quit of them, if this can be done truthfully. He will not shut his eyes to any difficulty, nor retire to his tent while the battle is going on, nor pretend there is no confusion, for the sake of light and sweetness. Truth to himself first — then he will be fit to see the Truth itself, if it be possible. But it is his aim, his hope, his impassioned desire, even in despair, to see it at last. That Truth *is*, he believes; and he sets himself to work his way to it through the tangled forest of life.

> It fortifies my soul to know
> That, though I perish, Truth is so:

> That, howsoe'er I stray and range,
> Whate'er I do, Thou dost not change.
> I steadier step when I recall
> That, if I slip, Thou dost not fall.

To a certain degree then, he was above scepticism. He did not think it a fine condition; the last thing he imagined was that there was any reason for being proud of it; nevertheless he would not move one inch out of it till his reason and conscience together told him he might leave this or that question behind. The only thing he knew was that there was a clear solution to be found somewhere, sometime, in the Truth itself. Even the star of that knowledge was sometimes overwhelmed in clouds. He kept his head and heart however; he was finally master in his soul. He moved amid the disorganised army of his thoughts and emotions, like a great captain who sees and knows the troubled state of his army, and the desperate and broken ground over which it has to advance; who visits every regiment and knows the wants of each; who has entered every tent, who is aware of the fears, doubts, failures, and despairs of every man—but who is determined to lead the army on, because he knows that, far away, there is a safe and quiet resting-place—soft grass and clear streams within a fortified defence — where he can camp them at last, order them, and restore their spirit. Sometimes he is all but hopeless; whence he has brought the armies of his soul he cannot tell; whither they are going he cannot tell; all is doubt and trouble; but again, there are hours of rest when

the place whither he is going and its far off light are
clear ; at times he feels a proud joy in the fighting for-
wards ; at times nothing lives but exhaustion, yet he
never thinks of surrender.   Here is a poem which puts
this life of his into clear, gentle, but impassioned form :

> Where lies the land to which the ship would go?
> Far, far ahead, is all her seamen know.
> And where the land she travels from ?   Away,
> Far, far behind, is all that they can say.
>
> On sunny noons upon the deck's smooth face,
> Linked arm in arm, how pleasant here to pace ;
> Or, o'er the stern reclining, watch below
> The foaming wake far widening as we go.
>
> On stormy nights when wild north-westers rave,
> How proud a thing to fight with wind and wave !
> The dripping sailor on the reeling mast
> Exults to bear, and scorns to wish it past.
>
> Where lies the land to which the ship would go?
> Far, far ahead, is all her seamen know.
> And where the land she travels from ?   Away,
> Far, far behind, is all that they can say.

Whence and whither our ship came, and goes, and the
ship of all humanity, we cannot know, though we may
hope to know.   We live by faith, not knowledge.
Sometimes the battle is illuminated and rejoiced by
sudden outflamings of faith ; again it is darkened by
absolute despair.   Faith in God rushes up one day
through the crust of doubt and drowns every sceptical
thought ; the next day, there is no God.   Christ is not
risen ; the day after He is risen.   There is no rest, no
clear heaven, no knowledge of whence and whither—

nothing but tossing to and fro. Even when he falls
back on duty, a voice in his heart tells him it is not
enough. He must find the unknown Perfect his soul
desires.

At last, he is enraged with his condition. Life is
slipping away in overthinking, in this way and that
dividing the swift mind. The soul, while he is young,
is growing old in a diseased confusion. Is this life, he
asks, this the end of our stay on earth?

PERCHÈ PENSA? PENSANDO S'INVECCHIA

> To spend uncounted years of pain,
> Again, again and yet again,
> In working out in heart and brain
>   The problem of our being here;
> To gather facts from far and near,
> Upon the mind to hold them clear,
> And, knowing more may yet appear;
> Unto one's latest breath to fear
> The premature result to draw—
> Is this the object, end, and law,
>   And purpose of our being here?

There are those who are not troubled by any such
questions, simple folk who believe and have peace, and
Clough praises their life and thinks them true and
happy; at moments he can feel with them, but not for
long. There are others who find peace and power to
live and work by giving up all questions of this kind
as hampering life and useless for good. But Clough
was not of that temper, and could not enter its regions.
He did his duty, but a tender intensity of passion

urged him beyond it to find the rest in perfection. He was the image and the expression of thousands who lived in that disturbed time, when criticism and science set the battle in array against the old theology. It is the image and the expression, even now, after the battle has raged for sixty years, of the condition of a number of persons who are impassioned to find a truth by which they can live, who desire to believe but are unable, who are equally unable to find peace in unbelief. Thus moving, like a Hamlet, through the strifes of theology and religion, he resembles Hamlet in another way. When the Prince is suddenly flung into the storm of action, he takes momentarily a fierce part in it, and enjoys it, till overthinking again seizes on him. Clough repeats this in his life, and his poetry is touched with it.

These are the causes of the pleasure with which we read Clough's earlier poetry—its clear image of a certain type of men and women in a spiritually troubled time, its close contact with and intimate expression of the constantly debating soul, its truthfulness, its sanity amid scepticism, its statement of all sides of the matter in hand, its personal humanity, and its sympathy with man, its self-mastery and its clear aim. There is also plenty of good matter of thought and of emotion worthily controlled—great things in poetry, provided they are expressed poetically. But the poetry itself is not of a high quality; its level is only a third of the way towards greatness; it is imaginative, but the imagination in it never soars and never is on fire, never at a white heat; on the contrary, its play is gentle, soft, touched, like an autumn evening when summer has just died, with tender, clear, brooding light.   The greater number of these poems are such as a man who lived in a constant atmosphere of trouble and battle might write, when, wearied with the strife, he enjoyed an hour of forgetful rest after trouble, and of sheathing of the sword after battle; and I do not know of any other poet of whom this may be said so truly.   In that he is alone—that is the distinction of these early poems.   And this clear, soft, brooding note is just as clearly struck in the poems which have nothing to do with the trouble of the soul, but with matter of the affections.   I quote this little idyll: how grave it is, and tender; what an evening light rests upon it; not the light of Italy, but of the northern sky among the mountains.   What self-control breathes in it; what a quiet heart, quiet, not by the absence of passion, but by self-restraint, and by that on which Clough so often dwelt and which subdued his poetry so often—by the sense of the inevitable, of a fate which, hemming us in on every side, imposes on us its will, and ignores our struggle and our pain:

ITE DOMUM SATURÆ, VENIT HESPERUS

The skies have sunk, and tied the upper snow,
(Home, Rose, and home, Provence and La Palie.)
The rainy clouds are filing fast below,
And wet will be the path, and wet shall we.
Home, Rose, and home, Provence and La Palie.

Ah dear, and where is he, a year agone,
Who stepped beside and cheered us on and on ?
My sweetheart wanders far away from me,
In foreign land or on a foreign sea.
Home, Rose, and home, Provence and La Palie.

The lightning zigzags shoot across the sky,
(Home, Rose, and home, Provence and La Palie.)
And through the vale the rains go sweeping by ;
Ah me, and when in shelter shall we be ?
Home, Rose, and home, Provence and La Palie.

Cold, dreary cold, the stormy winds feel they
O'er foreign lands and foreign seas that stray.
(Home, Rose, and home, Provence and La Palie.)
And doth he e'er, I wonder, bring to mind
The pleasant huts and herds he left behind ?
And doth he sometimes in his slumbering see
The feeding kine, and doth he think of me,
My sweetheart wandering whereso'er it be?
Home, Rose, and home, Provence and La Palie.

The thunder bellows far from snow to snow,
(Home, Rose, and home, Provence and La Palie.)
And loud and louder roars the flood below.
Heigh-ho ! but soon in shelter shall we be :
Home, Rose, and home, Provence and La Palie.

Or shall he find before his term be sped,
Some comelier maid that he shall wish to wed ?
(Home, Rose, and home, Provence and La Palie.)
For weary is work, and weary day by day
To have your comfort miles on miles away.
Home, Rose, and home, Provence and La Palie.

Or may it be that I shall find my mate,
And he returning see himself too late?
For work we must, and what we see, we see,
And God he knows, and what must be, must be,
When sweethearts wander far away from me.
Home, Rose, and home, Provence and La Palie.

The sky behind is brightening up anew,
(Home, Rose, and home, Provence and La Palie.)
The rain is ending, and our journey too ;
Heigh-ho ! aha ! for here at home are we :—
In Rose, and in Provence, and La Palie.

There may be, he thinks, inevitable partings, however true men and women be to one another. Life
moves us to an end of which we know nothing, which
we cannot master.

This is a favourite motive of his, as indeed it was
of Matthew Arnold. They must have discussed it
a hundred times at Oxford. We may exercise our
will on circumstance, but it is of no avail. We try,
and try again and yet again, but a little thing, of
which we take no note, turns us from the goal. At
last we grow wearied of being baffled, and give up the
thing we desired ; and then, in the hour when we
have released ourselves from pursuing, we wonder, as
we look back, whether we really cared for the thing
we pursued, or whether the person we pursued cared
for us. A series of slight pressures of circumstance on
a dreamy and sensitive soul drifts the will away from
its desired goal, and each of the drifts is accepted.
Clough must have felt that this was the position of a
part of his soul, perhaps with regard to matters of
thought, certainly so far as the affections were concerned ; or, if that is assuming too much, he must at
least have sympathised keenly with this position in
others. At any rate, he knew all about it. It is a
frequent motive in his poems, and one whole poem,

the *Amours de Voyage*, is a careful study of this matter of the heart. Clough seems to take a personal
delight in the slow, subtle, close drawing, week by
week, of the wavering, wandering, changeful drifting
of the heart of the hero in love, into pursuit, and out
of love — never one moment's resolution, never an
hour of grip on circumstance, never one bold effort to
clench the throat of Fate. Many are involved in
similar circumstances, and have a similar temper; and
the result in the poem is the exact result of a soul in
that condition. And it seemed, I suppose, to Clough
that it would be well to paint their condition, to show
its folly, its evil, and its end. " Go, little book," he
says—

" Go, and if curious friends ask of thy rearing and age,
Say, 'I am flitting about many years from brain unto brain of
Feeble and restless youths born to inglorious days.' "

Of course, we need not believe in the inevitableness of
the position, nor indeed did Clough finally. When he
recorded it, he recorded what he had felt and known
in himself, but he had passed out of it. Only, what
he had then attained—for I think he speaks of himself
—" that happiness was to be found in knowledge, that
faith passed, and love passed, but that knowledge
abided "—was not, it seems, a much better position.
Knowledge, to be sure, is a good thing, but it is a
foundation for life which is always shifting. Its abid-
ing is only for a short time, and its professors have to

relay their foundations. And in the moral realm, in the conduct of life, to say nothing of the spiritual realm, knowledge, or what passes for knowledge, is frightfully insecure, and is attended with one fatal comrade, with pride in itself.

This is always true: "Knowledge puffeth up, but Love edifieth"; and if I may judge from the bulk of his poetry, Clough came to that at last. As to this insistence on fate, on the inevitable in circumstance, it is not an image of true life. Man is not master of the whole of fate, for he is not able to see all, but a great deal of what he thinks inevitable is in his hands. If he cannot climb over obstacles, he can get round them; that is, if he have courage, and chose to exercise his will, to be what he was made to be—a cause in the universe. Fate, as they call it, seems herself to remove the obstruction, if we take her gaily and boldly. If we march up to the barrier, we find it to be mere cloud through which we go easily to the other side. It is always wise to disbelieve in obstacles.

If the gentleman in the *Amours de Voyage*, when he found that he had just missed his love at Florence, had not waited to analyse his feelings, and then arrived too late at the next town where she had been, and then paused to analyse again his sensations, and then was the victim of a misdirected letter, and then gave up his pursuit; had he knit his heart into any resolution, instead of saying "Whither am I borne," he would easily have found the girl, and found his happiness. Fate? nine-tenths of fate are in our own hands, but we let the other tenth master us, and then fate fills the nine-tenths which was in our power with her own sombre self. This is our punishment, and we deserve it.

Well, it is a good thing to have the whole matter laid before us with such remarkable closeness and veracity as Clough has done in this poem. Its hero is a characteristic type : cultivated, retiring, disliking society. He has been thrown in the past, like Clough, into a world of jarring strife and noise, of mental and spiritual disturbance. Sensitive, refined till he thrills at a touch, angry with the circumstances of life which call him to act—when action, which forces him into contact with vulgar reality out of philosophic dreams, is as repugnant to him as it was to Hamlet " a cursed spite " of fate—he welcomes any change, any chance, which takes him out of the world of strife and effort. This also was the case with Clough himself, from whom the hero of the poem partly drawn.

He was wearied with the strife within ; he sought the world without ; he welcomed the chance of employment elsewhere. He left Oxford, and afterwards went to America. There he gathered pupils around him at Cambridge, and wrote for the reviews. The things he wrote were not of any high quality ; they have not even subtlety ; they have no distinction. Uncontent still, he came back to England, his friends having found him a place in the Education Office.

And then, his career being decided for him, and his drifting boat anchored by another hand than his own, he settled down to the prim ways, and regular work, and consistent routine of a government office, with its pleasant holidays. And then, too, he married, and loved his wife, his children, and his home ; and gathered love around him, and found that love *did* abide and edify. His humour was set free from sorrow. The questions which had so deeply perplexed him were still subjects of careful thought, but they tormented him no more. He passed, we are told, "from the speculative to the constructive phase of thought," and would have, had he lived, expressed his matured conceptions of life in a more substantial way. He was happy and useful. He was always oppressed with the "sadness of the world, and the great difficulties of modern social life," but he turned his mind steadily, in this atmosphere of love and happiness, and with the deep experience they gave him, to help towards this solution. I wish he had had time to record in poetry his conclusions, but office work is a great disintegrator of poetic creation, and very little was done, and that not good as poetry, before the blind Fury came with the abhorred shears, and slit the thin-spun life.

He was only forty-three years old. The tales published under the title of *Mari magno* were written during the last holidays of his life, while he searched for health, and the last of them when he was dying. They

are for the most part concerned with the question of
marriage : its true end, its trials, fitness for it, and
other matters. They have their own interest, but their
main interest, like that of all the poems, is Clough's
revelation of his character. He was, with that sensitive nature of his, a reserved man ; but when he wrote
poetry, the unconscious disclosure of his soul—the
piece of human nature he knew best, and in which he
was most interested—was so fine and accurate and all
the more attractive because it was done unawares—
that it fascinates even those readers who do not think
highly of the poetry.

There is, however, another element in it which has
its own fascination. This is the ceaseless change of
mood within one atmosphere, like the ceaseless change
of cloud scenery in a day of the same kind of weather
from morning to evening. We never can tell what is
coming in a poem, what the next verse will bring out,
what new turn will be given to the main matter. Moreover, from day to day his mood varied. He might
be sarcastic on Monday, depressed on Tuesday, gently
humorous with life on Wednesday, despairing on
Thursday, joyous with hope and strong in fortitude on
Friday, idyllic on Saturday, sceptical on Sunday morning, religious on Sunday evening, and subtle, delicate,
and tender every day. This has its own attraction for
certain people, and those who like him, like him dearly.

Then, he had an excellent, light-flitting, kindly
humour. Sometimes it was broad enough, as in that

poem about money, written in Venice, in the character
of a vulgar rich man, two verses of which I quote:

As I sat at the café, I said to myself,
They may talk as they please about what they call pelf,
They may sneer as they like about eating and drinking,
But help it I cannot—I cannot help thinking
How pleasant it is to have money, heigh-ho,
How pleasant it is to have money.

I sit at my table *en grand seigneur*,
And when I have done, throw a crust to the poor ;
Not only the pleasure, one's self, of good living,
But also the pleasure of now and then giving.
So pleasant, etc.

Sometimes his humour touches lightly and softly the
comfortable, thoughtless life, as in these two verses on
the gondola :—

Afloat ; we move.   Delicious !   Ah !
What else is like the gondola?
This level floor of liquid glass
Begins beneath us swift to pass.
It goes as though it went alone
By some impulsion of its own.
How light it moves, how softly !   Ah,
Were all things like the gondola !

With no more motion than should bear
A freshness to the languid air ;
With no more effort than exprest
The need and naturalness of rest,
Which we beneath a grateful shade,
Should take on peaceful pillows laid.
How light we move, how softly !   Ah,
Were life but as the gondola !

So live, nor need to call to mind
Our slaving brother here behind !

Sometimes it is a humorous mock at his own want of decision and force, as in that poem which wonders how Columbus could ever have conceived, or, rather, ever have carried out his conception of a world beyond the apparent infinity of waters. " How in God's name did Columbus get over," is the first line of the poem, and it ends by insisting that no one who had guessed that there was a world beyond the great waters would ever have gone sailing on, and that he himself could never have done it. " 'T is a pure madness, a pure wonder to me." The *Bothie* also is full of quaint, observant humour. All the Oxford elements of his day are there; liked, even loved, but held up to gentle, subtle ridicule, delicately touched, but touched home. Oxford's young enthusiasm is pictured in the pupils, its quiet temper in the tutor, its dress, its ways of talk, the beginning of its æstheticism, its hereditary self-satisfaction, its variety of youthful intellect, its high sense of honour and morality, its manliness, its noisy athleticism, its sense that Oxford is, on the whole, though a doubt may now and then intrude, the mother, and the father, too, of the intellectual universe; and its reading parties, with a tutor, the incubator of states-men, poets, philosophers, radical emigrants, and con-servative squires, all fitted to replenish the earth and subdue it, to counsel and lead the world.

The poem, written in broken-boned hexameters, belongs to his early time. It is his longest effort. Four young men, with a grave tutor, form a reading party in the Highlands. They go to a sporting function at the Laird's, and Philip Hewson, the radical and revolutionist of the party, in whom Clough, no doubt, sketched his own opinions at this time, meets there a Highland girl, the daughter of a small farmer near Braemar. The farmer invited Hewson to visit him if he should come that way. He falls in love with the girl, begs her to marry him, and sends for the tutor to guarantee his character. The girl refuses at first; their stations in life are different. She will be, she thinks, in his way. The farmer doubts on the same grounds. Will his daughter be happy? But Philip does not desire to live in this burdened, denaturalised England; his opinions (and they may represent a dream of Clough's) lead him to a freer life, close to Mother Earth, in a new land. Will she come with him, taking a plough, a tool-box, a few books, pictures, and £500 to New Zealand? The tutor thinks he could not do better; the girl is charming, intelligent, a true-hearted woman; both are in love, love based on mutual reverence; and Philip is a hard worker, who will put all his theories to the test in an eager life in a fresh country. So they marry; and Clough, whom the social subject of marriage engaged all his life, airs his views in tender converse between Philip and Elsie, mixed, as is always the case in his work, with a certain high reasonableness which their love idealises.

There is a true love of nature, especially of Highland

scenery, in the poem. Clough loved the mountains. Wales and the Highlands were dear to him. He wandered alone, meditating, among the glens ; it was his great pleasure to have his contemplation broken by nature's sudden shocks of mild surprise, and to weave what he saw into what he thought. His friend, Frank Palgrave, who wrote a gentle, distinguished memoir of him, said that his mind was " haunted like a passion " by the loveliness of poetry and scenery ; that by his " acceptance in the natural landscape, he had inherited a double portion of the spirit of Wordsworth. He loved nature, not only for its earthly sake, but for the divine and the eternal interfused with it." This seems too strongly said, but it is the judgment of a friend. Clough may have loved nature as much as Wordsworth, but he had not Wordsworth's power of expressing his love. His descriptions are ill-composed ; the spiritual passion he felt slightly appears in them. In the *Bothie*, the halting metre mangles the description ; indeed, here, as in the whole of his poetry, the execution lags behind the conception. Art had not thrown her mantle over this man; the language does not enhance or uplift the thought; it rather depresses and lowers it ; and, though we always understand him, which is a blessed gift to us, considering what we suffer from others, we wish that the clearness of the poem had been accompanied by a finer composition and workmanship. Palgrave even goes so far as to say that "one feels a doubt whether in

verse he chose the right vehicle, the truly natural
mode of utterance.'' If that means that Clough would
have perhaps done better to write in prose, I am sure,
though it sounds bold to say so, that the critic is
wrong. I have been surprised by the inferiority of
Clough's prose to his poetry. His prose does not rise
beyond the level of the ordinary review; his soul is
not living in it. On the contrary, in his poetry,
though it does want art, and does not seek for it, there
is a spirit always moving—a delicate, fantastic, changing spirit; a humanity, with a touch here of Ariel,
and there of Puck; a subtle sound and breathing such
as one hears in lonely woods and knows not whence it
came, and a melody of verse which his friend Matthew
Arnold never arrived at; and these qualities prove,
as I think, that prose was not the true vehicle of his
thought, and that poetry was. I cannot conceive that
even the mocking arguments of the Fiend in *Dipsychus*
would be half as well expressed in prose. There is a
short prose dialogue at the end of that poem. To read
it and compare it with the poetry is proof enough of
this. As to the impassioned utterances of the soul in
Dipsychus struggling to hold its immortal birthright
against the tempter who cries: '' Claim the world; it
is at your feet,''—some passages of which are quite
remarkable in spiritual, I do not mean religious, poetry
—they would be impossible in prose. Prose could not
reach their feeling, nor the delicate interlacing of their
thinking. It is in describing the half-tones of the

spirit's life as well as of the life of the heart, in touching with the delicate finger the dim, delicate regrets and hopes and fears which flit before us like moths in twilight, in following with soft and subtle tread the fine spun threads of a web of thought, in recording the to and fro questions and answers of our twofold self within, and passing from one to another, each different as light and darkness—with distinctive power and pleasure in the play—it is in these remote, unsailed-on seas of feeling and contemplation that Clough's best work is done, and very few have done the same kind of work so well. The best of this kind is written in the region of the spirit, but he loved also to write of remote and unvisited regions of the affections, where Destiny, as it were, played her part in bringing together, and in parting, lovers and friends; and the pathetic quiet, the still submission to the parting, and the silent, sorrowful hope that Destiny may again unite those she has divided, are as simply told as they are tenderly felt. Here is a poem which uses a common occurrence—one of his favourite methods—to enshrine a sad, and not too common an experience in life:

QUA CURSUM VENTUS

As ships, becalmed at eve, that lay
  With canvas drooping, side by side,
Two towers of sail at dawn of day
  Are scarce long leagues apart descried;

When fell the night, up sprung the breeze,
    And all the darkling hours they plied,
Nor dreamt but each the self-same seas
    By each was cleaving, side by side:

E'en so—but why the tale reveal
    Of those, whom year by year unchanged,
Brief absence joined anew to feel,
    Astounded, soul from soul estranged?

At dead of night their sails were filled,
    And onward each rejoicing steered—
Ah, neither blame, for neither willed,
    Or wist, what first with dawn appeared!

To veer, how vain! On, onward strain,
    Brave barks! In light, in darkness too,
Through winds and tides one compass guides—
    To that, and your own selves, be true.

But O blithe breeze; and O great seas,
    Though ne'er, that earliest parting past,
On your wide plain they join again,
    Together lead them home at last.

One port, methought, alike they sought,
    One purpose hold where'er they fare,—
O bounding breeze, O rushing seas!
    At last, at last, unite them there.

I may have quoted more of this poetry than is in proportion in a short essay, but I feel that Clough has been too much neglected; and the reading of the whole of this intimate history of a soul, struggling to light in a time of great spiritual trouble, is likely to be of use to many who, in our changed circumstances, are going through a similar kind of trouble, and for similar reasons, which Clough went through.

The trouble did not last all his life. He attained a harbour of peace when he took life by the right handles. The inward storm retreated over the mountains, and at eventide there was a clear quiet. Had he lived, he might have made music for us out of the peace as soft and clear as his earlier music was sad and harsh, and yet, in the harshness, tender. When he was less within his own soul—that ill-fortuned dwelling for us—and moved in and out among men, his hopes for man, his faith in God, his love of natural humanity, revived, and with them came restoration of the calm he had lost. Even in 1849, about the year he left Oxford, where self-contemplation has her natural seat for those who care for it, he had begun to look beyond his inner soul to humanity, and to think that if he did not get on, others might; if truth did not dawn on him, it might have risen on others; that in the world there might be fighters who had won the field, though he had been put to flight; that his strife might have unconsciously helped them to their victory; that the struggle, though so dark and despairing, was not without its good;—and he used concerning this more hopeful thought a noble image in the poem I now quote. What the image suggested became true as the years of the century went on. It is even truer now. We have a closer, more faithful grasp on truth than Clough could have; we have a diviner and a clearer hope. And what the last verse says was realised also, one is glad to think, in his own life.

Say not, the struggle nought availeth,
  The labour and the wounds are vain,
The enemy faints not, nor faileth,
  And as things have been they remain.

If hopes were dupes, fears may be liars;
  It may be, in yon smoke concealed,
Your comrades chase e'en now the fliers,
  And, but for you, possess the field.

For while the tired waves, vainly breaking,
  Seem here no painful inch to gain,
Far back, through creeks and inlets making,
  Comes silent, flooding in, the main.

And not by eastern windows only,
  When daylight comes, comes in the light;
In front, the sun climbs slow, how slowly,
  But westward, look, the land is bright.

These happier, more hopeful words belong to 1849.
He died in 1861. A kinder, gentler, more delicate
soul has rarely lived among us. The Tennyson children used to call him the Angel-child. His fantastical
spirit, his finer thought which would have liked to
have danced on life's common way, the Ariel in him,
would seem to have fitted him for fairyland, were it not
that the sore trouble of the world, and the mystery
of God's way with it, were, in that tempest-tossed
time, too much for him. He was forced to enter the
battle with eyes which saw too many things at the
same time. The confusion might have overwhelmed
him, but the other side of his nature came to his help.
His light-heartedness, it is true, departed, save at
happy intervals, but he never allowed its absence to

injure his association with his friends. And then, to meet his distress, he had great allies within—profound love of and belief in truthfulness, no self-deceit ever touched his soul; a set and honest manliness, a rooted scorn of the temptations and the base things of the world; a great love of freedom and a deep sympathy with men who strove for it; a soul which honoured the ideals and the vital causes of humanity; a love of natural life and a longing to see the divine in it; a fresh delight in the sweetness and beauty of earth and sky and sea; and a humility which touched with its grace all whom he met. His sarcasm, which grew out of the bitterness of his struggle, out of his silent, passionate, tormented inner life, bit only on himself, and spared the world; and when it fell on the world's follies, it was so mixed with happy humour that it half-healed the wound it gave. He had his martyrdom, but he was martyred for us, and the blood of these martyrs is the seed of that invisible Church which rises yearly, beyond all our creeds and scepticisms, into fuller weight and power.

His literary position is rather a solitary one. He has no parents and no children. I seem, however, to trace in some of his religious poems the poetic influence of Keble. What is plain is : that he stands between the absence of art in poetry which marked men like Bailey and Alexander Smith—in their long, uncomposed, intemperate, and self-conscious poems— and a man like Matthew Arnold, who made a study of his art, who was excessively conscious of being an artist, who worked out a theory of his art on the bed of which, like Procrustes, he strained out or shortened his poems ; who rarely, therefore, was spontaneous ; who questioned his emotion till it grew cold instead of yielding to the angels of impulse whose wings brushed his shoulder, and whose celestial colours glimmered before his eyes. Arnold's act was too conscious of itself to be great art, but he forced the lesser poets of his time to study and practise their art with conscientious care. In our own time we have had somewhat too much of the art of poetry pursued as if it were a science. In many ways it has passed into the artificial ; but also since his time no poet has dared to neglect it, dared to write without care and study of what has been done in the past by the great masters. But he did this more by his art-criticism in prose than by art-example in his poetry. He was an artist in poetry more by study than by nature.

Clough wrote side by side with Arnold, but was not influenced by Arnold's demand for artistic excellence. He wrote what came to him with all the carelessness, but without the natural genius of Walter Scott. He did not obey, though he knew, what noble art demanded. Yet, he reached a certain place among the poets. And he owed this, I think, to the steady, informing, temperance-insisting culture of a great university. He was a scholar and had studied and loved the Greek and Roman models of what

high poetry is. He might—since he had no poetic genius, only a gentle and charming talent—have been enslaved by a scientific art, a slavery from which genius saves a man, and have become one of the literary prigs of poetry who prate of art but cannot practise it; who gain the whole world of a clique's applause and lose their soul as poets. He was saved from this by the strength of the passion with which he wrote, by his truthfulness which did not condescend to modify his work and by his love of clearness. But though he had this one artistic merit of clearness, he was, unlike a true artist, indifferent to beauty, to excellence, to delicate choice and arrangement of words and music. He spent no trouble on his work. His poetry, therefore, with all its personal charm, remains in the porch, not in the temple of the Muses.

That was his position, and it was just as well, for the sake of the minor poetry of the time, and for the sake of the poets who were to follow, that Matthew Arnold set himself deliberately to ask what art ought to do in poetry, in what it consisted, what was its right aim, and what were its fitting subjects. His poetry, then, its relation to his time, what he was as a poet, what ideas and what delight were in his poetry, is the matter of the following essay.

MATTHEW ARNOLD

MATTHEW ARNOLD, who is loved as a poet by so many of us, and justly loved; whom we do not read continuously as we read the greater poets, but who suits us so well in certain circumstances of the inner life; who, in them, reflects and strengthens us; whose poetry, always unimitative and underived, rose clear out of his own soul; who stood alone with an ill-hidden scorn for other English poetry in his eyes—was worthy of more acceptance as a poet than he received in his lifetime, and has his own distinct chair in the general assembly and church of the first-born of England.

He was unfortunate in the time in which be began to be a poet, if any man who has a strong will, a clear aim, a joyous temper, and a bold faith, can be called unfortunate at any time. Arnold had a strong will, but it was not strong enough to master within himself the sceptical spirit of his age (which, however useful, is not poetical), or the unpoetic spirit of self-analysis, which, in men of the poetic temperament, naturally accompanies the habit of scepticism. Inquiry is a good thing, but it is prosaic. It is true that Arnold grew into a clear aim, but he was at first too contemptuous of the world in which he lived, and too apart from it to give it that sympathy with its goods, which is one of the needs-be of a poet's power. He had courage, but it was not the courage of faith or of hope; he had little firm faith or hope in God, or in man, or, I may say, in himself. He had insight into the evils, the dulness, the follies, the decay, and death of the time at which he wrote; but he had little insight into its good, into the hopes and ideas which were arising in its darkness, or the life which was collecting itself together under its decay. His temper, therefore, was not joyous, nor was it in sympathy with the temper of the whirling but formative time in which he began, and continued, to write poetry. I do not say he was at daggers drawn with the elements of his world; he did not fight with them in the fierce way in which Byron and Shelley fought with those of their day; but he sat apart from them in a silent, brooding, wrathful, even contemptuous opposition. When he spoke against them in poetry, it was not so much to attack or vilify them, but to glorify the spirit which was the enemy of their turbulence. He did not see the elements of life and of far-off peace in the turbulence, and he never gave it sympathy. At times he could not bear it, and he fled away, like Obermann, into the solitudes of nature to commune with his own soul. It was not a wise thing to do, but he thought it eminently wise; and perhaps it was the only thing he was then capable of doing. In later life he modified his view and felt that he had been too quick to condemn his world. But he was too proud to say that he had then been too blind to be able to divide the good from the evil in the turmoil, or that he had not then seen its good.

His earlier poetry then—since he and his world were so inharmonious—was, with a few exceptions, too much a poetry of opposition. He could not sufficiently disentangle himself from the pressure of his age, and he hated that pressure. Under it his poetry contended, mourned, and analysed. And it suffered, as poetry, from this perturbing element. Had he possessed the animation, like that of birds in spring, which marks the great poets, he would have neutralised this element. But he had it not; he could not lift himself into that bright, magnanimous air, in whose clearness a poet sees, and is able to love and help, the good as well as the evil, the joy as well as the trouble, of humanity.

Arnold sat by the tomb where he thought the true life of England lay dead, and mourned over its disappointed hopes. He did not hear the angel of the nation say, "What is best in England has arisen, and has gone before you into Galilee." It was not his to understand—"Let the dead past bury his own dead." Only at intervals the clouds lifted for him, and he saw through mist the flush of dawn; but he had not heard enough to follow that gleam. He had settled down in these early days into a stoic sadness, as yet unilluminated by humour. It had a certain moral force, a grim tenacity of duty, a stern resolution to fight on, were the heavens themselves to fall ; and this makes his poetry dear and useful to men and women even now who may still be in his condition. But the condition did not develop his art, as it might have been developed in a happier world. Absence of joy limited, it even maimed, his creative energy. It repressed in him the powers of faith and hope. And the want of these powers, without which creativeness is weak, prevented him all his life long from being as complete or as great a poet as either Tennyson or Browning.

Without the full energy of these powers, his poetry suffers in melody, in charm, in unconsciousness, in natural exquisiteness of expression (there is some art-exquisitiveness of expression), in imaginative ardour, except when he was writing mournfully. In the elegy, where his genius was quite at ease, he is excellent. Nothing better has been done in that way for two centuries than the *Scholar Gipsy* and *Thyrsis.* Indeed, all his best verse has this elegiac note, or nearly all. I should like, among a few others, to except the *Strayed Reveller*, into the inconsequence of whose enchanted intoxication I wish he had oftener wandered.

It was a pity, then, he was so unfortunate in the time at which he began and continued to write, for had he not been burdened with its fierce questionings and turmoil, had he found himself in an age of sweetness and light, when life was keen and keen for high things, he had been a greater poet. He might then

have spoken to the universal in man, " seen life
steadily and seen it whole," as he said of Sophocles.
Steadily he did see it, but not as a whole. That he
could not do. He is the poet of a backwater, of a
harbour, of a retired garden, not of the full, swift river,
not of the open sea, not of the king's highway.   He is
so far like Hamlet that he was not able to grasp the
nettle of the world so that it should not sting.   The
sad, philosophic, poetic imagination of Hamlet was
also his, but he had more moral power, a closer grasp
on realities, than Hamlet.   And he had this power
because he clasped stoicism—which Hamlet could not
do—to his breast.

   The power of stoicism lies in the appeal it makes to
the moral endurance of the soul in resolute, unviolent
resistance to the tyranny of outward and inward evil.
It bids us claim our moral individuality as the con-
queror of fate and of the outward world.   The claim is
high, and uplifts the character of the claimer.   " The
fates are hard on me," the stoic says, " but they shall
not subdue my soul.   Things are dark as night, but
there shall be light within.   Pain is here, but it does
not touch my real self.   It is not I that suffer, but the
shell of me.   I do not understand why the world is so
wrong and so troubled, but one thing I do understand,
that *I* need not be wrong or troubled, and that I will
not be.   The furies of the gods may hunt me down,
but my soul remains unconquered, even by the gods."

   There is no doubt of the power which is hid in that

position, and it has transferred itself to a great deal of Arnold's poetry. It makes his language resonant, clear ; his thought, his matter, weighty ; and it brings into his poetry a moral passion which at times reaches a lofty exaltation. Moreover, its spirit proceeds outward from the poetry, as should be the case with any fine art work, into the lives of a number of men and women who are battling with fate, who do not understand why things are so awry, who find no brightness in life, but whose soul passionately answers the stoic's appeal to keep themselves, in spite of fate, unsubdued in right, clear in their own thought, and unconquered by evil. "I am I," they say, "and everything else is indifferent." It is to that class of men and women that Matthew Arnold speaks with power, and will continue to speak, it may be, for centuries to come.

But this power has the weakness which follows on pride. It thinks itself powerful, and in the thought loses some of its strength. If it belong to an artist, it makes him not only intrude it into his art, but also over-conscious of the artist-elements in his nature. Arnold shared more than was fitting in this weakness, and it lowers the excellence of many of his poems. It helps to place him below the poets who are unconscious, in the rush of their creation, of themselves ; who, lost in the glory and grief of what they see, break into song without knowing why or how they sing ; whose work is prideless, for they behold face to face the infinities of that they try to express ; who leave any work they have finished behind them without considering it, and pass on, unconcerned, to new things. Rarely, if ever, does Arnold's poetry make that impression upon us. It has too much pride in itself; it is too self-conscious of its artistic effort, and this lowers its imaginative power; and too conscious of its being moral and teaching morality, and this lowers its influence as art.

Then, again, the stoic position which gave him the power of which I have spoken, made him weak, on another side, as a poet. It often isolated him too much from the mass of men, very few of whom are stoics either in philosophy or practice. A certain touch of contempt for ordinary humanity entered into his work. His appeal was so far to the few, not to the many; to a class, not to the whole; to the self-centred, not to those who lose their self in love. In this way also, he became too self-involved, and, troubled with the restlessness and noise of man, took refuge in the solitudes of his own heart. Owing to this self-involvement—which, though it was modified towards the end of his poetic life, was an integral part of his nature— he was very rarely, if ever, swept by any high passion out of himself altogether. He could not feel, till later in life, the greater waves of human emotion, save once perhaps with regard to England's vast imperial toil, breaking upon his heart. Into the infinite hopes, the infinite possibilities of man—into that country where the greater poets live, his early poetry entered only for moments, and then his sceptical self-consciousness

recalled him from it, and bade him consider how little
the history of his own soul supported the far-off hopes
for man into which he had been momentarily hurried by poetic imagination. The highest, the most
inspiring passion which can thrill a poet was therefore
not his in the first years of his poetry. This self-
involvement and this isolation from the universal hope
of man are the great weakness inherent in stoicism,
and when they belong to an artist, they enfeeble his
art. Only by drinking incessantly at the deep wells of
common humanity does a poet win the power to rejoice
in his creative work, and the love which enables him
to continue it till old˙ age. Arnold, in the end, even
though he did gain much self-forgetful sympathy with
humanity, found his poetic power fail. His vein was
exhausted. He took to prose. But the greater men,
not isolated from but intimately mixed with all men,
if not in life, yet by the imagination of love ; not self-
involved but self-forgetful—love the whole movement
of mankind, even the noise and restlessness of it,
appeal to and win the universal love they give, are
always impassioned by the divinity which they see
everywhere in man, think nothing common or unclean,
and live, eagerly creating to the close.

However, there is something to say on the other
side. Arnold was too human to be the finished stoic.
The stoic demand for duty, for obedience to the eternal
laws of right, was always with him. It often fills his
poetry with an austere beauty. It keeps much of its

dignity, even in poems where, like a serpent round the witch it loves, he winds round and round himself and saves them from failure. So far he was pure stoic.

But the stoic demand of indifference to pain and trouble, of the independence of the soul of all the fates of men—Arnold could not fulfil. His stoicism broke down into sadness for himself and for the world. The pain was too great not to cry out, not to afflict the soul. It sought expression, and it found it in his poetry.

The stoic might think this a weakness, unworthy of a philosopher. But in a poet, this deep emotion of sadness, felt in himself and for himself, but felt far more for the labouring and laden world, is not a weakness but a strength. A poet may have a philosophy, but the proper mistress of his house is poetry. If his philosophy seek to be mistress, poetry shakes her celestial pinions, and flies away. But when Arnold, violating his stoicism expressed his pain with cries, his philosophic weakness became poetic strength. He came back to high natural art and feeling; he did the natural thing; and, indeed, it is one of the paradoxes of life, the truth of which the stoic forgets or does not know, that till pain is expressed, it cannot be fully conquered. The stoic who hides it in his breast or pretends that it does not exist, never conquers it or its evil. But the poet, expressing pain as well as pleasure, becomes at one with all who feel pain. Conscious then of his brotherhood with man, and far more conscious of it than by sympathy only with man's pleasure, strength and passion flow into his poetry. Men feel themselves expressed, sympathised with, and empowered by the noble representation of their trouble, and send back to the poet their gratitude and sympathy, till he, conscious of their affection, is himself uplifted and inspired. Then his poetic power, fed by human love, increases. A fuller emotion, a wider thought, a knowledge of life, deepened by imagination into something far more true than any intellectual philosophy of life can give,—fill his verse with the unsought for, revealing phrases, which seem to express, with strange simplicity, the primary thoughts of Being, to speak from the secret place where the laws of the universe abide.

The stoic tends to be unhuman, but is continually like Arnold self-humanised; and the breakdown of Arnold's stoicism into sadness for the world, and his expression of it, was a progress in him, not a retrogression. The higher levels of song, where joy lives because of the presence of faith and hope, he did not reach; but this mingling in his poetry of stoicism and of the sad crying which denies stoicism, of the spirit which isolates itself from the crowd of men in lonely endurance and the spirit which breaks down from that position into sympathy with men, gives to Arnold's poetry a strange passion, a stimulating inconsistency, an element of attractive surprise—the atmosphere changing from poem to poem and within the same poem—and a solitary distinction. No other poet is built on the same lines. Few have been so self-centred, and none pleases us more whenever we are in that mood in which, dividing ourselves from all mankind, we choose to cherish our own personality, to sit in its silent chambers, to reject the Not-me, to believe that in our own being is the universe, that nothing exists beyond ourselves. To that strange mood, which may have its good if it last a short time, but which has certainly its own naughtiness, Arnold speaks, and has revealed its thoughts in a poetry full of subtle and impassioned charm. It came out of the depths of his nature; but he could not always remain in these solitudes of the soul. He fled from them into sympathy with the sorrow and confusion of men; and the mingling of these two opposites—and they are frequently mingled, even in single poems—gives this uncommon note of distinction to his poetry; a human cry, shrill and piercing as of a soul divided, beating between two moods, and angry with the indecision. The instrument on which he plays is like a violin played by a regretful artist in a lonely room.

These are considerations concerning his poetry which arise out of his character. There are others which arise from the condition of the world when he began to write. It was a time (and I repeat what I have already said in writing of Clough), when the old foundations of the Christian faith were no longer accepted without inquiry. They were dug down to, exposed to the dry light of science, and to a searching investigation. The criticism of German scholars had thrown the gravest doubt on the history of the Gospels; scientific discoveries and historical criticism had invaded the Old Testament; and both had begun to shatter that belief in the inspiration of the Bible on which so much of English religion reposed in peace. The stormy waves these investigations awakened had reached Oxford when Arnold and Clough were students, and they were first disturbed, then dismayed, and finally thrown into a scepticism which profoundly troubled them. Their skies were darkened; the old stars had gone out in the heavens, and no new stars had arisen. They staggered blindly on, and at last fell back on their own souls alone, on the unchallengeable sense of right they felt therein, on the imperative of duty and on resolution to obey it. Nothing else was left. But much more had been; and it was with bitter and ineffable regret that they looked back on the days when they were at peace, when the sun shone upon their way. With what intimate naïveté Clough expressed this trouble, and what cure he found for it, has been already considered. With Clough it was extremely personal. Arnold generalised it far more; he extended its results all over life; it drove him in after days, not now, to consider world-wide questions, the fates and fortunes of the whole race.

Fifteen years after his earliest book of poetry he emerged from the trouble I have described. His long strife ended in a quiet force which looked steadily on the problems of life. He looked with eyes, purged from personal consideration, at the pressure of every kind of trouble on the human family, and asked why it was and to what end. And he never let the question go till he found his solution for it, and gave it to the world in hope that it might help and comfort others. In the process, he reconstituted, for himself, the theology of his youth. And then, feeling, as he did, that in faith in God, in worship, in a right and graceful spirit of love, and in righteousness of conduct, was the true foundation of life, he devoted himself, in prose, to clear away from religion those forms of it which violated intellectual or moral truth, and to establish what was eternal in it, beyond controversy, and fitted for God to be, and for man to believe and love. With that, into which he passed from poetry, we have nothing to do here. What we are in contact with now is his early religious trouble, and its distress breathes through all his youthful poetry.

Again—and this belongs to his personal feeling against mob turbulence and chattering theories—Oxford, when he was there, was filled with the noise of controversy between the High Churchmen and their opponents. Both were intolerant one of another, and the battle raged with confused tumult, not only between these two hot-headed parties, but also between both of them united against the Neologians, as the critical school was then called. Clough, greatly disturbed by the loss of his faith, was not much disturbed

by the noise of the contest in which he lost it. He
rather liked the smoke and the roar of fighting; the
revolutionary atmosphere he breathed with pleasure.
But Arnold was of another temper. He hated noise,
quarrel, confusion ; he loved tranquillity, tolerance,
clearness, plainness, moderation, ordered thought,
and passions brought under control, especially those
passions which belong to theological contests of the
intellect. He had much ado to keep down his natural
abhorrence of this tumultuous shouting about things
which even then seemed to him to have nothing to do
with the weightier matters of the Law or the Gospel.
" It is a sorrowful time," he might have said, " to live
in ; the outward noise about things indifferent doubles
my inward trouble."

Then again, the year before he published his first
volume of poems, the whole continent was disquieted,
and even England shared in that disquiet. France,
Italy, Germany, Austria broke into revolution ; the
Chartist movement threatened revolution in England.
The accredited order which in 1815 had restored so
many of the evils the French Revolution had shaken,
was again (to leave out 1830) broken into by popular
fury, and with a confusion of thought and an ignorance
of what was to replace the old, which jarred on everything which Arnold thought wise and practical.
Clough liked it ; he wrote rejoicingly from Paris, with
whose revolution he lived ; he stayed at Rome when
the people set up a republic and fought the French.

But Arnold had no belief in the popular cries, and he
hated the disturbance and the noise. Out of these, he
thought, no salvation comes. And weariness of the turmoil fell upon him, and desire that he had been born at
another and a quieter time. By this also his personal
sadness was deepened, and it drove him into a longing
for solitude and calm outside the tortured world.

We can trace these impressions all through his first
three volumes of poems; and we can read what was
his temper with regard to revolutionary Europe in
the two sonnets addressed to Clough, entitled *To a
Republican Friend.* The first says how far he agrees
with his friend, and it would not have been thought
worth much by the enthusiasm of Clough. The second says where he parts from his friend; and it is full
of his suppressed anger with, and disbelief in, the
revolutionary movement. More impressive than these,
more personal, expressing that which was deepest in
him at this time, that which he most desired—and
more important for our knowledge of him, because he
chose it as a preface to his third volume, published
three years after his first—is the sonnet with which
the volume of 1849 opens :—

> One lesson, Nature, let me learn of thee,
> One lesson which in every wind is blown,
> One lesson of two duties kept at one,
> Though the loud world proclaim their enmity—
> Of toil unsevered from tranquillity!

To work with Nature's constancy, but without
turbulent passion ; like her sleepless ministers " Their

glorious tasks in silence perfecting." To stand apart from fierce explosions like the Revolution was his desire, but he forgot that Nature sometimes works by explosions, relieving by them her over-burdened breast, and that revolutions are in a strict analogy with her volcanic outbursts. Yet Arnold would have disliked Nature's catastrophes and blamed her for them. His work was to be, he hoped, done with patience, trusting his own soul, choosing one clear aim, and confident that in following it sincerely he would best assist the world. It was for that he praised the Duke of Wellington. He had a vision, Arnold thought, of the general law, saw what he could and could not do, and followed the one thing he saw. That made, among all the fret and foam of Europe acting without sight of a clear goal, the splendour of his place in history. But to fulfil this resolve clearness of vision was the great need, that clearness which all his life was Arnold's deep desire. In a noble sonnet, *To a Friend*, he asked who are they who support his mind in these bad days? They are Homer, whose clear soul, though his eyes were blind, saw man and life so well; and, for the inner strength of the soul, Epictetus, whose friendship he had lately won; and, for the just and temperate view of life, Sophocles—

> Whose even-balanced soul,
> From first youth tested up to extreme old age,
> Business could not make dull, nor passion wild;
> Who saw life steadily, and saw it whole.

all Greeks; for Arnold bent his poetic effort to that
Hellenic spirit which, by temperance and the clearness
ensuing from it, and by the desire to make the world
better, made the artist-work of the Greeks so nearly
perfect.

But to return to the sonnet on Nature (*Quiet Work*).
It is plain that its view of Nature is quite different
from that of the poets who preceded Arnold. It contains that scientific conception of Nature, already far
more than half embodied, which declared that all its
developments could be correlated under one energy
and were forms of that energy, ourselves included.
Belief in this theory made a mighty change in all
poetry written by men who were sufficiently educated
to realise it, and it influenced a good deal of Arnold's
poetry from the beginning to the end. Not altogether;
he slipped out of the theory where it pleased him. At
one point, even now (and this is illustrated in another
sonnet—*In Harmony with Nature*), he rebelled against
it, at the point where it subjected man, as only a part
of Nature, to its law. He was willing to be taught
by the course of Nature. He was not willing to be
mingled up with her.

> Know, man hath all that Nature hath, but more,
> And in that *more* lie all his hopes of good.

We are different from her; we move on in a straight
line, he might have said, Nature goes round and
round. "We begin," he did say, "where Nature
ends"; and he recurs elsewhere to the same thought.

These are some of the cries of his first poems, when he was but twenty-seven. It is plain, then, that the racking trouble of man's disobedience to law, his necessary restlessness, and the confused noise that attended it—in contrast with Nature's obedience, tranquillity, and steady toil—were heavily pressed on Arnold by the circumstances of his time. He found no solution of the problem now, none in reasoning, none in warring religions and philosophies. "I will listen no more to them," he thought; "I will fall back on my own soul; know the worst and endure it austerely, holding fast to the power of righteousness within. Of that I may be sure. The will is free, the seeds of Godlike power are in us. Within, we may be what we will."

This did not solve the question, but it gave a noble basis for life, and the worry of the question might be laid by. What we can, we will secure. Then wait, and as the world goes on the question may solve itself. At least, if the solution come, those who wait quietly in patient righteousness obeying law, will be capable of seeing it. Even if we are mixed up with a blind Nature, with matter alone, have ourselves no divine origin, and no end beyond the elements, there is that in us which is ready for either fate, and which is above both, and can choose how to meet the one or the other. There is a remarkable poem—*In Ultrumque Paratus*—which, on a higher poetic level than most of the other poems in this first volume, puts this view before us.

It begins by supposing that the universe has its course
in God's thoughts—

> If in the silent mind of One all pure,
>   At first imagined lay
> The sacred world ; and by procession sure
> From those still deeps, in form and colour drest,
> Seasons alternating, and night and day,
> The long-mused thought to north, south, east, and west
>   Took then its all-seen way.

If this be true, and thou, man, awaking to the consciousness that the world of Nature is thus caused
of God, wishest to know the whole of life and thine
own life in it, oh, beware.   Only by pure and solitary
thought thou shalt attain, if thou canst attain ; and
the search will sever thee from the pleasant human
world into a painful solitude.   The verse in which
Arnold tells this is so prophetic in its excellence of
his best poetry, so full of his distinctive note, that I
quote it :—

> Thin, thin the pleasant human noises grow ;
>   And faint the city gleams ;
> Rare the lone pastoral huts—marvel not thou !
> The solemn peaks but to the stars are known,
> But to the stars, and the cold lunar beams ;
> Alone the sun arises, and alone
>   Spring the great streams.

But if this be not true, and Nature has never known a
divine birth, and thou, man, alone wakest to consciousness of a great difference between thyself and Nature—
thou, the last and radiant birth of earth's obscure working—oh, beware of pride.   Think that thou too only

seemest; art, like the rest, a dream. Yet, since thou canst think *that*, since thou mayst control thy pride, thou standest clear of Nature.

So, once he saw the problem of human life. Then, tossed as he was from thought to thought in those days when evil things held sway, he recurred, in another sphere of thought, to his view of the necessity for the steady pursuit of one aim, clearly conceived in the soul. Here, he mingled it up with one of the common angers of men who suffer and know no reason for their pain—an anger which no doubt, had stirred in him at intervals. He took the story of Mycerinus, and treated it with a brief nobility of imaginative and sympathetic thought which was rare in so young a poet. The king's father had been unjust, cruel, a wicked king. He had lived long and happily. The son had believed in justice, kindness, good government, and practised them; yet the gods condemned him to die in six years. He had governed himself, sacrificed himself, and this was his reward for giving up the joy of life. "Then have I cleansed my heart in vain." There is then no justice, no morality in the gods. Or they are themselves slaves of a necessity beyond them, or careless, in their leisured pleasure, of mankind. I scorn them; and, men of Egypt, if you wish to please them, do wrong, indulge in injustice, be like my father, then they will give you length of days. For me, I will give my six years to revel, to youthful joys, and so farewell.

Nor does Arnold, in that passing mood, altogether

blame him. At least, the king knew his aim and followed it. It is curious to read the lines in which
Arnold expresses this. He would not have approved
the life, but he approved—since the king had deliberately chosen that life—the firmness and clearness of his
choice, the settled purpose of his soul—

> he, within,
> Took measure of his soul, and knew its strength,
> And by that silent knowledge, day by day,
> Was calmed, ennobled, comforted, sustained.

But this was the only point at which he approved
the king's life of pleasure. In *The New Sirens*, which
fine as it is in parts is feeble as a whole, he seems
to express, with obscure length, the gloom, sati-
ety, and sorrow of the soul in which mere pleasure ends, the reckless following of impulse after
impulse.

Another poem of far higher quality, called *The
Voice*, dwells, in the two last verses, on the same
thought with a noble brevity and imagination. It
records an hour when the ancient cry of youth to fulfil
all joy came to him out of a forgotten time, came
to him when his heart had been long sobered by
dreary and doubtful thought, by heavy circumstance.
Sweet and far, in strange contrast with his present
trouble, like a wanderer from the world's extremity,
it asked again to be listened to. And his answer is
given in lovely poetry, in passionate revelation of
himself:—

In vain, all, all in vain,
They beat upon my ear again,
Those melancholy tones so sweet and still.
Those lute-like tones which in far distant years,
  Did steal into mine ear—
Blew such a thrilling summons to my will,
  Yet could not shake it ;
Made my tost heart its very life-blood spill, *
  Yet could not break it.

In these many ways he turned the problem of life. One would think that among them there would be, brought up as he had been, a cry for freedom and salvation, an appeal to the Power who is with us in the night. Once at least, and suddenly as it seems, Arnold, in the mouth of Stagirius, a young monk to whom St. Chrysostom addressed three books, made this cry. We cannot miss the personal passion in these verses, nor fail to feel that they are the outburst of long-endured distress which having tried many ways of escape in vain, fled at last to the fatherhood of God. "I do not know Thee clearly," they seem to say, " but there is that within me which bids me take my chance with Thee."

Finally, to close the eventful history of this volume, there is the last poem, entitled *Resignation*. It represents that to which the struggle had brought him, what he thought the wisest manner of life, the groove in which he desired to move onwards.

* *Note*.—In the first edition this line is better said :
  Drained all the life my full heart had to spill.

He wished it, but in vain. But it never ceased to be one of the moods of life in which he desired to live at intervals. Yet it was well that it could not be a continuous desire. Resignation is fitting for age, for the man who has fought in the battles of the world for fifty years, but not well for the young who go forth to battle. And, in spite of Arnold's wish for patient peace, he had the just spirit of impatience with the evil ideas which were oppressing the world in which he lived. When he became a man, he was always a fighter. Yet those who fight the most, most long at times for the rest of resignation. And this poem is his record of that desire, even in youth, as many other poems record its recurrence in the years that were to come.

The subject is worthy of poetry, and Arnold has made it worthier by the fine composition of the poem, and especially by the imaginative fusion in it of the mental and natural scenery. The illustrations, the episode of the gipsies, the phantom grace of Fausta, develop and enhance the main thought. The verse is flowing, and the scenery of that walk between Wythburn and Rosthwaite which many know so well is drawn with its own distinctive touch and feeling. We see, as we read, that it made on him a new impression on this day. But we also feel, that in and through the new impression, the old impression of the years before is mingled, bringing with it another tenderness and light,—and this is a delightful piece of fine art.

Ten years before, as a boy of seventeen, he had taken the same walk with Fausta. What ten years had done we read in these verses; and the many changes and wanderings of his soul during this decade of life are well represented by the windings in the poem of various thoughts within the unity of its main thought. The lines I quoted are full of the soul of Arnold at twenty-seven. Their quiet, self-controlled, and solitary note, with their love of peace and obedience, and of union not with quarrelsome particulars but with the still movement of the general life to an ordered and luminous end, is no unfitting close to the struggle I have endeavoured to describe. "Blame not," he cries, "Fausta, the man who has seen into life, and who has attained tranquillity, but for thyself "—

> Rather thyself for some aim pray
> Nobler than this, to fill the day ;
> Rather that heart, which burns in thee,
> Ask, not to amuse, but to set free ;
> Be passionate hopes not ill resign'd
> For quiet, and a fearless mind.
> And though fate grudge to thee and me
> The poet's rapt security,
> Yet they, believe me, who await
> No gifts from chance, have conquer'd fate.
> They, winning room to see and hear,
> And to men's business not too near,
> Through clouds of individual strife
> Draw homeward to the general life.
> Like leaves by suns not yet uncurl'd ;
> To the wise, foolish ; to the world,
> Weak ;—yet not weak, I might reply,
> Not foolish, Fausta, in His eye,

> To whom each moment in its race,
> Crowd as we will its neutral space,
> Is but a quiet watershed
> Whence, equally, the seas of life and death are fed.

The second volume of Matthew Arnold's poems was published in 1852, and its title was *Empedocles on Ætna, and other Poems, by A*. Empedocles, a Greek of Sicily, one of the last of the religious philosophers, is supposed by Arnold—in a preface to an after-edition of the poem—"to have lived on into a time when the habits of Greek thought and feeling had begun to change, character to dwindle, the influence of the sophists to prevail. Into the feelings of a man so situated there entered much we are accustomed to consider as exclusively modern : the calm, the cheerfulness, the disinterested objectivity of the genius of the earlier Greek have disappeared ; the dialogue of the mind with itself has commenced ; modern problems have presented themselves ; we hear already the doubts, we witness the discouragement of Hamlet and of Faust."

This is a sufficient description of the poem, and suggests its motive. It enabled Arnold to express, on the lips of Empedocles, the problems which confronted him in his own time, to tell with a certain passion how he felt concerning them, to relieve his heart by giving words to the profound discouragement and confusion into which they put his soul, and to suggest what means of escape from their tyranny occurred to him. Empedocles escapes by flinging himself into the crater of Ætna. Had Arnold been a Greek he might, perhaps, have shuffled off his trouble in the same easy fashion. When a man is brave, is sick of mankind, and recognises no duty to God, suicide is almost too facile a business.

The representation of a man beset by such feelings and pains, if he is stern enough with himself to represent them truly, cannot be without interest, or even without passion; but their representation, if too elaborate, becomes wearisome. And Empedocles goes over his troubles at such a severe length that it is fortunate he is alone save with Pausanias, who is only a shadow. Callicles would have tired of him. Moreover, he sings them in so lumbering a metre that we begin to conjecture that the entangled melancholy of his mind had unconsciously influenced his ear, and dulled it out of tune. These were the real reasons, I think, why the poem displeased its writer. But they were not the reasons he gave for leaving it out in the volume issued in 1853, and issued, for the first time, under his own name. He left it out, he said, because, though the representation was interesting, it did not inspirit and rejoice the reader, and poetry was bound not only to add to the knowledge of men, but also to add to their happiness.

"The Muses," said Hesiod, "were born to be a forgetfulness of evils, and a truce from cares." This happiness may be felt in the representation of the most tragic, even tortured, situations, provided they are full of the permanent, noble, and primary passions of human nature, passing onwards into magnanimous action, whether of endurance of, or of resistance to, human or divine oppression—into action which awakens high passion and action in others. Such action, represented in poetic form, kindles high pleasure in us, however painful the situation.

In *Empedocles* there is no such action. A " continuous state of mental distress was prolonged in it"; the atmosphere was morbid, and the unhappiness monotonous. It was not then a fit subject of poetry and Arnold excluded the poem from his next book.

This is a very grand reason for so simple a matter as the poem of *Empedocles on Ætna*, and indeed it might lay itself open to some slight ridicule. It is an example of that overweening self-consciousness of himself as an artist which sometimes deprived his poetry of naturalness and of spontaneity. The real reason was that Empedocles bored him, and no wonder; and that Arnold, under the mask of Empedocles, exposing all his present woes, confusions and wanderings of thought, his hatreds and scorns of his time, had begun to bore himself. Again, the Empedocles of the poem is quite petulant with the Universe, and especially with that state of man which, having vast desires and conceiving noble ideals, is disenabled by the gods, and apparently on purpose, to realise them. It may be that this petulance, when Arnold came afterwards to read of it, displeased his proud taste: it certainly did not fit in with his stoicism.

Two years after he wrote *Empedocles*, in 1853, he was in a more healthy state of mind. He wrote about the problems of life and their trouble, but he wrote about them in short lyrics, some of which ended with hope, even presaged joy. Later on, many years later, when his foot was on firmer ground, and some sunlight in his sky, he restored *Empedocles* to its place in his collected work, at the instance of Robert Browning. When he left it out, his soul was too near the shipwreck of Empedocles to relish its representation. He was tossed to and fro on the deep, close to the rocks. But when he had escaped, it was not unpleasant to see the picture he had made of old of the storm and the labouring ship, and to hang it up as a votive tablet in a shrine of the gods of the sea.

Again, Empedocles accuses, and with all the weakness of his type, the hopeless confusion to which the gods have brought the soul of man; and then, remembering his philosophy, scoffs at himself and all the complainers whom the course of nature and their own thought have enslaved. At last, in a transient excitement, having persuaded himself that he is free,—and before the persuasion fails him, and lest it should—he finishes his worry by the medicine of the volcano. Arnold did not. He fought his way through to no petulant conclusion, to no excited, hurried surrender of the battle. In 1867, when after an interval of fifteen

years, he republished *Empedocles on Ætna*, he had
grown into a wiser but sorrowful calm. It was not
the calm of the stoic, but of one who, realising with
passion the sorrow of humanity yet looked forward
with hope, even at times with a chastened joy, to its
redemption. Life at least was worth the living; the
battle was to be without despair. It pleased him then,
now that his feet were set on a rock and his goings
ordered, to republish this picture of his youth and its
disordered wavering, to realise afresh how much he
had gained. Moreover, it pleased the artist in him to
feel through all the wailing of the poem, the freshness
of youth in it, its intensity and the pleasure of its pain.

Even when it was written, the poem was not all
melancholy or monotonous. Callicles lives in it as
well as Empedocles—Callicles, the lyrist and the poet,
young and exulting in his youth, inspired by the
beauty of Nature and the romantic stories of Greece,
loving women and song, feasting and the dance—
incarnate joy—yet tender of heart, wise through reverence of wisdom, and with that deep common sense
which born of love and imagination is one of the first
attributes of genius. When Arnold created him he
was half way to a higher region of thought, feeling,
and action than he could ever have attained by stoicism on the one hand, or by wailing and indignation on
the other. But he did not create him excellently. It
is a thing half done—half flesh and blood, half marble,
like the poor prince in the *Arabian Nights*. Callicles

is but a voice, not a living young man ; the voice only of the half-reaction in Arnold's mind towards life and untroubled joy. Callicles sings of what he sees ; of the pleasant outside of things, of the loveliness of Nature, and of the natural life of men and animals, but the descriptions are a little too literary. He sings, and better, of the beautiful legends of Greece, of Cadmus and Harmonia, of Apollo and Marsvas, of the Ætnean giant, of the singing of the Muses, with youthful sentiment and artist charm ; and Arnold thought these songs and the temper of them so good, that when he repressed the poem, he extracted and published some of them as separate lyrics. Indeed, these two regions, the beauty of the common world and the great stories, were the homes where Arnold found some comfort in his trouble, some hours of refreshment. They saved him from himself. In the physical peace of the one, and in the moral peace he was conscious of in the other, he attained so much of the resemblance of rest that he believed in its possibility. When he speaks of natural beauty, he loses his self-inquiring self. When he tells a fair or noble tale, the intellectual snake which was gnawing at his entrails goes to sleep, and the frigid weight of his stoicism was lifted off. He forgot himself—that blessed remedy for all the afflictions of the world. In the *Strayed Reveller*, the *Forsaken Merman*, the *King at Bokhara*, in *Sohrab and Rustum*, *Balder Dead*, *Tristram and Iseult*, the *Church at Brou*, the weary, self-inquiring, self-controlling Arnold does not appear. We are freed from him, and he is freed from himself.

This is the noble power which the great stories of the world have upon us, this, their healing and exalting good. They release the soul from its own despotism. They hush the heart into self-forgetfulness. They fill our being with sorrow and with joy which are not our own. And it was well for Arnold that he felt their power. It was one of the enabling elements in his battle towards peace and light. It took him away not only from the turmoil in his own soul, but also from the turmoil without, the evil of which he grossly exaggerated. He was fortunate in that ; far more fortunate than the great number of persons whose souls, even now after so many years, are sensitive to, and whose reason is troubled by, the bitter problems of life which afflicted him. They have no means of expression ; they fight alone and in silence the grief that would, but cannot speak. Arnold at least had the gift of expression, and he rid himself by his art of a great deal of his distress. No sooner did some aspect of the human question rise threateningly before him, and mock him, than he put it into a poem. It is really curious how many of the short lyrics in this second volume are dedicated to fragments of that problem. One would think he would, after *Empedocles*, have been a little anxious to throw off the yoke of inquiry, a little tired of walking up and down the alleys of yew within his soul ; but it is not so. He had an undying interest in himself as an epitome of man.

I will touch on a few of them. One, entitled *Human Life*, glances, in spite of its important title, at only one experience of life. We would fain steer our ship as we please, and not by the inward law. But we cannot live, we are compelled not to live, by chance impulse. As the ship leaves behind it the waves it divides, so we leave behind the joys not designed for us, the friends not destined to be ours. Unknown powers direct our course as they will, not as we will. This is only one small fragment of the riddle of human life. Its title is a misnomer.

Then he asks himself in a well-written sonnet : Shall I be glad, when I am growing old, that the heats of youth are left behind and I at peace? No, I shall wish its agitations, fire, and desire back again, and sigh that nothing is left to youth and age save discontent. This is a common human cry, but it belongs only to one type of men, and even they do not feel its passion, save at intervals. Browning and Tennyson would not have come to that conclusion, nor the lovers of mankind. It also is only a fragment of the problem.

In *Self-Deception* we have another fragment. We think we have great powers, and expect to realise their ends. We may have had them in an antenatal world, and been as eager then to use them towards their perfection as we are now. But the Great Power who gave us them, imposed on us a rigid law, and the

law baffled us.   And when He sent us here He left us
only the stress of them, and yet their full desires.   And
we know we shall never win their fulfilment.   Yet,
there *is* a power which rules us, and there is a chance
in that, the vaguest of chances, but a chance.   This is
the Empedocles' argument over again, and it is interesting to contrast it with Browning's view of the same
aspect of the problem.   Browning, looking out of himself with love upon humanity, saw far and clear the
certain end which the inabilities of life suggested, and
to which they led.   Arnold, loving the personalities of
his own soul more than man, saw at this time of his life
only one dim chance for man.   Gross is the film which
self-consideration draws over the eyes of the spirit.

Take another, *Lines at a Death Bed.*   The face of
the dead is calm.   The settled loveliness of rest is there.
Is this the end of life ? this the attainment of its desire ?
Is youth so fresh and bright because of the hope of rest
in death ?   No, youth desires light and joy, life and
passion, here, on this side of death—

> Calm 's not life's crown, though calm is well.
> 'T is all perhaps that man requires,
> But 't is not what our youth desires.

This, too, is but a fragment of the problem, enough for
a lyric, and an unfinished one.

Take another—take *Courage.*   Our business here is
to tame the will to Nature's law.   Renounce, or endure, keeping the soul free from fear or shame.   That
is his stoicism ; but there is room, Arnold thought, for

another side of the question ; he could not altogether
fix his thought into the stoic limits. Now, in these
bad times, he cries, when fate and circumstance are
strong, praise the strong for their defiant courage, even
though they do not live under the law of right—and
here he recurs to the motive of *Mycerinus*—praise the
younger Cato, praise Byron, for their dauntlessness.
For what we want now is force of soul, even in the
things which in themselves are blameable. Our bane
is faltering, indecision. We may see clear, but can we
act forcibly ? That, too, is only a fragment of the
problem of life, a little lyric cry.

Then there is the poem of *Self-Dependence*—a piece of
modern stoicism. I say modern because the Nature
Arnold dwells on—Nature as the revealer of law moving in the universe in quietude, and teaching us obedience and its calm—is a thought the ancients only
conjectured. They had no knowledge of the constancy
of energy. The close applies to himself the teaching of
Nature.

> O air-born voice ! long since, severely clear
> A cry like thine in mine own heart I hear :
> " Resolve to be thyself ; and know that he,
> Who finds himself, loses his misery."

It is a thought which grows out of the stoic position,
out of that weary reference to the soul alone as the
source of strength, that pride engendering self-consideration, which, isolating a man, enfeebles love, and,
if the gods do not interfere, slays it altogether.   Who

finds himself loses misery ! Nay, I answer, gains it. Who loses himself, he alone loses misery, and it is the only way to lose it. That, too, is the poem of a fragment of the problem.

Kensington Gardens, a lovelier poem, has the same thought at its root. He contrasts the peace of the quiet meadows, trees, and water with the impious and raving uproar of men, the sound of which he vaguely hears. Here is quietude, always new ; the sheep, the birds, the flowers, the children sleep. Calm soul of all things, he cries, give me—

> The will to neither strive nor cry,
> The power to feel with others give;
> Calm, calm me more ; nor let me die
> Before I have begun to live.

Peace! Like Dante, but without his power, Arnold sought for peace. Could he now have loved more, could he have more fulfilled his prayer to feel with others more than with himself, could he have not had that foolish desire to know himself—the utmost thing the Pagan reached—he would soon have gained it. " Know thyself," said Socrates, and man, because this dictum flattered his pride, thought it the ultimate wisdom. It is rather the ultimate foolishness. The true thing to say is this—" Know Nature, man, and God ; get outside of thyself into their glory and beauty. Only then, thou canst begin to justly know thyself ; only then, at union through love with all that is without thee, lost in joy, beyond self-disturbance, self-inquiry, canst thou, in humility, attain to peace."

Then there is another poem—*The Buried Life*—it too, touches only one aspect, one fragment of the problem of life. The poem, full of imaginative beauty, has also its deep interest; it touches what we imagine in the mysticism of the heart of the subconscious stream of our being the unexplored tracts of our nature, the revealing of which we wait for so long and so vainly. Even two lovers, Arnold thought, cannot tell each other what they are. They would if they could, but their buried life flows on, unseen, unknown. Fate, knowing how we are led astray by the apparent and confused, has ordained it thus, in order that our truer life should not be mastered by the apparent; but live within itself, independent of the world. We are beset with longing to find our actual self. In vain we strive; yet could we find it, we should be at rest. Only at times, fallings from us, vanishings, airs, floating echoes, "as from an infinite distant land," reveal or seem to reveal the heart of the life which beats within :—

A bolt is shot back somewhere in our breast,
And a lost pulse of feeling stirs again.
The eye sinks inward, and the heart lies plain,
And what we mean, we say, and what we would, we know.
A man becomes aware of his life's flow;
And hears its winding murmur; and he sees
The meadows where he glides, the sun, the breeze.
    And there arrives a lull in the hot race
      Wherein he doth for ever chase
    That flying and elusive shadow, rest.

And then he thinks he knows
The hills where his life rose,
And the sea where it goes."

Another aspect of the same thought is to be found
in the poem—*Palladium*, where the soul, as far apart
from our outward life as the Palladium was from the
battle round Troy, is pictured on its lonely height.
When it fails we die, while it lives, we cannot wholly
be a victim of the world.

The best of all these battling, fragmentary poems is
A Summer Night. Its composition is good, its arrangement clear, its thoughts well-shaped. It does
not wander like the rest. It is passionate throughout,
and it soars to a climax from which it descends in
peace, like a still sunset after storm. The natural description with which it begins is done with a delicate
purity of touch. It represents Arnold's temper at the
point where it was changing from unmixed sadness
and a somewhat fierce contempt of the world, into a
better and wiser mind, into a greater harmony with
mankind, into pity for men with a touch of love
in the pity; into some hope, some faith for them, and
therefore into some hope and faith in God.

There are yet other poems which illustrate this
story of a soul in those troubled years, but enough has
been said of these fragments. The essence of the history is concentrated in the *Stanzas in Memory of the
Author of Obermann.* This poem places Arnold as he
was in 1852. Fifteen years later his position was not

the same; and he records the change in another poem
in 1867, addressed to the same person. *Obermann
once more.* The similar titles make it plain that he
intended to reveal the change that had passed over the
temper in which he viewed the world.

Obermann, as Arnold conceived him in 1852, had
fled from the world, in which, like Arnold, he moved
a stranger, to find what peace he could in the pastoral
life of Switzerland, and in a chalet on the lower hills,
whence he saw the solemn snows of the high peaks
rise in ethereal purity and calm. Nature, in her quiet
order, might heal his heart ; and though Obermann's
pain did not leave him, yet he saw his way to as much
peace as he could find ; and for that threw everything
else away. And that was some attainment. Only
two others, Arnold thought, had been as bold, as
self-certain in the whole of Europe—Wordsworth and
Goethe ; and Wordsworth saw only half of human life,
and Goethe's clear and lonely soul few of the sons of
men could follow. But our time, he says to Obermann,
is worse than theirs—a hopeless tangle—and we turn
for help to the immovable composure of thy icy despair.
Thou hast renounced the world and thy life in it ; at
least thou hast the peace of renunciation, and the
majestic pleasures which Nature brings. Half my
soul I leave with thee and Nature, but the other half
Fate takes, and forces it to abide in the world. May I
live there, like thee, unsoiled by wrong, unspotted by
the world, and bear the pain of these miserable days.

Rigorous is the line on which the unknown power drives us ; we cannot

> when we will enjoy ;
> Nor when we will, resign.

That is his position in 1852. Many years passed by, and he remembers at the same place, where Glion looks down on Chillon and the lake, Obermann once more, and slips, in a moment of thought, back to his old desire to be in solitude and calm with him, out of the warfare he has waged so long. He recalls the infinite desire of his youth—that he and man might reach harmonious peace in union with the universal order.

And as he mused night came down, and Obermann stood beside him—

> And is it thou, he cried, so long
> Held by the world which we
> Loved not, who turnest from the throng
> Back to thy youth and me?

Dost thou turn *now* to me, now when the world is being new born, when hopes and hearts are blossoming? The history of the world is the history of the Rise and Fall of Ideas. We lived, of old, when one set of ideas was falling into fragments. In the turmoil and confusion we could find no sure aim for life. We despaired and fled from the world. But now, is not the Power at hand which will reanimate humanity? I died wrapped in gloom, but thou, who sought me of old, do not thou despair. The

sun is risen on the earth. The present I despaired
of held in it resurrection power. But thou—

> though to the world's new hour
> Thou come with aspect marr'd,
> Shorn of the joy, the bloom, the power,
> Which best befits its bard—
>
> Though more than half thy years be past,
> And spent thy youthful prime ;
> Though, round thy firmer manhood cast,
> Hang weeds of our sad time
>
> Whereof thy youth felt all the spell,
> And traversed all the shade—
> Though late, though dimm'd, though weak, yet tell
> Hope to a world new made !
>
> Help it to fill that deep desire,
> The want that rack'd our brain,
> Consumed our soul with thirst like fire,
> Immedicable pain ;
>
> Which to the wilderness drove out
> Our life, to Alpine snow,
> And palsied all our word with doubt,
> And all our work with woe—
>
> What still of strength is left, employ
> This end to help attain :
> *One common wave of thought and joy*
> *Lifting mankind again.*
>
> The vision ended. I awoke
> As out of sleep, and no
> Voice moved ;—only the torrent broke
> The silence, far below.
>
> .   .   .   .
>
> And glorious there, without a sound,
> Across the glimmering lake,
> High in the Valais-depth profound,
> I saw the morning break."

This is a higher strain, but the redemption was not yet fully attained. There were still hours of deep depression, following on noble vision. Men recover from illness of the soul with relapses. The tide ebbs before it floods the strand. Oscillation is half of our convalescence. And in the same book—*New Poems*—in which these second *Stanzas to Obermann* appear, are the *Stanzas from the Grande Chartreuse*, 1867. The high emotion and thought of a heart, worn more by sorrow for the world than by its own pain, fills these verses to the brim. The wisdom of joy is not in them, but the wisdom of pain is. Yet, they look forward; waiting for light with weary eyes, with a faint hope which has at least slain despair. Meanwhile, he cries, while we wait and hope, allow us our tears, our solitude, our absence from the gayer world. Let its bright procession pass. Leave us to our monastic peace.

Another poem, *Dover Beach*—one of the finest he ever wrote—is also a poem of relapse into depression, but so profoundly felt that, both in thought and expression, it rises into the higher regions of poetry. He hears the "grating roar of pebbles which the wave sucks back" with the ebb, and the return of the waves that bring

> The eternal note of sadness in.
> Sophocles long ago
> Heard it on the Ægean, and it brought
> Into his mind the turbid ebb and flow
> Of human misery.

He hears in it, as in the silence he lives over again
the religious tempest he had suffered—the retreat of
the ancient faith in unconquerable sadness, and in the
sadness the whole world is dark. And so great is the
darkness that while he lives in it he can do no good to
the world, and none to himself.

> Ah, love, let us be true
> To one another! for the world, which seems
> To lie before us like a land of dreams,
> So various, so beautiful, so new,
> Hath really neither joy, nor love, nor light,
> Nor certitude, nor peace, nor help for pain;
> And we are here as on a darkling plain
> Swept with confused alarms of struggle and fight,
> Where ignorant armies clash by night.

This temper, now in 1867, was not a constant one.
Hope for the world and for himself had grown almost
into flower within him; and he attained through
hopefulness a new strength, even some rest. And
then, having found a haven where he could anchor,
and looking out on the storm, but not of the storm, he
used his quiet to give warning and counsel to the new
and excited world.

The present, he thought, may be full of vigour and
of a dancing life; but when its noise is loudest, retreat
for a time; remember the past and its quiet beauty.
Do not lose its power; and his *Bacchanalia, or the
New Age*, contrasts the dance of Manads, breaking in
on the shepherd's still enjoyment of the hush of Nature, with the wild orgie of the New Age, scattering

the charm, the dignity, and the peace of the past. "Rejoice in this," the new men cry, as the shepherd was bid to rejoice in the stormy riot of the Bacchanals. "Ah," says the poet, "the shepherd thought the hush and quiet beautiful, and I feel the past while I live in the present. Lovely was the silence, the hush of the world, when but a few were great, and men loved them ; when what was excellence was known."

And *Progress*, another poem of warning, tells the new world (which has thrown the old religion overboard) to take care not to lose with its loss the fire within, not to perish of cold. There is no religion which God has not loved, which has not taught weak wills how much they can do, which has not let soft rain fall on the dry heart, and cried to self-weary men, "Ye must be born again." Keep these things. It is not in the pride of life that the New Age should excel; it is not for its noisy movement that we should be chiefly glad :

> But that you think clear, feel deep, bear fruit well,
> The Friend of Man desires.

These things are written in a loftier. truer, wiser music than his melancholy, troubled harp could sing twenty years before. I trust I have not dwelt on them too long for my readers' patience. But the story is valuable because it is not only the history of a single soul, but the history of thousands of thoughtful English folk in those days between 1840 and 1870, when the discoveries of science and criticism, and the new developments of democratic ideas, changed all the habits of men's thinking, shook the old fabrics to their foundations, and did not, as yet, build new temples. Science changed its front, so did History, Literature, and Art. Theology and Philosophy strove to preserve their old formation, but as the years went on were forced, if they were to exist at all, to change it also. And in'the wildered disorder of men running to and fro, searching in vain for some foundation of the mind, there were only a few who found it or who believed it would be found. The greater number doubted like Arnold, were restless like him, or like him fell back on stoicism, or fled away from the noises into silence and solitude. There are many who remember those days. They lived in the thick of the battle, and most of them, being serious in that serious time, did their duty as they could. There are many now who are too young to have partaken of that strife or endured its confusion of hustling thoughts, of multitudinous efforts to find truth, but they ought to know something of its history, and be grateful to those who fought so well the battle of progress, and who suffered in the battle. It is because Arnold's poetry concerning his own soul and the soul of man reflects and embodies so much more closely that time of thirty years than either the poetry of Tennyson or Browning, that I have dwelt on it so long. It is history, an interesting history.

Looking back, we see that the times were not so

bad as Arnold thought them to be, nor was their restless movement really evil. The turmoil was not caused
by want of ideas, but by new ideas surging into the
sleepy elements of the time. It was not the seething
of decay and dissolution, it was the heating upwards
into force of new creative powers. Big, formative conceptions were cast into the world, and every element
in that vast caldron boiled up and over in resistance
or agreement. Only after years, did the ebullition
settle down, did another world of thought begin to
arise into a temple in which men could rest and live.
It is not yet half finished. Every year it is being
built into harmony. But we owe its beginnings, and
we shall owe much of its beauty and of the peace of
its aisles, to the wild creative turmoil which Arnold
thought so evil, which filled him with trouble and dismay. He began to see the truth of this in 1867. It
was clearer to him in 1877, when he collected his
poems. But by that time he had drained dry his poetic
vein. Weary when he began to write, he was far more
wearied as a poet when he had gone through the
storm. His imaginative power was tired out. His
intellectual power was not. On the contrary, the
sword of his intellect had been tempered in the fight,
ground down to exceeding sharpness, and if he used it
with too little mercy on his foes, it was always with a
certain humour, sometimes grim, sometimes gentle,
which made even those whom he satirised smile, and
forgive him after their pain was over. Men who loved

his true poetic note, who felt a new and lovely charm in such poems as the *Scholar Gipsy*, were sorry when poetry fled away from him, when the practical reason sat in the throne of imagination; but consoled themselves by thinking that he had done all he could do in poetry, that the gold of that mine was exhausted, and that if he had gone on, it would only have been silver that he could have given us. And *Westminster Abbey* and *Geist* are only silver. And then they felt how clear-eyed and sensible it was of him to put aside with so much ease and dignity his commerce with the Muses. It is not every day that we touch a man who, having reached some excellence in one of the great arts, knows when he can be excellent no more, and lays it by; and, moreover, takes up new work, in other realms altogether, conscious of new powers, pleased to exercise them, and exercising them with a sure hand. In this new work Arnold followed his own advice to others. He kept his eye fixed on his subjects. He realised his aim, and saw it, for the most part, distinctly. He worked with a deep anxiety to help the world forward to clearer views of life. He lived far less within himself, and far more for the sake of his fellow men. He took his share in the daily drudgery of the world and brought to it "sweetness and light." He believed in the new age while he deprecated its sensational elements, and he used all his powers to lead it into a simpler, quieter, and truer life. Much might well be said of his prose work; of its uniqueness, of its excellence, of its keen fitness for these later times, even when he still retained somewhat in it of his old apartness—but that is not my business in this essay. I pass on to those other poems of his which are outside of the struggle I have described, which belong to subjects more or less independent of its pain. Moreover, as I have written of the poems in their relation to the time in which he lived, so now it is their poetry itself which, as far as I can, I shall try to estimate.

" The eternal objects of poetry," said Arnold in his Preface to the Poems of 1853, " are actions, human actions." Excellent actions! he goes on to say,* "and excellent actions are those which most powerfully appeal to the great primary human affections, feelings which are permanent and the same in the race, in all climes, and at all times. Poetical work belongs to the domain of our permanent passions; let it interest these, and it does not matter whether the subject is ancient or modern. But, as in the ancient subjects the action is greater, the personages nobler, the situations more intense, those critics are wrong who say that the poet must leave the ' exhausted past ' and draw his subjects from matters of present importance."

No wise critic would ever say that the poet should not take his subjects from the past, or that the subjects

---

* I do not quote the whole statement, only passages from it, but I refer my readers to the book. It is too long to quote *in extenso.*

of the past are exhausted. But he would say that the poet who wrote *only* of the past, ignoring the present, would find that after a time his poetic enthusiasm would lesson and finally die away ; or that he would be forced to introduce, probably unconsciously, modern feeling or a modern atmosphere into his record of the ancient subjects; or, at least, that he would bring the subjects nearer to us by mediævalising them, as Morris did the Greek tales. Moreover, he would certainly add to Greek or to mediæval tales, as both Morris and Keats did, the modern feeling for nature and the modern subtlety of passion. Try as he will, the poet cannot divest himself of the spirit of the time in which he lives. However, to support his point of view, Arnold chose some of the great stories of the past for poetic treatment. He took the fine subject of Merope, and made it into a drama in the manner of the Greek. He selected *Sohrab and Rustum*—a tale common to the Eastern, Teutonic, and Celt peoples. He folded in his net the story of *Tristram and Iseult*. He tried to put the Norse mythology and sentiment into the poem of *Balder Dead*. And then he went no farther into the great subjects of the past. The present seized on him. Having carefully laid down his theory of the greater excellence of the ancient subjects, he made three-fourths of his poetry belong to the age in which he lived. His great, his dominant subject, up to 1855 (*New Poems* was published in 1867), was himself face to face with his age.

His theory then faded away before the pressure on his modern soul of the modern time, the modern pain. But the present, at least at first, seized on him in the wrong way. Afterwards, in poems which we may call poems of transition, his self-isolation was modified. But now, the present did not urge him outside of himself to live in the thoughts and emotions of the movement which surged around him. It drove him into his own soul to consider and reconsider what thoughts and emotions the movement outside awakened into life within himself—what his soul suffered from it, what hatreds, what fears, what clashing ! And he closed the windows of the inner house, that he might not hear or see that which disturbed his peace. I will know myself, he thought, alone, and then I may be able to understand and help the world. This was his early mistake as a poet. It was putting the cart before the horse.

I have said that had he lived with the movements of his time, with some hope and faith, and with some joy in the strife, he would have been a greater poet. But here there is a special thing to say, in this connection, with regard to the poems he wrote on the great ancient subjects. Had he not been too self-involved to enter with living interest into the movement of the world around him, he would have treated those great subjects with a fuller mastery. They are treated with a certain remoteness and coldness which can only be explained by the tyranny which the storms and woes of the time in which he lived exercised over his self-questioning spirit. He is less in the tales than in himself. He is not rapt away by *Sohrab and Rustum*, *Balder*, or *Tristram* as Keats was by *Lorenzo* or *Porphyro*, or Morris by the tales of the *Earthly Paradise*. *They* truly escaped from their age, and brought passion to their subjects. Their subjects were more to them than their self.

Nevertheless, Arnold did partly escape from himself when he handled the noble stories of the past. His poetry then, partly freed from self-inquiry and its restlessness, rose into a clearer, sweeter region and reached a higher level of art. When we read the *Strayed Reveller*, the *Forsaken Merman*, *Sohrab and Rustum*, the *Scholar Gipsy*, the *Church at Brou*, in all of which he more or less escaped from self-consideration, we say, feeling their excellence, " What a pity he was so worried ; what a greater pity that he worried himself; what a greatest pity that he allowed himself to be so tormented by his age or by himself. Yet, after all—for everything has two sides—we have seen how interesting as history as well as poetry he has made his age to us through himself. When he looked into its mirror he saw his own tired face, and the waves of thought that passed over it. But the reflection was also that of thousands who then lived and suffered and strove to find their way, but who could not, like Arnold, formulate their thought, or crystallise into words their feeling. And in this indirect fashion he may be said to have joined in the battle he hated, and to have helped the world.

Might he not have escaped from the trouble of the present, and his own in it, by falling in love? Most men, most poets certainly, pass in youth through a period in which love leads them out of themselves, and opens the gates of that vast and shining realm of self-forgetfulness where art has built her noblest palace. We may not say that youthful love-passion brings a man into that excelling realm, or leads an artist into its inner shrine. A larger, a mightier expansion of love is needed for that high citizenship— a love which passes beyond one woman or one man to embrace nature, and man, and God; but we may say that love-passion opens the gates of this kingdom, gives us our first experience of loss of self, and affords a fleeting vision of the glory it may be to lose ourselves in the whole of Love.

Arnold had but little, it seems, of that young experience. It was not the natural outcome of his character or of the character of Clough. This, too, was a pity. Had they had more of the usual love-passion of youth, they would much sooner have learnt the great lesson they needed so much, of not thinking of themselves. Only here and there, by fits and starts, and always mixed with retreats on his own soul, love seems to have come to Arnold in his poetry. And his few love-poems, half of the woman and half of himself, form a sort of transition between poems about himself and the others about subjects beyond himself. These poems then I shall briefly discuss.

It was not only the youthful passion of love which, if we judge from his early poetry, was of small force in Arnold. He seems also, in his desire for almost a stoic temperance, to have felt less than other poets those eager enthusiasms for natural beauty, for human causes, for universal ideas which stir into great emotion, whether of joy, aspiration, or pity, poets in their youth. The intense glow of young life, of which love-poems are only one result, was either weak in him, or repressed ; and in consequence, his poetic life was sure, sooner or later, to suffer from the exhaustion at which it did arrive. He ceased to write poetry.

But when that youthful fire is strong in a poet, it does not burn out. It only changes the objects on which it feeds, and glows with a steadier heat around them. When it is not strong, it is easily put out by ill-fortuned circumstances, and the poet is then left without one of the elements which most feed, impel, and develop the youthful imagination. Such ill fortune, we have seen, did befall Arnold. The pressure of that noisy, sceptical time ministered to the chilling of what youthful fire he possessed. His training also chilled it. Rigorous teachers imposed on him and Clough moral and intellectual responsibilities, too early for their strength, too heavy for them to bear, and froze the genial current of their youth. His father's mind, his father's view of life, lay heavy on him, and all the more heavy because he reverenced him so much. Duties were not sufficiently mingled with natural pleasures. He carried to Oxford a somewhat austere solemnity ; and the love-poem, with its exalted note of ardour, may have seemed to him unworthy of a serious man. But he was not yet a man, and it is a misfortune to a youth, much more to a blossoming poet, to anticipate the gravity of manhood. Nevertheless, if Arnold had had more of youthful fire, he might have saved his life from these despondencies. And it is that want which makes his poem of *Tristram and Iseult* so inadequate. The story of Tristram is a story of passion between the sexes. The passion of the story is faded out in Arnold's poem. Thin, thin as the speech of the wailing ghosts Ulysses saw in Hades are the voices in that poem. Perhaps Arnold felt that the wounds of Tristram, the long lapse of time since the lovers had met, excused, even insisted on the presence of a weakness in the expression of passion. But had he known more of true passion in love, and felt the story and the atmosphere of its time more truly, he would not have made this artistic mistake, which he probably thought was an artistic excellence. The note which is sounded in the poem might suit the temper and situation of Iseult of Brittany. It does not suit those of Tristram and Iseult of Ireland. The poem is cold.

There are other poems which may be called, each with its own difference, love-poems, of which the most remarkable are *Faded Leaves*, *Euphrosyne*, *Calais Sands*, and the series addressed to Marguerite. The poems entitled *Faded Leaves*, in which all the love is unhappy, "too late or separated, or despairing or longing," should not, I think, have been kept among the collected poems. The subject is plainly worked up and chosen from the outside. Their workmanship is weak; unfortunate phrases jar the lyric sense; there is none of the naturalness of love in the series, save in one verse of the last poem. His artistic sense is scarcely born in these poems, and his longing for quiet intrudes its philosophy curiously and unhappily into them. They must have been a very youthful effort, yet, if they were so, what a curious youth! As to *Euphrosyne*, it is better done. Browning would have liked its motive. This is sufficiently given in the last verse :—

> It was not love which heaved thy breast,
> Fair child !—it was the bliss within.
> Adieu ! and say that one at least
> Was just to what he did not win.

Calais Sands comes nearer to reality, but its close remains obscure. Whether the lover is to live always apart in a silent worship, as in one verse—or to be happy in meeting his sweetheart, as in the last verse— we cannot know. One motive or the other should have been chosen and completed.

No one can tell whether the series addressed to Marguerite, and entitled *Switzerland*, records a real

passage of love in his life when he loved for a time
a daughter of France who lived in Switzerland, or
whether he invented the subject in order to write on
the matter of a love-passion which was born, lived
for a time and died, in a heart too restless, too un-
tamed, too feverish with the trouble of the world, too
unable to forget itself, for unforgetful happiness in
another. I do not like to think that the subject was
invented, but there are passages—it may be they were
added afterwards—which are chill with that intellectual or moral analysis both of which are apart from
love in its passionate mood. On the other hand, if
anywhere in Arnold's poetry there is youthful passion,
it is here.

They begin with a poem of the first volume, 1849,
A Memory Picture, and record his first meeting and
parting with Marguerite. It ought to have been collected with the others. The poems of 1852 record the
progress of this love affair. Three years had not
dimmed his occasional passion for this girl ; and they
close with a poem written ten years afterwards, in
which he remembers her, and wonders where she is,
as he muses on the terrace at Berne.

The second in the series as finally brought together,
entitled *Parting*, is the most interesting. Like Goethe,
when he fled from his slavery to Lili—and Arnold
imitates here the motive of Goethe's poem—he calls on
the mountains to receive him and release him from the
storm of love ; but the vision of Marguerite, passing to

and fro in the house, will not let him go.   At last, he
seems to break away, but the next poem brings them
together again, only to part.   His love and her love
faded for different reasons, and they slid away from
one another.   It is no wonder she ceased to care, for
he mingled too much of his unquiet soul with his love;
and women, in the matter of love, have no patience,
and for good reason, with a lover whose psychology is
engaged with his own soul, and not with theirs.   It is
no wonder, on the other hand, that he ceased to care,
for her nature was unfitted to his, and, moreover, as
we are unartistically informed, she had a past.   Indeed, it is a melancholy business.   There is none of
the natural self-forgetfulness of passion in the poem.

As to the closing poem, which has its own grace and
charm, it is spoilt by the verse which wonders whether
she has not perhaps, in these ten years, followed her
light and flowery nature, and returned to Paris to live
an immoral life.   That verse should be expunged;
and I do not think that the poet could ever have really
loved the girl, else memory of tenderness and of passion past would have spared her that conjecture.   The
greater artist would have left it out, even had he
thought it.   But Arnold, though an artist, was not
a great artist.

I have said he was more of a careful artist in the
poems which he wrote on subjects apart from his own
time and his own self.   He took great pains with
them, sometimes almost so much self-conscious pains

that he lost, if he ever possessed the capability of it, the natural rush of a poet in creation. There is an occasional artificiality in poems like *Sohrab and Rustum* and *Balder Dead*, which bears the same relation to art that Rochefoucauld said hypocrisy bore to virtue. And it is especially displayed in their direct imitation of the similes of the Homeric poems and of their way of introducing similes. He seems like Homeric writers, to fetch them from other poems, and fit them in unfitly. He introduces far too many of them, and—sometimes excellent, sometimes too far apart from the thing they are supposed to illustrate, sometimes hopelessly wrong in the place they occupy, sometimes contradictory in detail,—they weaken the passion of the poem and delay its movement. In this, Arnold does not show the moderation he was so fond of preaching. Then, again, the just simile should only be introduced when the action or the emotion is heightened, when the moment is worthy, and when as it were in a pause, men draw in their breath to think what may happen next, for the moment has reached intensity. The simile fills that pause and allows men time to breathe. But Arnold introduces his similes often lightly, about unimportant matters, where the action should not pause but be rapid, when the moment is not weighty. This is an artistic frivolity.

Moreover, the Homeric tradition is out of place in *Sohrab and Rustum*. Arnold takes great pains with its local colour. We have all the geography of the

district, and he has used the names well. He describes
the Tartar and Persian dresses, armour, tents, the different aspects of the warring tribes, their manners and
much more in great detail. But in this fully Oriental
poem the similes and the whole manner of the verse
are Greek. It is a mixture too odd for good art.
Either have no local colour or keep it pure.

The story of *Sohrab and Rustum*, of the father who
unknowingly fights with and slays his son, and dis-
covers the misery too late, is a wide-spread tale. It
exists in two forms at least, in one of which the discovery is made in time, in Teutonic saga. We find it
in Celtic saga. It was attached to the Cuchullainn
tale, and the rash hero, like Rustum, slays his son.
The subject is simple, full of a terrible pity, and a
natural horror, capable of passionate treatment, and
of leaving in our minds, when wrought according to
nature, a sympathy with the fates of men which softens
and heals the heart. Arnold has not missed its opportunities. The brave, lovely, and tender-hearted youth
is well contrasted with the worn, haughty, austere
warrior ; and the pathos swells from point to point,
deepened by memorial allusion and description, till it
culminates in the discovery that the father has slain
the son. That crisis is simply and passionately
wrought by Arnold, and both the characters, made
beautiful by love and endurance of fate together, stir
that high pleasure in us which is compact of honour
for human nature and of pity for its sorrow — man

weeping for, but enduring with a constant mind, the worse the gods can inflict; till we feel that man is nobler than the gods—till we know that the gods whom man has previously created must be replaced by a new creation. The poem closes in a lonely beauty. The son and the father lie alone on the plain as night falls, between the mourning hosts, none daring to intrude. The dark heaven alone is their tent, and their sorrow their shroud. And we hear the deep river flowing by, the image of the destiny of man that bears us on, helpless, on its breast, until, with it, we find the sea.

Balder Dead is by no means so fine a poem. It is almost absurdly Homerised. It is far too long, and made too long by irrelevant matter and descriptions, and by repetitions. It is curiously inartistic. In it, however, Arnold had found out that he was too lavish of his similes. Moreover, his temper of mind was quite apart from that of the North. He must have been incapable of apprehending it, or he would never have written this poem in this fashion. He tries for the masculine simplicity of the North, but he does not gain it ; there are even times when his elaborate simplicity verges towards the ridiculous, as in the description of the daily battle and feast in Valhalla. Odin —and it would be to his blank amazement—is turned into the Zeus of Homer, and Frea speaks like Hera grown very old; and excessively curious this talk sounds to any one who cares for the northern sagas or the early northern poems. It is not a true Norse poem, yet it drags in so much of the northern mythology that the mind of the reader is dissipated away from the main subject. Some of the descriptions, however, like that of Hodur visiting Frea when night had fallen on the streets of Asgard, have a pictorial excellence. What Arnold has well seized—in spite of the excess of description—is the human emotion in the story, the bitter grief of Hodur for his unconscious slaying of Balder, the grief of Balder's wife, and Balder's love for her, the eagerness of the gods to get Balder back, the union of Balder and Nanna in Hela's realm, their happiness together in that shadowy place where even passion is thin; the farewell of Hodur to Balder when they part to meet no more till the Twilight of the gods. The last ride of Hermon to Hela's reign, his meeting with Hodur, the prophecy of Balder, his weariness of blood and war which half reconciles him to the world of the dead, the picture of the new world of peace for which he waits—this is the finest part of the poem, but, on the whole, the subject was outside of Arnold nor has he at all grasped its significance. Nevertheless, being thus outside of him, we are saved in it from the trouble of his soul.

Tristram and Iseult I have partly characterised. It does not cling and knit itself into its subject as ivy round and into the oak. It swims about it like a fish, hither and thither. Anything — the tapestry, the storm, the firelight, the bed curtains, the dress of the

queen—leads it away from the central passion. It is a
pretty poem, with charming descriptions, but sentimental, which Tristram and Iseult never were. The
most important part of it is where his ancient love
comes to visit him. There, if anywhere, Arnold should
be vitally clear, and in the subject. He is miles and
miles away from the time, the temper, the characters,
and the passion of the matter in hand. The conventions of modern society and morality rule the irritating
speeches of the lovers. Its ending is curious. Iseult
of Brittany is left with her two children, and goes out
to walk with them, just like a modern widow in a
sentimental novel, along the cliffs, and tells stories to
the boys. Among the rest she tells the story of Merlin
and Vivien, and with this, which has nothing in the
world to do with the subject, the poem closes. This
dragging in of a new tale is the most inartistic thing
that Arnold ever did, nor is the tale well told. Indeed,
it is scarcely told at all. Three-fourths of this closing
part are natural description, but natural description of
great charm and clear vision, quite modern in feeling,
and strangely apart from the atmosphere which sur-
rounds the story of Tristram. It reads as if Arnold,
unable to invent fresh matter, fell back on his remembrance of a visit to Brittany, and inserted a description
of the landscape, in order to fill up his space. *Tristram
and Iseult* must be a youthful piece of work, and I am
the more driven to that opinion by its distant imitation
of Coleridge and Byron, notes of both of whom sound

clearly in its verse and manner. These are the three long poems.

We turn from these long poems, for which his genius was unfitted, for he had not the capacity of either copious or continuous invention, to the lyric and elegiac poems in which his genius is at its best, and in which —unlike those already discussed—the subjects have carried him away from himself. A few of them belong to the Greek cycle of tales, a region where he loved to dwell.

He tried to write a tragedy in the manner of the Greek drama on the subject of *Merope*. It really is a failure. Its worst fault is dulness, and though he strove hard to make a great moral impression emerge through the action of the drama, and leave its power on the audience—an end his friend Sophocles desired —he did not succeed in this because the action of his play had not enough of life in it. "Good wine needs no bush," we say when we read his long, interesting, explanatory preface ; but here is an enormous sign hung out over the tavern door to lead us to try the wine. The landlord must have himself doubted its quality.

The songs, or rather the recitations, of Callicles, published in 1855 under the title of the *Harp-Player on Ætna*, are pleasant, but only one of them—*Cadmus and Harmonia*—is of the finest quality. *Philomela*, which recalls the old sad tale of the palace in the Thracian vale, is half English, half Greek, and full of

a passion rare in Arnold, half for himself, half for the
sorrow of the world.   But far the best of these Hellenic
things is the *Strayed Reveller*.   This is a piece of pure
creation with full invention flowing through it in happy
ease.   The scene is vividly pictured.   The palace, the
court, the fountain, the forest, and the hills around the
palace, are clothed in the Greek beauty and clearness.
We breathe that pellucid air, and see the Reveller
in the dewy twilight, and Circe in the palace porch,
and Ulysses, "the spare, dark-featured, quick-eyed
stranger" coming from the pillared hall.   This pictorial power charms us through the poem.   The Reveller,
half drugged into vision by Circe's wine, describes,
with a conciseness and illumination which save it from
the merely picturesque, a bright procession of countries,
men, and the works of men—a "wild, thronging train
of eddying forms" sweeping through his soul.   But it
is not mere description.   Good matter of thought lies
at the centre of the poem.   The youth tells what the
happy gods see :—Tiresias the prophet, the Centaurs
on Pelion, the Indian drifting on the mountain lake
among his melon beds, the Scythian on the wide
steppe, the merchants ferrying over the lone Choras-
mian stream, the heroes sailing in Argo ;—and the
gods rejoice, pleased as men in a theatre with the
stream of human life passing them by, where, unconcerned, they sit at ease.

The poet sees the same things, but not in the
same way.   He has to bear what he sees, to feel

with the pain and the fates of men, to share the
agony :—

> These things, Ulysses
> The wise bards also
> Behold and sing.
> But oh, what labour !
> O prince, what pain !

The gods exact this price for the gift of song, that the
poets become what they sing.

The poet, it is often said, by depth of sympathy,
suffers more than other men, a part of their pains
as well as his own. And this is a self-flattering theory
that poets hug to their breast. I have little sympathy
with the conceit. If the poet, being more sensitive
than other men, feel the pain and ugliness of the world
sorely, he also is just as sensitive to its joy and beauty ;
and he has greater rapture than other men. All things
are set over one against another, and the poet has no
business to enlarge on his pain and to ignore his joy.
He is, in reality, very well paid for his trouble. Moreover, he has a great advantage over other men. There
are thousands just as sensitive as he, who are obliged
to suffer in silence ; but the poet, having the gift of
expression, can shape his pain into words, cry loudly
his lyric cry, make the world the sympathetic witness
of his woes ; and then, having expressed his trouble,
forget it, or get rid of it and go on, if that please him,
to shiver with another pain, shape it in its turn, and
forget it—and this he can do all his life long. It is a

pleasing amusement, and one need not have much sympathy with his sorrows. Those whom I do sympathise with are those who have no voice, who appeal to no public, who live in lonely trouble with the troubled world. Yet they, too, have their outlet. What the poet sings truly expresses them to themselves. There is always a way to the common-sense of joy if only we look for it. These silent souls can read and be relieved: but that makes it all the more incumbent on the poet to take care that his muse should also prophesy joy and be the refreshment of care as well as the revealer of sorrow.

Arnold, though he cried out a great deal, did not hold this sentimental view of the poet. There is a fine passage in *Resignation* which enshrines another view. It is too long to quote, but it illustrates his poetic aim— and it belongs to his earliest poems.

> The poet, to whose mighty heart
> Heaven doth a quicker pulse impart,
> Subdues that energy to scan
> Not his own course, but that of man.
> Though he move mountains, though his day
> Be pass'd on the proud heights of sway,
> Though he hath loosed a thousand chains,
> Though he hath borne immortal pains,
> Action and suffering though he know—
> He hath not lived, if he lives so.

He sees the great ruler wisely sway the people, and the just conquests of beauty, and the populous town ; the whole movement of life ; rejoices in it, but does not say : *I am alone.*

Matthew Arnold 121

He sees the gentle stir of birth
When morning purifies the earth ;
He leans upon a gate and sees
The pastures and the quiet trees.

.   .   .   .

He gazes—tears
Are in his eyes, and in his ears
The murmur of a thousand years.
Before him he sees life unroll,
A placid and continuous whole—
That general life, which does not cease
Whose secret is not joy, but peace ;
That life, whose dumb wish is not miss'd
If birth proceeds, if things subsist ;
The life of plants and stones and rain
The life he craves—if not in vain
Fate gave, what chance shall not control,
His sad lucidity of soul.

But that does not contain all the thought on the matter. He tells in a sonnet of that young Italian bride, lovely, gaily garmented, who, perishing in an accident, was found to wear a robe of sackcloth next her " smooth white skin."

Such, poets, is your bride, the Muse ! young, gay,
Radiant, adorn'd outside ; a hidden ground
Of thought and of austerity within.

Again, we are told in the *Epilogue to Lessing's Laocoon*, the poet is to tell of Life's movement ; all of it from source to close. It is Life's movement which fascinates the poets. But it is too much for them to bear or to tell. Only a gleam of it here and there can they see, only now and then can they hear a murmur of it ; not the whole light, not the full music. A few, a very few, have seen and heard—Homer, Shakespeare—and these are the greatest of mankind.

Again, Arnold says — the poet is a priest of the wonder and bloom of the world. We see with his eyes and are glad. But he does not see all. As human life is wider than he, so Nature is greater, vaster than the singer. Her mighty march moves and will move on, when all our poetry of her is dead ; nor can it ever express the thousandth part of her over-brimming life. Yet if the poet love, he has charm ; and to charm the heart of man, to loose our heart in tears and joy, to give us the freshness of the early world, to heal the soul, to make us see and feel and know,—this is the poet's dignity and use.

But he takes another view. The poet is, by his nature, alone (and here the personality of Arnold intrudes), and solitude oppresses him. He flies from the noise of men which jars him. But can Life reach him in the solitude, and he is to express Life ; and fenced from the multitude, who will fence him from himself? He hears nothing then but the mountain torrents and the beating of his own heart. Wherefore, tormented in exile, he flies back into the world of men. And there he is again unhappy. Absence from himself (for in the turmoil of men he cannot hear the voice of his soul) tortures him. Again he refuges in silence, and again the air is too keen to breathe, the loneliness unendurable. Thus, miserably bandied to and fro, only death can heal the long disease of his life.

It is in that way that Arnold, in *Empedocles*, paints the Thinker and the Poet, nor is it only in *Empedocles*. It was a picture that he afterwards changed for a brighter one ; but it represented truly during periods of depression, his view of his own, and of a poet's, life.

Of all these poems, written apart from himself, one of the most delicately felt is the third part of the *Church of Brou*, where the young prince and his duchess lie together, carved on their tomb ; and in the silent night when the soft rain is on the roof, or in the sunset when the rose and sapphire glories of the great western window fall on pillar and pavement, wake to cry—This is the bliss of Heaven, this is eternity. That is a fair poem, but the most charming, the most romantic, most in the world of the pure and tender imagination is *The Forsaken Merman*. To read it is to regret that he could not oftener escape into that ideal region where, at least for a time, our sorrows seem dreams, and the soul is healed of its disease. Moreover, this poem is sweeter in melody than most of his poems, as if his ear had been purged in that loftier and brighter air. There is nothing stranger in a man who dwelt so much on excellence in the poetic art, and who criticised failure in form so sharply, than Arnold's inability to recognise the harshness, the broken sounds, the want of harmony in his own verse. How he could have left unchanged verses so frequently out of tune I cannot understand. His ear was not sensitive, but in the *Forsaken*

Merman it was in tune. It may be that it derived
this excellence from the good composition of the piece.
When the composition is good, the melody of the
verse is also good. One excellence induces the other.
And this may be said of the *Scholar Gipsy* and of
Thyrsis. They are both well composed, and the
melody of the verse in them is always good and sometimes exquisite.

The mention of these two pieces brings me to the
elegiac poems. I have said that Arnold, having sorrows at the root of his life, wrote with peculiar excellence the elegy. To excel in the elegy is not easy.
Of course, it is easier to write than an ode of triumph
or a song of rapture like the *Epithalamium* of Spenser;
but there are many pitfalls into which a poet may fall
in building an elegy, and into these Arnold, being
austere in thought and hating excess as much as he
loved temperance, and always mingling thought with
feeling, did not easily fall. There is a severe beauty,
an intellectual force, in these elegiac poems which
strengthens, as it intensifies, their emotion, and is, as
it were, the skeleton round which imagination com-
pacts their living body.

The first of these is *Memorial Verses*—written on
Wordsworth in 1850—and they contrast in soothing,
healing power with Byron's force and Goethe's calm.
Few things have been better said, or with more delightful finish, than these on the influence of Wordsworth,
and the roots of his power. Not quite so well said,

but said with more personal feeling and with Arnold's
long affection for the Lake country made for the moment more tender by the death of Wordsworth, are
the verses in the beginning of the poem, *The Youth of
Nature*, where those strange lines occur which say that
the age can rear no more poets, so blind Arnold was to
the real significance of the time in which he lived.

Then there are the verses on his father—*Rugby
Chapel*, 1857. They are written like the others without rhyme, in the form which Arnold often used, and
which can only be perfectly used by an artist who,
unlike Arnold, is a master of melody. Else he falls
into prose, or, being unlimited by the austere rule of
rhyme which ought to force concentration, he lets his
thought run more loosely than it should. Into both
these errors Arnold is sometimes betrayed in these
rhymeless verses. Yet the deep, controlled, filial feeling with which he wrote this poem, and the steadfast
matter of thought concerning human life which was
born of the depth of his feeling, give to it so great a
sincerity and so serious a spirituality, that no one can
read it without being thrilled into sympathy by its
moral power, and by its prophetic passion bettered in
soul. It is an influence for life ; and the close is noble
—that close in which he paints the worn and weary
hosts of mankind dispirited, scattered, and lost in the
waste, but uplifted, cheered, and knit together by the
great souls he always thought so few, but who are
many more than he imagined :—

Then in such hour of need
Of your fainting, dispirited race,
Ye, like angels, appear,
Radiant with ardour divine!
Beacons of hope, ye appear!
Languor is not in your heart,
Weakness is not in your word,
Weariness not on your brow,
Ye alight in our van! at your voice,
Panic, despair, flee away,
Ye move through the ranks, recall
The stragglers, refresh the outworn,
Praise, re-inspire the brave!
Order, courage return.
Eyes rekindling, and prayers,
Follow your steps as ye go.
Ye fill up the gaps in our files,
Strengthen the wavering line,
'Stablish, continue our march,
On, to the bound of the waste,
On, to the City of God.

The poem on the Brontës, *Haworth Churchyard*, is
scarcely up to the level of its subject, but that on
Heine is of a different and a finer quality. It does
not seize the whole of Heine, but it touches his youth
and happiness with grace, and his manhood, in its
mockery and agony, with so sympathetic a pity that
the very censure seems part of the pity. The misery
of Heine's life made most impression on Arnold, and
he seems to trace it to an inborn root of bitterness.
He quotes, with approval, Goethe's phrase concerning
some poet, and applies it to Heine, "that he had every
other gift, but wanted love," love which is "the
fountain of charm—charm, the glory that makes the

song of the poet divine.'' And in a strange close to his poem—in a thought of which Arnold seems to think far more highly than he ought to think, for it is intolerably fantastic—he makes Heine to be the incarnation of a momentary bitter mood of the Spirit of the world.

> The Spirit of the world,
> Beholding the absurdity of men—
> Their vaunts, their feats—let a sardonic smile
> For one short moment, wander o'er his lips.
> *That smile was Heine !*—for its earthly hour
> The strange guest sparkled; now 't is pass'd away.

This is not as true as he thinks. Heine was much more than that. Far more than half of his bitterness was born of lovingness the fulness of which he could not exercise, of natural and excusable feeling against his terrible fate. He cried aloud at it ; the poet must speak ; but, in reality, no man could have borne that fate more resolutely, nor did he lose love in it. Nor could Arnold, when he wrote these lines, have known the poems where Heine's better soul went forth to feel with man and to fight man's battle, to stand as a lonely sentinel when he could fight no more, and to die alone, in the night at his outpost, for the cause of the whole army. I cannot quote the whole of the poem, the *Enfant perdu,* but here are the first and the last verses—

> Verlor'ner Posten in dem Freiheitskriege,
> Hielt ich seit dreissig Jahren treulich aus.
> Ich kämpte ohne Hoffnung, dass ich siege,
> Ich wusste, nie komm'ich gesund nach Haus.

Ein Posten ist vacant !—Die Wunden klaffen—
Der Eine fällt, die Audern rücken nach—
Doch fall'ich unbesiegt, und meine Waffen
Sind nicht gebrochen—Nur mein Herze brach.

And now I touch on the two best poems he wrote—
the *Scholar Gipsy* and *Thyrsis*. Both are engaged
with Clough, and they are suffused throughout with
the tenderness of that deep friendship between man
and man, which, begun in youth, keeps in it the purple
light of youth; which, continued in manhood, wins the
strength of the love which perseveres through sad
experience, and the beauty which is born of, and nour-
ished by associated memories. These fill the poems
with sweet emotion, enfold them in an air of tenderness.
Then, though in this tenderness of friendship he has
escaped from self-consideration, yet they are filled
with thought concerning the time they had both lived
through, the needs of their age and its remedies. In
this region, on which I must dwell further, the poems
ought to be read together. They illustrate and supple-
ment one another ; and whatever is said, both in retro-
spect and prospect, however different may be the
momentary turn of thought, all is brought into unity
by the pervasiveness of the one emotion of memorial
and loving friendship.

Then, too, another emotion fills the verse—that love
of Oxford as the home of his youthful heart, as the
nurse of intellect, the mother of fine causes, the teacher
and cherisher of the wisdom and beauty of the ancients,

the lover of the masters of humane learning and art. That flows through these poems, and is supported by so rich a local colour that not even Tennyson has ever laid more fully a whole countryside before us. From every field and hilltop crowned with trees we see Oxford in the verse, her ancient colleges, her "dreaming spires," lovely in her peace, romantic in her memories, classic in her thought. Over every hill we wander in the verse, in the well-known woods, through the quiet villages, in the deep meadows where the flowers love their life, by the flowing of the Thames; in poetry so happy and so loving that each name strikes itself into a landscape before our eyes. And to add to the charm, Arnold has filled the landscape with humanity and its work, with shepherd and reaper, gipsies and scholars, hunters and oarsmen, dancing maidens and wandering youths, among whom, alive and gay, Thyrsis and the Scholar Gipsy, and a meditative Arnold, alive and serious, move and speak of the true aims, the just ideas, the grave conduct, of human life. The picture is delightful, and the urging power of it is love—the life-long love of an Oxford scholar for the shelter and inspiration of his youth. In no poems that Arnold wrote is his natural description better than it is in these.

His natural description to which I now turn, is always vivid, pictorial, accurate, done, to use his own phrase, with his eye on the subject. The adjectives which he chooses so carefully are so apt and striking that they have the force of facts.   What can better words like these—

> So have I heard the cuckoo's parting cry,
> From the wet field, through the vext garden trees,
> Come with the volleying rain and tossing breeze :

or these from *Dover Beach*—

> The sea is calm to-night.
> The tide is full, the moon lies fair
> Upon the straits ; on the French coast the light
> Gleams and is gone ; the cliffs of England stand,
> Glimmering and vast, out in the tranquil bay.
> Come to the window, sweet is the night air !
> Only, from the long line of spray
> When the sea meets the moon-blanch'd land,
> Listen ! you hear the grating roar
> Of pebbles which the waves draw back, and fling
> At their return, up the high strand,
> Begin and cease, and then again begin,
> With tremulous cadence slow, and bring
> The eternal note of sadness in.

This, as accurate as it is poetical, is finer but not truer—with "its melancholy, long, withdrawing roar" —than Tennyson's verse, describing the same thing—

The scream of a maddened beach dragged down by the wave.

At least, it enables Arnold to make a more human use of the natural fact than Tennyson could have done. Tennyson's phrase makes the sea and the stones of the beach be and feel like men, and, having done so, he cannot use them as illustrating the large movement of human life.   But Arnold seeing and hearing them as pure nature, not humanised nature, transfers the scene

into an image of the spiritual life of man ; and with an
imagination and force which, by their passion, reach
splendour of thought and diction. This is a frequent
way of his with nature, and no one has done it better
in English poetry. I quote it :

> The Sea of Faith
> Was once, too, at the full, and round Earth's shore
> Lay like the folds of a bright girdle furl'd
> But now I only hear
> Its melancholy, long, withdrawing roar,
> Retreating, to the breath
> Of the night-wind, down the vast edges drear
> And naked shingles of the world.

Always it is the same in his poetry of nature. He
describes the thing he sees, flower or bird, stream or
hill, exactly as they are, without humanising them,
without veiling them with any sentiment of their own,
without having concerning nature any philosophy that
spiritualises nature as the form of thought or love,
any belief that she is alive or dwelt in by living beings.
Nature to Arnold is frequently the nature that modern
science has revealed to us—matter in motion, taking
an inconceivable variety of form, but always, in its
variety, acting rigidly according to certain ways,
which, for want of a wiser term, we call laws. For
the first time this view of nature enters into English
poetry with Arnold. He sees the loveliness of her
doings, but he also sees their terror and dreadfulness
and their relentlessness. But what in his poetry he

chiefly sees is the peace of nature's obedience to law, and the everlasting youth of her unchanging life.

He contrasts her calm with our turmoil, her quiet changes of action day after day, her rest after action, with our hurry, our confusion, and our noise. Calm soul of things, he cries, make me calm, let the human world, like thee, perfect its vast issues "in toil unsevered from tranquillity." Again, he contrasts the immortal life of nature with our decay and death. That life existed before us, will exist after us, fulfilling pauselessly its pure eternal course. Oh, he cries, to be alone with that intense life, and in its youthfulness, to be clear, composed, refreshed, ennobled; to have its steadfast joy ! *Calm, with life*, that was the ideal he drew from nature.*

Then, he also contrasts her joy and freedom with the sorrow and the slavery of our struggle towards any perfection. She obeys law silently and therefore

* Once he drew from this a strange corollary. Such vast life, ever evolving new things and old things in new shapes, may bring us (who are in that life) back hereafter into another conscious life—may even bring together again in better circumstance those who have been together here in sadness and pain. At least, so I read the meaning of a curious epilogue to *Haworth Churchyard* :

> Unquiet souls !
> —In the dark fermentation of earth,
> In the never idle workshop of nature,
> In the eternal movement,
> Ye shall find yourselves again !

is free. We do not obey, or we resent the law, and suffering from its rigid restrictions, are enslaved by it. This is the motive of a great number of passages in Arnold's poems. In this view of nature, he has slipped out of his view of her as seen by science. Science could not talk of the joy or freedom of nature. And indeed, he was not faithful to the scientific view of her. His conception of her wavered with his mood. He sometimes, in a sort of reversion to Wordsworth, speaks of her as powerful to help him, as having, like a mother, the heart to help him. He appeals to her to fill him with the healing qualities he vainly imputes to her. He is happily inconsequent in his conceptions of her.

For example, there is a half-outlined conception of nature, quite different from the rest, which obscurely appears in a poem entitled *Morality*. He seems to imagine that behind nature there is a self-harmonious, self-conscious Life, as it were a Demiourgos, who, putting the thoughts of the Eternal Intelligence into form, has made the Universe and the intelligent beings who inhabit it, and therefore, being in nature and in man as thought, can bring them into communion and cause nature to work and feel with man ; and the lines which close *A Summer Night*, seem to be filled with that idea—

> Ye heavens, whose pure dark regions have no sign
> Of languor, though so calm, and though so great,
> Are yet untroubled and unpassionate ;

Who, though so noble, share in the world's toil,
And, though so task'd, keep free from dust and soil!
I will not say that your mild deeps retain
A tinge, it may be, of their silent pain
Who have long'd deeply once, and long'd in vain.

This thought which I suggest he conceived, is in
these lines obscure and wandering.   It takes a clearer,
indeed another, consistency in *Morality*.   Nature there,
in her freedom and joy, looks on our agony, and, while
we think she censures or despises our strife, does really
nothing of the kind, but, on the contrary, is emo-
tionalised by it, set into self-wonder and questioning
by it.   Did I ever feel, she asks, the eagerness to perfection, to realisation of thought in form, which gives
to men that earnest air?

See, on her face a glow is spread,
A strong emotion on her cheek!
    " Ah, child!" she cries, " that strife divine,
    Whence was it, for it is not mine?

"There is no effort on *my* brow—
    I do not strive, I do not weep;
I rush with the swift spheres and glow
    In joy, and when I will, I sleep.
        Yet that severe, that earnest air,
        I saw, I felt it once—but where?

" I knew not yet the gauge of time,
    Nor wore the manacles of space;
I felt it in some other clime,
    I saw it in some other place.
        'T was when the heavenly house I trod,
        And lay upon the breast of God."

This self-conscious communion of nature with her own heart, this questioning of her own being in contrast with man's being, this dim remembrance of herself elsewhere, hold in them a philosophic idea of nature we do not find elsewhere in the poets, and the philosophic imagination is charmed to play with it. It seems as if Arnold thought of the creative Logos, by whose being outward nature is and continues, as able to pass back momentarily from his existence in the natural world, which is subject to the conceptions of time and space, to a remembrance of the eternity when there was neither time nor space to him, when there was no material universe into which he had shaped the thoughts of God, when he was himself the Logos in God as yet unexpressed in form, but desiring eagerly towards form. This is Arnold playing with the obscure conceptions of Neoplatonism.

Again, he puts into two poems, the *Youth of Nature* and the *Youth of Man*, his contrast of the everlasting life of Nature with the decay and fleeting of our life. The beauty, charm, romance we feel in nature, are they, he asks, in nature or in the poet ? In nature, he answers, and far more than in the poet ; the singer is less than his theme. They were in the poet when he was conscious of the immeasurable glory of Nature's life. And what they were in him no pencil could ever paint, no verse could ever fully tell. The depth, the force, the joy, sadness, and longing of them which in youth he felt were nature's depth, force, joy, sadness, and longing ; and only a shred of them could he ever put into all his verse. Yes, cries Nature, when all the poets who, because they were part of me, thought that my life was theirs, are dead dust, I remain as living, as young as ever. This is the law. Nature, rich and full in us when we are young, we think to have no life but that which we give her. But as years pass by, our energy fails, and, like fools, we think our decay is a decay in nature. But she watches us, silent and contemptuous. Her living beauty never sees our corruption. Therefore, cries Arnold, while we are able, get into vital union with the calm, and obedience and life of nature, order the soul into the spirit of her life—

> Sink, O youth, in thy soul !
> Yearn to the greatness of nature ;
> Rally the good in the depths of thyself !

That is his conclusion. It would not be mine from the premises, and it belongs to that part of Arnold's thinking which he derived from stoicism. It were better to rise out of one's soul into love of the soul of the world, to lose oneself in its beauty and joy and peace by self-forgetfulness, to see the perfect good outside of one's self, and spring off one's own shadow into union with the infinite light. No man can change his yearning to the greatness of nature into possession of that greatness who is sunk in his personal soul. But outside of that prison, ravished by the love of the perfect—he retains in decay, in old age, in death, not the misery Arnold paints in the poem, but delight and life, even rapture.

I say no more of his poetry of nature. I pass to his poetry of man, and here I must risk repetition, and take up, in this new connection, poems on which I have already written. He cared for the beauty of the natural world, but he cared far more for the landscape of the soul of man. It was at first the landscape of his own life—its rivers, its buried life,

> The hills where his life rose
> And the sea where it goes,

the voices which called it in the night, of which he first wrote with his serious stoic passion. But the time came when the landscape of the soul of the world, of humanity at large, engaged him far more than that of the little world within him. He sang of man's history in the past, but chiefly of his own age and country, and of the battle for life and God in which he moved; yet, even now, he still remained more of an interested spectator than of a fighter. It was only when he gave up verse that he became a warrior hotly engaged in the fray. But whether spectator or not, it is when he is writing not about himself but about the soul of man travailing through its foes to the City of God that he is at his best as a poet. The larger subject makes the lovelier verse, when one is a poet at all. Even in the earliest poems, as in *Resignation* and in the passion of *Philomela*, he began, as also in some of the sonnets of that time, to look out beyond himself over the world of man. The close of *Dover Beach* marks how despairing and pitiful was sometimes that outlook. The world, he says,

> Hath really neither joy, nor love, nor light,
> Nor certitude, nor peace, nor help for pain;
> And we are here as on a darkling plain
> Swept with confused alarms of struggle and flight,
> Where ignorant armies clash at night.

Then, in another mood, hope for the world emerges at the close of that noble and frowning poem, *A Summer Night*. And then, changing again, he can stand apart, and give advice to the confused and toiling world. *The New Age* bids men keep reverence for the past, and *Progress* bids them keep religion. Guard the fire within, lest the heart of humanity perish of cold. *The Future*, a poem as full of imagination as of thought, paints first all that man has lost of the insight, the freshness, the calm, the vigour of life which filled the past; and then, the hoarse roar of the present, the huge cities, the black confusion of trade, the peacelessness. What was before man neglects, of what shall succeed he has no knowledge. But haply, the river of Time, as it grows, may gain, not the earlier calm, but a solemn quiet of its own; and as it draws to the Ocean, may, at last, allure peace to the soul of man out of the infinite sea into which it flows.

This is a higher, a more hopeful strain; and it is continued and strengthened in the *Elegiac Poems*. I have said something of them already, but more must now be said. I dwell now on their deep interest in the life and history of humanity. Their poetry, with a few lyric exceptions, is the best he wrote. They are weighty with interesting, novel, masculine, and often surprising thought. They extend their sympathy over wide areas of history and are in close contact also with the limited time in which he lived. They contain admirable drawings of men and women whom he admired and loved; of their characters and their influence on the world. Weighted with grave and clear thought, their imagination moves with power, and with a grace which results from the power. It grasps the higher nature of one division of the human race, as in these celebrated lines which describe the Orient when Rome had ceased to disturb it; yet the phrase is only partly true:

> She let the legions thunder past,
> And plunged in thought again.

With as much forceful insight, when he pictures the Scholar Gipsy flying from the fevered world and pursuing still the unreachable ideal, he describes another whole class of men. And with the insight and the force of it, what beauty of words, what intimate love of the lovely world!

> Still nursing the unconquerable hope,
> Still clutching the inviolable shade,
> With a free, onward impulse brushing through,
> By night, the silver'd branches of the glade—

Far on the forest-skirts, where none pursue,
    Or some mild pastoral slope
Emerge, and resting on the moonlit pales
Freshen thy flowers as in former years
With dew, or listen with enchanted ears,
From the dark dingles, to the nightingales.

I rejoice to feel in these elegies, the delicate, sensitive art, the careful strength which, combined with a winning grace and serious love of quiet beauty, affect the soul as a still, fair autumn Italian day in lands full of human history affects the senses. Quietude, power, beauty, and tenderness pervade them.

The appreciations of Byron, Goethe, and Wordsworth, which in a poem on Obermann he carries further, are not only good in themselves, but they are applied to the story of man, and to the criticism of the time in which he lived. And the tenderness and gratitude with which he remembers the work of Wordsworth pass into gratitude to him for the healing which his verse has brought to the heart of man. A greater tenderness, a deeper reverence, a personal love and honour fill, as with sweet waters, the verses to his father's memory. But they also pass from personal feeling into feeling for the fates of man. What is the course of the life, he asks, of mortal men on the earth ? Most men eddy about, blindly strive, achieve nothing, and perish. But some a thirst unquenchable fires, and they move to a clear goal ; and of these he writes in a noble and imaginative passage, with a splendour of description. Only one out of many pilgrims reaches

the desolate inn and the gaunt landlord on the ridge of
the snow-clad pass. The rest have perished. But his
father would not be saved alone, but gave his life to
bring those that were lost safe to the goal. And from
this he passes to describe in lofty phrase those others,
servants and sons of God, through whom it is that
mankind still has faith and strength enough to march
on to the City of God. This is indeed a change from
the days when he only thought of his own soul.

Then the famous passage in the poem on *Heine's
Grave* on the Titan toil of England shows how he felt
beyond himself the building pains of a nation. This
dignified passage is lightened and enlightened by his
delicate description of Heine's youth and his sympathy
with his joy ; and finally all the poem is made to thrill
with its final thought concerning all humanity (thrown
back from the end into all that precedes it)—that the
Spirit in whom man exists has made each of us the
revealer of one or more of His thoughts, discloses
through us the infinite variety of His Being. It is a
leading thought of Fichte's, a thought that arises in
many, and that arose, I have no doubt uncommuni-
cated, in the soul of Arnold.

The *Stanzas from the Grande Chartreuse*, represent,
as I have already said, a partial reaction from the wider,
brighter view he now takes of the world to the trouble
of his own life and spirit ; but as they develop, they
also pass from self-consideration into consideration of
the fate of the world of men, and of those who shared

in and were broken by the strife. Ah, he thinks at
the close, with that constantly recurring thought of his
in which so much of his inner life and of ours is hidden,
let the new world thunder on its noisy triumph and
use its powers, be proud of its turbulent life or of its
eternal trifling—yet there are a few who would in
quiet take their bent towards unwearied pursuit of the
perfect, who like Glanvil have "*one* aim, *one* business,
one desire," who wait in joyous unconcern for the
celestial light; and they, in these unthinking days,
are the refuge and light of the world.

Then the two poems to Senancour, the writer of
Obermann, mingle their personal and self-revealing
verse with so wide a human interest that in all who
read them a hundred questions rise—of their own soul,
of the age in which they live, and of the fates of man.
On the great difference of the second from the first I
have already written, but I may dwell here on their
charm—charm of grave thought, ranging far and wide,
charm of happy word and phrase, and charm of natural
description. The very atmosphere of that lovely land,
where so many hearts have been healed, the flower-
haunted meadows, the shimmering lake below, the
blue hills, the far-off snows—is in the loving verse,
and it is mingled with the soul of Arnold and Obermann, till each mountain slope and every flower upon
them, and the waves of the lake as they break on the
shore, are of men, and through men, and in men.

Of all these elegies, the *Scholar Gipsy* and *Thyrsis*

are the most delightful, delightful even though their
subject be sad. I have dwelt on the tenderness of
their sadness. I have not dwelt on their contemplative
beauty. They are pervaded by that retired contemplation of life a man may have who, flying from the
storm of cities for a brief holiday, thinks the brief time
into an eternity, and in the eternal hermitage of his
soul muses on earth and human life.

These poems reach excellence, that rare thing Arnold
himself loves so much, to whose lonely summit, the
artist, climbing through rocks and mist, so seldom can
attain. They are pure poetry, moving in a dance,
serious and bright, graceful and grave in turn, to the
Dorian pipe, "the Dorian strain." The soft recorders
accompany the pastoral, the idyllic song, wise with
thought, happy with noble phrase, filled with accurate
and loving description of nature ; and in it lives from
line to line the contemplation of humanity.

Virgil and Theocritus have been infused into their
manner and their verse, nor has *Lycidas* been quite
forgotten. Yet they are not imitative ; the atmosphere,
the thought, the music, and the subject are Arnold's
own. Although this classic echo is heard in them,
they are modern, of the tempestuous age when they
were written by one who, while he wrote them, looked
on the tempest, but for their meditative hour was not
tossed upon its waves. Some of the classic episodes
seem a little out of place, especially that of the Tyrian
trader and the Grecian coaster at the end of the *Scholar*

Gipsy, but we are glad to forgive this for the sake of their charm. Indeed, whenever Arnold's poetry touches Greece, we meet an especial music and grace; but nowhere is this clear, lovely, and sweet air so lucid and so pure as in the classic scenery and life which glide in and out of these two elegies. Oxford, while we read, seems not far away from the flowers of Enna or the silent stream of Mantua, nor is the wandering student then surprised to hear Theocritus piping near the Iffley mill, or see, as he passes by, Virgil dreaming under the shade of the Fyfield tree.

But Glanvil's scholar, the gipsy-hearted wanderer, a shy shade that comes and goes, who loves the lovely, quiet world, pursuing ever the ineffable, is brought, in a beautiful variety, into contrast with Arnold's own life, and with the feverish life of his time. Beyond the elegiac cry is the greater cry of humanity. *Thyrsis*, too, closes with the same personal, ever-recurring strain. Thyrsis loved the country, so did I. He felt the storm of his world and went to meet it. It was too much for him and he died.

Too quick despairer, wherefore wilt thou go?

But I was forced into the world. The way is long and the Alps of truth unclimbable. I too am going; but I wander on, like the shy Scholar, like Thyrsis, on the quest. The light we sought is shining still.

DANTE GABRIEL ROSSETTI

IN the course of the history of all the arts, and perhaps most plainly in the history of poetry, similar conditions recur, not in particulars, but in general outline. The different circumstances of each age naturally modify the conditions away from accurate similarity, but in the main development of the art, a time comes when it follows lines resembling those it has previously followed, and this analogous condition has been produced by similar causes. I have already in other places noticed such a similarity between the creation of a literary poetry—to use an inadequate term—by Keats, and that of a similar kind of poetry by Rossetti and Morris. Both poetries have little to do with the age in which they were written. They reject, on the whole, the present and abide in the past. Their subjects are not the subjects of their day, nor are they influenced to any great extent by the thoughts or emotions of the world around them. Their main desire is to live outside of that world, to assimilate a different realm of thought and feeling, to find beauty as she was in the past not as she seems to be in the present, to live in the imagined not in the actual world ; and yet to keep the imagined world true to the main lines of nature and human nature. "Let us escape," they cry, "into a lovelier earth, a purer air, a simpler and more natural life."

We can trace, in the middle of the nineteenth century, the beginnings of such a cry in Arnold's passing endeavour to find his subjects in Greek, Norse, and mediæval story, in his reiterated longing for beauty and calm, apart from the noise of warring thought and low desires. We have looked back to the time when in the fifties and sixties of the last century the old faiths and theories of life were thrown into the hissing furnace of scientific and historical criticism, and no one knew what would emerge when the amalgam had cooled. We have seen how this confused world, and the tossed world of his own heart, were too much for Arnold. He could not escape from the trouble when he was young. He never quite escaped from it. But Rossetti did, and so did Morris.

The history of their poetry repeats the history of the poetry of Keats. It had no connexion with the thoughts concerning man and the war around them which so deeply influenced poetry from Blake to Shelley. The ideas Shelley sought to revive, those also which Byron drove at the heads of men, made the slightest possible impression on Keats. He does not, on the whole, seem to be aware of their existence. The controversies, furies, and passions which had collected round them in the realms of social, political, and religious thought, and which had lashed Byron and Shelley into poetic rage, were to him, if ever he deigned to be conscious of them, weariness and vexation of spirit. And the condition of the England in which he lived and of which he said, "Glory and loveliness have passed away," gave him no impulse. He did not go to Italy or Greece in the body, but he fled thither in the spirit.   He sought loveliness and young ardours in fable, in love's world of myth, legend, and tale. There, he thought, beauty lies asleep, and I will be the young prince who shall awake her. And through the deep undergrowth not of the briar-rose, but of thorn and thistle, hemlock and darnel, his fervid spirit pierced its way.   He kissed the princess and she awoke to life. Together they brought forth a new poetry. It was a lovely child, but, unsupported, unnourished by any emotion of the present, only living in the past, it never married itself to any vital power in the England of its day, and it had then no children. It was an episode in the great epic of poetry; and when the new movement, about 1832, began with Tennyson and Browning it did not follow Keats into the beauty of the past; it knit itself to living emotions and ideas of the present. For England had then, as I have already noticed in this book, awakened to fresh thought and national passion, to new ideas and their attendant emotions; and out of these proceeded powers of action which ran like fire through the whole body of men and women who loved thoughts, and thought out what they loved.

That is a slight sketch of the history of the poetry of

Keats. I have elsewhere expanded it, and do not wish
to repeat it. A similar history now unfolded itself.
By 1853, when Rossetti had finished the poems which
we find in his first volume, the ideas and their impelling
emotions which had begun to shape themselves clearly
in 1830, which had awakened in England a political,
religious, and social movement, and which, by their
passion, had stirred Browning, Tennyson, and others to
write poetry—were subjected to continual attacks,
rapidly developing through the following years, from
historical criticism and science. Doubt, especially in
the case of the religious ideas, collected round them.
So far as the history of poetry is concerned, the struggle took place over religious conceptions, both those
held by the orthodox, and by the more liberal theolo-
gians. The ideas accepted with joy from the school
of which Newman was the moving force, or from the
school which Maurice may be said to have founded,
were now denied or at least subjected to a cold investigation. And what had been their beauty was stained,
till there was little or no pleasure and peace left in
them for the imagination. Tennyson and Browning,
however, would not let their spiritual essence go.
Browning did not descend into the arena at all, nor
was he one whit disturbed by the noise of the contest.
He went quietly on, realising his own soul and what it
had to say. Tennyson did enter into the fight, and
was somewhat disturbed by it. *In Memoriam*, published in 1850, records what he thought of it during

the years between 1842 and '50. Later on, his description of that dim grim battle in the West where Arthur died, himself in doubt, and where friend and foe were shadows in the mist,

> And friend slew friend, not knowing whom he slew,
> And some had visions out of golden youth,
> And some beheld the faces of old ghosts
> Look in upon the battle,

was his record of this time, and all it meant for those who, in its war, still held to their standards. Nor indeed, when he wrote the *Passing of Arthur*, was his own soul freed from the agony of the battle. Nevertheless, he did not give way. Like St. Paul, "cast down but not destroyed," there were certain heights of faith and thought in his secret soul to which, undismayed, and unheeding of the confused strife, he retired when he pleased. But the others—down in the heat of the contest, on the burning sand—we have seen in what a condition they were in the poetry of Clough and Arnold. Misery and restlessness; changing and divided thoughts; doubts and longing for peace and calm; nothing left but duty; faith retired to her interlunar cave; the noise and confusion of the battle driving men distracted who cared for the ancient ideals; even among those who had no poetic instincts a certain vague distress; beauty gone, ugliness and tumult filling the world of thought. And in common life, materialism growing; conventions and maxims again tyrannising over society; art, creation, imagination, and truth

utterly gone out of it. This was the state of things
even in 1847 when Rossetti began to write poetry,
much more in 1853 when his first poems were finished,
still more in the sixties of the last century.

It was a state of things which the artist nature
rebelled against, as, not in identical but in similar circumstances, Keats had rebelled. A whole tribe of
young men, to whom Rossetti and the Pre-Raphaelite
movement and afterwards Morris, Burne-Jones, and
others, gave expression, were weary to death of all
the turmoil round subjects which (as they were presented to them at the moment) did not interest them
at all, much less excite or impel them. All that Arnold
wrote about with so much intensity, all the waters of
thought in which he struggled, were as little to them
as all the ideas which Byron and Shelley wrote of were
to Keats. They broke away from them, like Keats,
into another world—a new world of beauty and art.

The theological contests were outside of their theology which was concerned, when it existed, and for
a time it did exist, not with doctrine and its battles,
but with the inner mystic relation between the personal soul and the divine, between the saints, angels,
and spirits of the universe and their own spirit here
on earth. They were, in their early career, and especially Rossetti, mystics by nature and grace. Doubts
did not trouble them at all. They either believed or
disbelieved. Historical criticism and science bored
them to extinction. They cried : " Away with these

follies and phantasms. That which actually is, is not
in them. They are in the apparent, not the real world.
Why should we walk through their mud and lade ourselves with their thick clay? The constancy of energy,
the correlation of physical forces, natural selection, the
struggle for existence, the descent of man, whether
the Bible be infallible or not—if it be beautiful and
instil peace is all we care for—are outside our world.
For us, they might as well be discussed in Sirius. Let
us get away from this vain disquiet to quiet, from
futile argument to fruitful contemplation, from materialism to the spiritual, from this ugly world to a
beautiful one, from theological squabbles to religious
symbols, from fighting sects to the invisible Church,
from Science and its quarrels to the great creations of
imagination, from convention to truth in art, from
imitation of dead forms of art to Nature herself. Let
us leave a world, noisy, base through money-seeking,
torn and confused with physical and mental ugliness,
worried with dry criticism of history and futile con-
tentions of doctrine, to the realm of pure faith, or, if
we cannot or do not care to believe, to that pure image
of beauty which we see once more rising from the Sea
of Time. And for that we will turn back to the bygone centuries, to their thought and their work, to a
world noble, lovely, joyous, full of passionate subjects,
close to Nature, thrilling with possibilities for the
imagination ; a world which believed in a spiritual
life ; which understood how to love, how to forgive,

how to live in honour, how to despise wealth for beauty's sake ; and which, inspired by great thoughts and yielding itself to natural passion and its joy, created with intelligent rapture, and day by day, beautiful things in all the arts.

Such was the spirit of these men and such their outlook on the world. It was a spirit and an outlook similar (except in its somewhat transient religious or mystic turn) to the spirit and outlook of Keats. And it is well that we should know,—and especially those who think sceptical criticism so vitally important, and science and its discoveries and the analytic intellect with its nose on facts, the master-powers of the world at whose footstool all should bow; and conclusions established by pure reasoning as the only truths ;— that there are still a whole class of men in this manifold world of ours who do not care one straw for all these matters ; to whom the talk about them and their discoveries are practically non-existent in thought ; who would not be very sorry if they were all forgotten ; who live outside of them altogether, and think them needless ; who abhor the money-making side of them ; and who believe that they are likely to do serious damage—as long as they are unbalanced by the things which make for imagination, beauty, and the spiritual life—to high morality, to the love of perfection, to man's happiness, and to the true progress of mankind. These persons, even in these extremes, it is to be hoped will not diminish. They provide a counterpoise to the tyrannies of the scientific intellect, they keep up the balance of power in human life. Silently, for they make no noise and only live their lives, they lead men into worlds where they can rest; and even in ignorance and poverty find inward wealth and joy and sweet content.

In his day Rossetti, ignoring the science and caring nothing for the contending faiths of the present, began a new phase of that ever-recurring movement, both in poetry and painting. Morris followed him into the realm of the past, but separated himself more determinately from a present he detested than Rossetti. He never touched for years a single political, religious, scientific, or social interest of his own time. Rossetti did; being, as a poet, more manifold than Morris. What interest they took in the present was taken in its arts, not in its theological, critical, or scientific work. Holman Hunt, Millais, and afterwards Burne-Jones, flung away, as artists, the traditions which ruled the art of their times, and went back to the early Italian painters for the spirit in which they conceived their art and the duty they owed to it. They filled their pictures with thought and imaginative symbolism, but they did this within the limits of a careful and steady obedience to truth—truth to their subjects and truth to nature. A fresh and living movement of art in painting and drawing was born from these endeavours.

At the same time, and filled with a similar spirit,

the new poetry arose. It was indeed new. No one can for a moment bring together on the same plane of thought or imagination, of passion or of the reception of sensible impressions, the poetry of Tennyson, Browning, Clough, or Arnold, and the poetry of Rossetti or Morris. The air is different, the landscape different, the manner of thinking and feeling different, the subjects different, the methods and the aims of art different, the inspiration drawn from different sources, and the material different. It was as new a poetical world as that of Keats was in his time. It was also an interlude. It had no children or none of any importance. Its apartness from the present made it delightful, but it condemned it to sterility. Its analogy in that to the poetry of Keats is striking. But it is much more striking in the poetry of Morris than in that of Rossetti. The revolt of Morris from the present was much greater. Indeed, Rossetti more or less maintained that "all work to be truly worthy"—and I quote words he has put into the mouth of a character in the unfinished story of St. Agnes of Intercession—"should be wrought out of the age itself, as well as out of the soul of its producer, which must needs be a soul of the age." He did not, from my present point of view, carry out that sentence fully in his work, but he came closer to it than was the case with the poetry Morris wrote before he became a Socialist. The modern element is plain in his treatment of *Jenny*, though the problem is universal. The *Burden of Nineveh*, welds together in his thought London and Nineveh, the religion, the future and the fates of both ; and outside his thoughts, as he sees the winged bull brought into the British Museum, the din and crowds of London go by. At times, the political interests of the world took hold upon him. The revolutionary movement of 1848 was hailed by him, when priests turned white and kings were in the dust. He hears the cry of Italy, and the *Last Confession*, in itself a modern poem, is thrilled throughout with the Italian hatred of Austria. On the *Staircase of Notre Dame*, on the *Place de la Bastille*, he feels the emancipation of Paris and the world. He denounced the atrocious business of 1851. He wrote a half-felt ode on the death and work of Wellington in 1852.

Then, there are short poems, of a delicate and majestic pity, on such sorrowful and heart-subduing incidents as he touched in daily life. *Between Holms-cote and Hurstcote* is a lovely example of this. More-over, even in poems which treat subjects belonging to a remote past, there is often a modern touch, a dim reference to the temper and thoughts of the modern world, which bring, floating into the antique tale, a breath, a wind, from the life of the nineteenth century. These wafts of modernism often give body to his mystic story, and a strange clearness to the past of which he writes.

Again, among a number of poems which treat of love and other passions, and belong to the common life of

man at any time, there are a few which are concerned
with the problems of life, moral and spiritual, and
which, in their mode of thought and expression, are
entirely modern—so modern that even now, nearly
fifty years after they were written, they paint our souls.
They are of our subtilty, our obscurity, our passionate
self-extension ; our hopes, fears, faith, and faithless-
ness. In many wandering ways of careful thought,
they ask what is our life. Of these are all the sonnets
which form the second part of the *House of Life*,
and poems like the *Card Dealer, Cloud Confines, Soothsay*, and a few others of less value. In these, love between the sexes which forms so large a part of his
poetry can scarcely be said to exist. They knit themselves with a singular force around the life of man, his
death, his pain, and his pleasure. They are weighty
with thought, very subtle, yet very clear. The thinking does not run along the known philosophic lines.
It avoids them, as if truth were not to be found on
their roads. It moves, on the contrary, through the
windings, impulses, passionate feelings of the self-
neglecting soul, thinking and feeding in its silences
around the memories, the regrets, the happiness and unhappiness of its past, around the hopes and fears of its
future ; searching into the fierce remorse and the stern
demands that come from conscience ; and questioning
those aspirations of the spirit towards the unattainable
perfection which deny and mock analysis. And, above
all, they ask, with reiterated force—Why are things as

they are? What shall we do, things being as they are? *Soothsay* is such a poem. The poetry belonging to these matters is perhaps the greatest, not the most beautiful, of all his work. It is marked by so masculine a concentration of thought and wording that it demands the closest attention and deserves it. It is not obscure save to inattention. On the contrary, in spite of all the infoldings of thought with thought, it is, by its anxious wording, as clear as a mountain spring. It is not only a poetical but an intellectual pleasure to follow its intricate involutions, made beautiful at every step by the play of a passionate imagination. And this is poetically enhanced by the careful art, by the technique which is not satisfied by anything less than perfection, and which, when perfection is not reached, makes us feel that it has been struggled for with the whole force and eagerness of the artist. One example of this, which is most patent in the sonnets, is the excellent use he makes of long Latin words which seem to open out and expand the thought and set it into a rush like a sudden flood over wide plains. Such words are chiefly adjectives, but they are so used as to have the force of a picture.

Another characteristic of this graver poetry is its unwearied symbolism—incessant images in words, in the sound of lines ; illustrations which awaken emotions or ideas ; images, created by the words, which leap into the vision of the soul, and bring with them a hundred meanings, suggestions, memories, and pict-

ures. Rossetti is a master of this, and it was done by
him in painting as well as in poetry. In poetry he
was freer than in painting, and he used his freedom,
sometimes too richly. He hurries one symbol into
another, he folds and enfolds them together ; they
are labyrinthine ; yet if we pursue them, we reach at
last their centre, and their central thought, with their
central emotion. Then, when we reach the centre,
all the involutions are understood. There is no one
clearer than Rossetti. It may be that some of this
clearness is owing to the music of the verse. That is
another characteristic of his poetry. And his music
does not seem to be the result of laborious art, but of a
native genius for sweet sound. Everywhere we find
this grace, in the lighter as in the graver poems. I
give one example from a serious sonnet. Its melody
flows like a soft stream—

> When vain desire at last and vain regret
> Go hand in hand to death, and all is vain,
> What shall assuage the unforgotten pain
> And teach the unforgetful to forget ?

Lastly, with regard to these serious poems which
meet the questionings of modern life, some have said
that the problems they treat of are similar to those
of which Arnold wrote, and are met in a similar way.
That is not the case. The Stoic solution, for example,
never occurs to Rossetti. Moreover, the problems
are not the simple ones Arnold meets and to which
the intellect naturally applies itself, but the subtle,

complicated questions of the spiritual and passionate life which are altogether outside of the sphere of the intellect, and ignore its methods. And, finally, the subjects are treated, without any special reference to his own soul or to his own time, from that universal point of view which considers human nature as it is independent of any personal feeling or of any isolated period. The later sonnets of *The House of Life* and other poems of a similar kind belong to the present of human nature, but they also belong to its past and its future.

I turn from this discussion of the modern element in Rossetti's poetry to other elements belonging to it. When we read the earlier poems, beginning with *The Blessed Damozel*, we must bring to our reading matters of thought imported from Italy in the thirteenth or fourteenth centuries, or from that ancient world where Lancelot and Tristram lived, or from that more sacred and earlier world which gathered its emotions, like flowers round a house, over the youth of Jesus, the days in Jerusalem after the Cross, and the legends of the Early Church. The elements of these worlds crept into the study of his imagination, were quick in his thought, and move out of his poems, even when they are outside of the Christian realm, into our reflection. They leave their spirit everywhere in his verse, like the distant scent of lavender in linen long laid by in oaken presses.

Of these elements Italy was the chief—the Italy of Dante, and the poets who with him created Italian poetry; nor was modern Italy forgotten or unrepresented. It could not have been otherwise. His mother was half Italian. His father, Gabriele Rossetti, was a native of the Kingdom of Naples, a man of letters, a poet and patriot; forced to flee from the tyranny of Ferdinand I., and well known in England as a commentator and exponent of Dante. From his childhood Rossetti was trained to love his father's land, and its greatest poet, and his poetry as well as his painting were filled with the subjects and redolent of the mysticism of the wisdom-worn Italian. Yet so strong was Rossetti's clear individuality that no one can say he was an imitator of Dante. Whatever he drew from Dante he passed through the crucible of his own soul, and so mingled it with his own material that the result was incontestably his own. His spirit was dominant in it, not Dante's. Moreover, it was not only the austere and tender spirit of Dante of which he drank deep, but the pleasanter and lighter spirit of the men who before and after Dante made poetry within his circle. With these also he sympathised, but he drank more of their manner, a manner which was common to them all, than of their matter. For Rossetti, like Dante, was always somewhat severe, serious, even grim at times, when he wrote poetry. There was, indeed, another side to Rossetti—a wild, mocking Bohemian side, full of grim sarcastic humour, but this did not intrude into either of the arts he practised. The solemnities of our earthly life and of its passions more than its gaiety or pleasure were in this poetry daily guests. And his methods of writing, his style, his correction and finish, were as severe, as strictly conscientious to his art, as those of Dante or Milton. Otherwise, I do not compare him to them. The limits of Dante and Milton extend beyond our ken. The limits of Rossetti are clearly within our ken. But within them his matter and his manner were nobly grave, severe, temperate, and controlled, almost too controlled at times to have the ease and naturalness of the greater poets.

The manner then of his work was largely influenced by the early Italian poets, even by their perversity of logic in amorous poetry, but was not imitated from them. His vivid, intense individuality burnt up the possibility of imitation. Whatever he gripped, he gripped in his own way ; and the way was original. And all that I have here said concerning the Italian influence in his poetry might be even more fully said of his works as a painter.

Again, one might expect that his poetry would be greatly influenced by mediæval romance, especially by the multitudinous tale of Arthur, with its dependencies. It may be said of him with truth that he was Galahad on one side of his nature and Tristram on another. But though he loved the tale, and oftentimes discussed it, it scarcely ever appears, even in allusion, in his poetry. The story seized on contemporary poetry ; it did not seize on his ; and this, like many other things, isolates the man. The Italian genius separated him from the Celtic and Teutonic elements in the cycle of Arthur. Indeed, I have observed that those poets on whom the shadow of Dante falls, with whom Italy dwells as a mistress, are not only freed from the Celtic glamour, but out of harmony with the Celtic temperament. The Latin nature does not agree with the Celtic. It is too serious, and life presents itself under too grave an aspect for such agreement. Moreover, all through the Arthurian tale—I do not speak of its later modifications in Germany—the passions, and above all the passion of love and the passion of war, are lightly felt in comparison with the profound and grim impetuosity of the way they are felt by the Italian people. And it was so Rossetti felt them. There was nothing Celtic or indeed Teutonic about him or his poetry. In this also, he wholly differed from Morris who, in spite of his being partly Celtic by descent, had Teutonic rather than Celtic elements dominant in his nature. Except in his intense individuality, his extraordinary eye for colour and his love for it, and in a certain, but not common, affection for the wilder forms of natural scenery, Morris was little of a Celt. The Arthur legend caught him, it is true, but it was in its mediæval, not in its Celtic, forms.

Then again, the Celtic genius is somewhat disordered. It does not willingly submit to the logic of the imagination, nor is its imagination ridden with a curb. But the Italian genius loves order, strict arrangement of thought, fixed and chosen limits wherein to exercise itself, well linked emotions bound together by one dominant idea. Its imagination is not fettered, but it moves of its own will, under self-chosen laws. It is also always controlled for the sake of the full and clear expression of the subject. And all this is sternly characteristic of Rossetti's poetry. It is a pleasant exercise, when one has leisure, to follow the intricate windings—as of some mediæval designer—of the imaginative reason through any one of Rossetti's sonnets. We cannot find anything more fiercely beaten into order, yet so closely set on beauty as an end, in English literature. It is not really English; it is Italian, and it divides Rossetti from his poetic comrades. There is not a trace of it in Morris or in Swinburne. Though he communicated to them a series of impulses from his originating genius, yet he gave them nothing of this; or rather they could not receive it. He was left alone with this part of himself, and severely alone he remained with it.

At another point he was Italian, not English—in his love-poetry. It was accused of sensualism, but all its tendency is, in truth, toward a noble chastity in the natural affairs of love. As to the accusation, and the controversy arising from it, I will content myself with saying—as most intelligent persons came to say, including his accuser—that the accusation was false and

unworthy. Yet I can partly understand how it came
to be made, though I cannot understand a brother in
poetry having either the heart or the want of intelligence to make it. It was really Italian and not English
love-poetry which Rossetti wrote, and so vitally different from the English way of feeling and speaking of
love-passion, that, when it fell on English ears and especially on Lowland Scottish ears where it touched the
ingrained puritanism of a Teutonic people, it was to
them like listening to a foreign tongue which because
folk do not understand, they think to be out of nature.
It was really the difference of national genius which
was at the root of the accusation.

The warmth, the glow, the white fire of Rossetti's
love-poetry, the concentration of the whole being for
the time of writing, to the exclusion of all else, on the
passion of the hour or the life, which is characteristic
of the Italian poets, and especially of Dante, who lays
all the realms of feeling, spirit, and intellect at the feet
of his love, astounded the English nature ; and whatever astonishes England revolts her till she slowly
comes to understand it. She had been for a long time un-
accustomed to love-poetry of this kind. We shall find no
parallel, not even in Burns, to Rossetti's love-poetry till
we get back to the Elizabethans, who themselves were
deeply influenced by the Italian poetry. Shakespeare's
sonnets are steeped in Italy, and there are no love-son-
nets in English Literature which in concentrated thought
approach those of Shakespeare, except Rossetti's.

Then, English love-poetry is chiefly concerned with the growth of love, its aspirations, the results it has on life while its end is as yet unattained; or with that which follows on the attainment of love—its regrets, its quiet pleasures, its miseries, its fancies or its ruin. Italian poetry and Rossetti's—even where it takes similar subjects of love as English poetry—is concerned with all these subjects raised to intensity; with love in all its forms at their height, and with all the world brought into fiery union with it. We see in English love-poetry all the landscape of love's country. We see in Italian, and in Rossetti, the sun of love itself which made the landscape. That is another reason, arising out of national difference, which made this poetry, at its first appearance, strange, and therefore objectionable, to English folk.

Moreover, and this is perhaps the most important thing, English love-poetry, when it is sensuous, which is rare, is for the most part unmixed with any spiritual feeling; and when it is spiritualised, which is common, is kept apart from the elements of sense. Except in a very few men—among whom I may instance Dr. Donne, and he insists on the sensuous too much for the spirit—there is little intense and complete admixture of the sensuous and spiritual elements of love in English poetry. There *is* such an admixture in the best Italian poetry; even in the lower poetry, in poetry frankly sensual, the spiritualising element steals in. But in Rossetti's love-poetry this complete

fusion of the spirit and the sense is expressed more
intimately than in any Italian poetry, because he was
partly English, and England gave him more reticence;
and more intensely than in any English poetry, because he was three-fourths Italian. Those times in
love between man and woman when the sensuous element is lifted by pure joy and emotion into the spiritual world and there transfigured; and when the
spiritual element is brought into the sensuous till it is
made, as it were, palpable, embodied, incarnated—
when both sense and spirit are fused into one fire—in
those love is best known, best felt and best expressed,
and they are of love's finest, purest, most exalted
power. No one in England has shaped them into
words like Rossetti; and he, feeling their clear purity
and beauty, thought himself licensed to express them.
They are a thousand years away from sensualism, but
the strangeness and uniqueness of them in English
poetry jarred at first the English nature, and especially
on its reserve. I am not, however, sure that this revelation of the central heart of love is not too intimate
for words. It is there, if anywhere, that I should
challenge the love-poetry of Rossetti.

The love-poetry is of the finest Italian quality in the
Sonnets, where he was forced to pack what he thought
and felt into fourteen lines, and to arrange its development in obedience to a strict rule. When he was not
thus limited his love-poetry is less excellent. It
wanders into so many side issues that its passion is

ravelled. It runs to so great a length in consequence that the reader who expected and almost hoped to be burnt alive, is only warmer by its ashes. This is the case with *The Stream's Secret*, with *Love's Nocturn* in spite of its many fascinating verses. *The Song of the Bower* is far better than these, true throughout to its subject. Its subject is common in experience, and its feeling deep, but more fitted perhaps for a woman than for a man. The strength of love in *The Blessed Damozel* is deeper, more speechless—all that is said is thought not actually expressed by the woman—and more united, than in any other love-lyric Rossetti wrought. Infinite regret, infinite hope mingle their emotions in it. It is illuminated by many images, many pictures, but these are so full of the one passion, that their number and variety concentrate rather than disperse it. Moreover, although they adorn it with a beauty not of the earth but of heaven, yet the emotions of the earth are intense within the heavenly loveliness. It is a mixture, strange, complex, and beautiful.

Again, there are many love-lyrics, some light, some sad, on transient phases of love—its memories of joy and sorrow, its regrets for lost opportunities, its broodings on happiness which might have been and was not, its ruins and its raptures, in the past, its despondent hopes, its changes and why they came, its false economics, its true extravagance—lyrics such as *First Love Remembered*, *Sudden .Light*, *Plighted Promise*, *Three*

Shadows, A Little While, Spheral Change, and others
a few of which are light and gay.

It is in the sonnets of the first part of *The House
of Life* that Rossetti's love-poetry ought most to be
studied. The atmosphere which they breathe and
which fills them is not English. It is chiefly Italian,
but not pure Italian. It is mingled with English elements, and this separates them into a class apart from
either England or Italy. They stand alone, and this
loneliness of theirs is part of their charm to those readers
who are fond of the unique in literature. Of course
they belong, therefore, to the particular, not the universal, and to the particularly particular, like those
specialised manufacturers of porcelain of which only
twenty or thirty examples exist in the world. This
rarity also pleases their readers, but restricts the number of them. They do not appeal, like the highest
poetry, to the multitude; and this particularity is
enhanced by the strangeness to English readers of
their Italian manner of thought and imaging. That
manner also, in its complexity of expression and its
multitudinous imagery, seems to us to disperse and
dishevel their emotion. It is only when we are accustomed to it, that we discover to our surprise that it
enhances it. Their elaborate thought, their subtle
logical intellectualism seems also to take them away
from the simplicity of love, to diminish its intensity,
even to chill it. But this is of the very nature of such
Italian sonnets as those of the *Vita Nuova* and, as

before, a little trouble enables us to feel that passion
has entered into the intellectual work, and is in it
like a fire. A sonnet itself demands concentration of
thought and emotion. Its form creates intensity, or
ought to create it. And in these sonnets of Rossetti
thought and emotion are packed as closely as the summer sprays and leaves are packed in the winter sheaths
of a beechen spray. Their concentration makes their
heat. It is too hot for flame—"each of its own arduous
fulness reverent."

Their subject is Love, but Love for the most part
in its momentary phases. They seem to spring from
any daily experience; from writing a letter, walking
in a wood, a flash of sunlight, from all his mistress
does and is, her hands, her voice, her eyes, from the
changes of the seasons and the weather, from dreams
which picture her, and moods which recall her moods—
yet, however, the subject changes, one Love is dominant over the changes and in it every subject glows.
And as the main subject is love, and beauty is the
form of love, each sonnet seeks at every point to be
and to secure beauty of form, of expression, in the
parts and in the whole. It is owing to this seeking of
beauty that their symbolism is so multitudinous, for
by symbolism beauty can most easily be suggested.
Into certain melodies of words, into adjectives which
awaken associations, into illustrations drawn from
nature, into impersonations of states of the soul,
Rossetti packs his symbols, so that not unfrequently

every one of the fourteen lines of the sonnet has its awakening symbol, each illuminating and intensifying the subject of the whole. I quote the following sonnet—*Soul's Beauty*. It illustrates what I have tried to say, and is itself a noble example of his sonnet-poetry:

Under the arch of Life, where love and death,
Terror and mystery, guard her shrine, I saw
Beauty enthroned; and though her gaze struck awe,
I drew it in as simply as my breath.
Hers are the eyes which, over and beneath,
The sky and sea bend on thee,—which can draw,
By sea or sky or woman, to one law,
The allotted bondsman of her palm and wreath.

This is that Lady Beauty, in whose praise
Thy voice and hand shake still,—long known to thee
By flying hair and fluttering hem,—the beat
Following her daily of thy heart and feet,
How passionately and irretrievably,
In what fond flight, how many ways and days!

It remains to say that this love-poetry is only of love between the sexes, and within a limited area of that love. It seems a pity that so much good poetry, subtle feeling, careful thought and art should be expended on a kind of love which, however varied its phases, is, when it is made the sole interest of life, so fleeting and so isolating. It is natural, even needful, to pass through its house in youth, but men and women have other and fairer houses to dwell in permanently. All the greater poets have felt this. They have written lyrics of this passion, but these are only incidental. Their real work is elsewhere in humanity. Rossetti

gave too much to this business of love.   Yet, if we are
to have it, it was well to have it excellently done, and
it is so done.

I pass on to the mysticism of his poetry.   It is
difficult to characterise it because it was so complex.
It was compounded of many elements, and they frequently contradict one another.   But he had a way, like
Ruskin and others, of inducing apparent contradic-
tories to live within him in an amiable harmony.   He
cherished, for example, at one time of his life, quite
an ascetic turn, but at the same time, thoroughly
disliking the principles of asceticism, he gave to the
body its full value in his work.   He had faith in a
divine love when he wrote his early poetry, and he
knew what he believed, and yet he had a curious turn
for superstition, which arises straight out of fear and
ignorance of the gods.   Such harbouring of contra-
dictories in one soul is characteristic of a certain type
of mysticism and has sometimes been tranferred to
philosophy.

It is difficult also to explain mysticism in Rossetti,
because it is difficult to define mysticism itself.   It
shows a different aspect in every man who is affected
by it.   But generally speaking it is that temper of
mind and feeling which considers the apparent world
and all its ways as not real, except relatively to our
constitution; and the invisible world of the spirit and
of life, outside of our world of sense-perception, the

real world. And that is Rossetti's position as a poet.
It makes his poetry difficult to that large class of
persons who have no mystic tendency, to whom all
mysticism appears impossible. The appeal then of
his mysticism is to a small class at present ; and though
his range within its circle over many and various subjects is remarkable, yet the circle itself is a small one.
On the whole, so widespread through his poetry is this
mystic element, that I doubt whether he will ever
come to be read extensively until the spiritual view of
the universe has conquered the materialistic view. At
present, in the midst of the loud yelling of the armies
of materialism, Rossetti's voice is not likely to be
heard at large.

At first there was a touch of asceticism in his mysticism, not that which crushes or despises the body on
the ground that all matter is evil (that was repugnant
to him), but that which restrains appetite and sense-
enjoyment in order to be able to contemplate more
quietly and to realise more fully spiritual ideas and the
spiritual world in an impassioned imagination ; and,
again, in order to feel his own soul in direct contact
with a spiritualised world. In his pursuit of the arts,
he made both painting and poetry partakers of this
endeavour. It would be easy to illustrate this effort
by self-control to rise above the apparent from his early
painting, but that is outside my subject. It is not easy
to illustrate this mystic asceticism from his earlier
poetry, because it only pervades it, is not defined in it.

It lingers in it like a scent of unseen flowers, like a dim
music heard over misty waters—and this almost sensible appeal to the world of the soul, chiming through
the verse, is especially comforting to those of the same
temper of mind, and secludes him as their poet.   Nor
was it unrepresented otherwise in his family.   In
another direction, with a clear religious passion, and
with that doctrinal foundation in which Rossetti had
no interest, his sister, Christina, was a mystic.   Her
unreligious poems are those of a mystic.   As to her
religious poems, and her treatment in them of the soul
and life of man, nothing so deeply felt, so poetically
conceived, so lyrically pure, has been written in
England.

If we wish to feel what Rossetti's mysticism was in
the early days, when he was nineteen years old, and at
the same time to know what his aspirations were as an
artist, and the foundations of his artistic thought, it is
well to read *Hand and Soul*, a little tale published in
1850 in *The Germ*, a magazine started to represent the
principles and spread the ideas of the Pre-Raphaelite
Brotherhood.   It is a literary jewel—opal, ruby, and
sapphire in one.   It is steeped through and through,
in every sentence, in every turn of expression, in
thought and feeling, with his personality ; written as
it were by the soul itself.   The little book then has one
of the elements of a fine style.   And in other points—
in clearness, in naturalness, in ease, in constant surprise, in excellent arrangement—the style is as good as

the stuff. Moreover, with all its mysticism, the mediæval time and the *mise en scène*, especially the fierce
swift outburst of the two noble factions into wild war
in the streets of Pisa, are given with a masterly realism
which makes a delightful contrast with the mysticism.
On that realism in Rossetti I shall touch hereafter.
At present I refer to one more element in his poetry
which is indirectly linked with his mysticism.

The love of the supernatural—in weird, uncommon
or ghastly forms, of witcheries and charms, apparitions
and ghostly enemies, of all that half-human, half-spirit-
ual world which hovers and works, as some think, in
a zone between earth and heaven—is an offshoot, in a
certain temper of mind, of mysticism. That it is so is
a matter of history. And Rossetti when it pleased him
to get into this world, did so with a peculiar pleasure.
It did not master him. He dominated it, otherwise he
could not have written about it with such imaginative
intensity, with so close a grasp, as he does, for example,
in *Sister Helen*. We feel, as we read, that the woman
and the vengeance were fact, that such a power exists, that her belief in her spell is justified ; but we
also feel that Rossetti is master of his realisation ;
stands without it as its maker, while he is within it, as
its conceiver. He believes, by imagination, in the
wasting of the woman's betrayer as the waxen figure
melts, but the high reason of the artist has no belief
in it.

Having this double power over his conceptions and

his art, he loves to imagine and shape art-subjects in
this supernatural world.   One of his favourite stories
was the story of Lilith and Adam, and he wrote a wild
poem upon it.   One of his favourite books was *Sidonia
the Sorceress*, a book of Meinhart's.   One of the grim-
mest, weirdest of all his designs was of two lovers
meeting their wraiths in a wood, and seeing their ghostly
presentment in a light half fire, half gold ; a mist of
fateful flame.   " How we met ourselves " is its title.
Rose Mary is full of black magic, of evil spirits in
precious stones, of unearthly beings that betray men
and women who trust in them ; and the poetry is, to its
very sound and movement, veiled by a supernatural
mist, like that which broods in *Christabel*.   The studies
in prose, like the *St. Agnes of Intercession*, and the
schemes for poems drawn up in prose—*The Orchard Pit*,
The Doom of the Sirens, *Michael Scott's Wooing*, *The
Philtre*, show how much his imagination loved to
wander in this distant land, and how well fitted he was
to cope with it and impress us with its atmosphere.

The only poet, at this point, with whom I can compare Rossetti—not in the poetry itself, but in a similar
love of this kind of subject, and a similar power of
creating its atmosphere—is Coleridge, for whose few
years of fine work Rossetti had a deep admiration.
The Ancient Mariner, Christabel, The Three Graves
move and have their being in this dusky, unhuman
world and breathe its air with magic ease.   Nor does
the parallel fail in other particulars.   Coleridge, too,

was steeped in mysticism of the noble sort; and this, with far more distinctiveness of religion than Rossetti knew, pervades his poetry. And Coleridge, also, like Rossetti, while he infiltrated his soul into the characters who made, or were subjected to, his supernaturalism, so that we must believe in them as we read, is yet, in his artist will and reason, in his shaping power, the master of the things he made; is on a higher mystic plane than they. In that higher, simpler, spiritual world he and the young Rossetti lived. From it they descended to touch and vivify the lower supernatural. Into it, when they had done that work, they easily re-ascended.

In curious opposition or contrast to this love of the supernatural was Rossetti's realism, his pleasure in facts, in things as they are in the present, as they were in the past; only, being an artist, he chose the facts he represented for the sake of their beauty and loving-ness, and composed them as his imagination saw them. The form was imaginative; but the materials used were so chosen and arranged as to be strictly true to nature. When Turner painted a landscape, the form he gave it was conceived from the impression the landscape made upon him. In accordance with the emotion of that impression he composed not only the whole but the detail of his picture. It might or might not resemble the place which had produced the impression, but it exactly resembled what his soul had seen and his im-agination had shaped within him. The beauty, the voice, the spirit of the picture, the intelligence which fled through it, were born out of his soul striving for beauty. That was the mystic, the spiritual, the imaginative part. It is analogous to that which Rossetti's imaginative mysticism did for the subjects of his mystical poems.

But the material which Turner painted into his picture was rigidly true to nature. The mountain lines and surfaces, down to the smallest detail, were true to existing mountain forms. The curves of running and falling water and of waves of the sea; the outlines of clouds in calm or storm, and the swirling and tossing of their masses, and their drifts of flying foam; the bending, leap, and sturdy strength of trees and their branches; the colour and the light, the mist and the distance, were all true, point by point, to what he had observed and recorded in note after note, of the facts of nature. This was his realism, and it could not be more sternly faithful than it was to truth. It is quite analogous to that which Rossetti's realism did in poetry and art. Mystic religion in art, mystic mediæ-valism and magical supernaturalism, were combined by him with a stern realism, a determined clinging to the actual both in nature and human nature. The aim of the Pre-Raphaelite Brotherhood laid down by Rossetti himself in *The Germ*, is this, "To enforce an entire, or rigid, adherence to the simplicity of nature, either in Art or Poetry." Holman Hunt did follow that rule from the beginning. He follows it now. He kept close, even in his largest designs, to the simplicity and

truth of nature. What he mingled with it was symbolism rather than mysticism. But the symbolism was
contained in accurate representation of natural fact,
selected and arranged to contain the symbols.

Rossetti did not completely follow the rule he laid
down. He was more complex, more unexpected than
the rest of his fellows, and while he painted on canvas
or described in words his details with truth to nature,
he did not cling fast to simplicity. He drenched his
work not only with symbols but also with mystic theology and mediæval superstition. The atmosphere he
had the genius to add to his poetry and his painting
was not in nature, nor in the intellectual explanation
men give to symbolism. It was above and beyond
both, drawn from the strange incursions of his imagination into unexplored lands of his own soul, into the
realm some call the subliminal consciousness ; drawn
also from a spiritual, often a præternatural, world.
This is true both of his poetry and his painting ; and
this distinguishes him from his brothers in art.

In 1848 the Pre-Raphaelite Brotherhood was formed
to carry this combined imagination and realism, symbolism and naturalism, into art. The two primal
movers in it were Holman Hunt and Millais, and
Rossetti became, at many points, one with them.
They were the chiefs, the men whose power grew and
lasted. And all the three, with the modifications
which naturally belonged to three potent individual-

ities, followed in their early work their law with consistent obedience; and, creating a new and living school, rescued the art of painting from the degradation into which it had fallen;* flung aside its vulgar conventions; infused into it ardour, imagination, life, and truth. They returned to Nature, and Nature, welling over into them from her perennial fires of life, day by day kindled and fanned their imagination into creative power, so that all subjects became new in their hands. There had not been such an art-awakening since Wordsworth himself returned to nature in his art, and, inspired by her, added to his realism the passion and mystery of the spiritual world, of the soul searching for beauty through infinitude. In poetry that was more easy of accomplishment than in painting. In painting it had chiefly to be done by symbolism ;—that is, the natural things in the painting, while they were painted with exact truth, were so arranged that they suggested the thoughts and emotions the picture was intended to convey. In the *Carpenter's Shop* of Millais the scene is realised as it was to the smallest detail. All conventions are thrown aside. The room, open to the country, is a poor carpenter's room; the bench, the lathe, the table, the tools, the furniture are painted directly from the things themselves. Joseph is a working man ; Mary, with her ethereal face, Christ and the Baptist, are such persons as might have been seen by passers-

*Art, that is, other than landscape art. Turner had long since done this work for landscape art.

by in the streets of Nazareth. Their dress is the dress
of the poor. Everything, down to the shavings on the
floor, is kept rigidly to the reality. But everything is
also so arranged as to be symbolic. The life, the mis-
sion, and the death of Christ are shadowed in the scene
and its accessories. The very landscape outside, where
the sheep are wandering on the hills, speaks of the great
Shepherd. The wound which Mary is binding up in
the hand of Christ, the sorrow in her face, tell the
story of the coming tragedy and redemption. The
very arrangement of the tools is symbolic. The mystic and the real mingle.

I take another picture, *The Scapegoat*, by Holman
Hunt. The acted parable, with all its profound meaning, of the animal sent into the wilderness laden with
the sins of the people, speaks from every part of the
picture, but is concentrated in the slow, heavy-burdened
Syrian goat who labours under the spiritual weight
through the salt crust of the Dead Sea shore. This
symbolic element is the soul of the picture. But the
animal is painted from nature with the utmost reality.
Nor is there a light or a shade on the Dead Sea waters,
nor a branch on the shore, nor a stunted shrub, nor
a cliff or valley on the sun-baked mountains of
Moab which was not painted with the most seeing
eye and with the most accurate pencil, at the place
itself.

There is a little unfinished water-colour of Rossetti's
which used to hang near Ruskin's bed in Denmark

Hill, and which was the first thing he showed me on the first day I visited him, very long ago. It is the *Passover in the Holy Family.* Under a rude porch, supported by unhewn doorposts made of young trees, Zacharias is sprinkling the wooden lintel. The blood of the lamb which Joseph had brought trickles down one of the posts of the porch, near which Jesus, a small boy, is standing, holding the bowl of blood, and looking at the crimson stream, rapt in thought. Elizabeth is lighting the pyre, and Mary gathering bitter herbs, and John fastening the shoes for departure, which he was not worthy to unloose. The whole drawing, and the figures and faces, are steeped in symbolism. There is scarcely a knot on the wood of the rude porch or a fold of the garments of the folk which has not a meaning addressed to the Christian supernaturalism ; but the landscape, the cottage, the dresses, the details are as close as they could be made to reality. They are conceived and drawn as they would be at the time in the dwelling of a poor family on the slopes of Nazareth. I might illustrate the same mingling of the ideal and the real, through a detailed symbolism, from Rossetti's impassioned picture of the Virgin in the house of St. John on the night of Good Friday, but I refer my readers, since the picture is to be seen, to *The Girlhood of Mary.* The girl, the bed, the room, the flower, the embroidery, the walls, every detail, are painted with the utmost reality direct from nature, but Rossetti has recorded their symbolism—

—On that cloth of red
I' the centre is the Tripoint : perfect each,
Except the second of its points, to teach
That Christ is not yet born.   The books—whose head
Is golden charity, as Paul hath said—
Those virtues are wherein the soul is rich :
Therefore on them the lily standeth, which
Is Innocence, being interpreted.
The seven-thorn'd briar, and the palm seven-leaved
Are her great sorrow and her great reward.

It was often his way to embody not only in painting,
but also in poetry, this mysticism and realism.   At
the beginning of his poetic life he mixed them in
religious poems on the Gospel history ; and the most
relevant example of this is the beautiful poem entitled
Ave, which is really three pictures translated into verse.
Only the three subjects, being here conceived and
worked by him as a poet, and not as a painter, are
radically different in the way the ideas and feelings
are represented, from any pictured representation of
them.   The poem supports, I think, my statement,
but whether it does or not, it ought to be read for the
sake of its beauty.

The realism in that poem is less than the mystic
supernaturalism, but it is clearly there.   Nor was his
realistic and symbolic treatment of the Gospel story
ever quite given up.   It arose in later years in another
form, when the realism was mixed with the supernaturalism, not of the Gospel story, but of the mediæval
Church.   The elaborate symbolism of the mediæval
religion and theology attracted him as strongly as

they did Dante. The beauty which gathered round the conceptions of Heaven and of its cosmogony, such conceptions as the Earthly Paradise of Dante which was all but Heaven, its mystic indwellers, and the Divine Pageant which accompanied the chariot of the Church, stirred Rossetti's imagination with a nameless joy. The mystic Rose of the Saints in the Empyrean, the angelic choirs of the Nine Spheres, adoring, and cloṭhed with unutterable loveliness of form and colour ; the companies of the Greek and Latin Fathers, the Virgin Saints and Martyrs who walked together in the green fields and beside the waters of Paradise, the serene beauty of their ideal shapes, each charged with the thought and emotion of centuries—these, and a hundred more imaginations, filled his soul with a heavenly pleasure and inspired his thought. His imagination walked in them like a queen singing to herself in a walled and secret garden. *The Blessed Damozel* is the best outcome of these attractions. It is mystic throughout. Yet it clings, as the mediæval painters and poets did, to realism. It is as clear as things are in Dante. The rampart of Heaven, the gold bar over the sheer depth of Space are described with close reference to place and appearance. The view of all the worlds below is given, even to the look, from Heaven's unfathomable height, of the earth and moon. The shrine of God Himself, the living, mystic tree of the Spirit, the groves where the Lady Mary walks with her five handmaidens, and how they sit garlanded and weaving into the white robes the golden thread for the dead, now new-born, the angels in their level flight—are made as visible to our eyes as if they were actually seen. They are close to reality, even down to the warmth of the golden parapet on which her bosom leaned, and the passion with which

> she cast her arms along
> The golden barriers,
> And laid her face between her hands
> And wept.

A last touch of this strong realism ends the poem—" I heard her tears."

If any poem of Rossetti's is known, that is known. It is a lovely thing, as exquisite in tenderness and sublimated thought as it is in form and finish. He was only twenty when he wrote it, and his art is as true and fine in it as in the best of the later sonnets, so swiftly does genius grow to its full height. The subject is noble, and appeals to universal feeling. No one who has loved and lost, and waits here below, or there above, but must have cherished its main thought and felt its main emotion. The ornament is beautiful, and is charged with human feeling. It is not the work of fancy but of imagination piercing with vital power into the heart of the subject, and radiating new thought, new feeling through every verse, even every line.

This kind of mediævalism, of which there are so few examples in the earlier poems and many in the painting, continued to appear at intervals in his poetry. It traverses *A Last Confession*, that remarkable piece of Italian modernism and fierce reality. It breaks out fully in the dream the murderer tells the priest :

> I know last night
> I dreamed I saw into the garden of God,
> Where women walked whose painted images
> I've seen with candles round them in the church.
> They bent this way and that, one to another,
> Playing: and over the long golden hair
> Oı each there floated like a ring of fire
> Which when she stooped stooped with her, and when she rose
> Rose with her. Then a breeze flew in among them,
> As if a window had been opened in heaven
> For God to give His blessing from, before
> This world of ours should set ; (for in my dream
> I thought our world was setting, and the sun
> Flared, a spent taper ;) and beneath that gust
> The rings of light quivered like forest leaves.
> Then all the blessed maidens who were there
> Stood up together, as it were a voice
> That called them ; and they threw their tresses back,
> And smote their palms, and all laughed up at once,
> For the strong heavenly joy they had in them
> To hear God bless the world.

That is a new imagination, built out of the conception of the mediæval heaven such as Fra Angelico took up from the middle age and painted, where the saints and martyrs and angels dance on the flowery meadows in a golden air ; but this is touched not only with the rude, peasant nature of the dreamer, but with modern thought expressed with modern turns of words. And the laughter of the maidens is not of the mediæval foundation. Dante was too serious for that.

Beatrice never laughs, but smiles; and her smile illumines heaven.

Then all through the *Staff and Scrip*—a story borrowed from the Gesta Romanorum—through *The World's Worth*, where Father Hilary climbs the steep-coiled stair of the church among the bells and hears the mass below, and finds his world in God alone—a beautiful short poem—the religious mediæval atmosphere is fully realised. But it is not only the religious atmosphere. A hundred touches in these poems bring the churches of the middle ages, the castles, moats, the gardens, the wild country round the solitary fortresses, the superstitions, the belief in magic and in evil spirits, the women, the lovers, the battles, the music, before the eyes of the mind. Nor is that neglected which is so vivid in mediæval Romance : the intense colour and fantasy in design, of glass and tapestry and raiment; the jewelled robes and shoes and belts; the love of gorgeous and heraldic dress and armour. I quote a few verses from *The Bride's Prelude*, which flame and glitter while we read :

> Within the window's heaped recess
>   The light was counterchanged
> In blent reflexes manifold
> From perfume-caskets of wrought gold
> And gems the bride's hair could not hold
>
> All thrust together : and with these
>   A slim-curved lute, which now,
> At Amelotte's sudden passing there,
> Was swept in some wise unaware,
> And shook to music the close air.

Against the haloed lattice-panes
  The bridesmaid sunned her breast ;
Then to the glass turned tall and free,
And braced and shifted daintily
Her loin-belt through her cote-hardie.

The belt was silver, and the clasp
  Of lozenged arm-bearings ;
A world of mirrored tints minute
The rippling sunshine wrought into 't,
That flushed her hand and warmed her foot.

At least an hour had Aloyse,—
  Her jewels in her hair,—
Her white gown, as became a bride,
Quartered in silver at each side,—
Sat thus aloof, as if to hide.

Over her bosom, that lay still,
  The vest was rich in grain,
With close pearls wholly overset :
Around her throat the fastenings met
Of chevesayle and mantelet.

It is not as good as it might be, but it illustrates
this element of mediævalism in his poetry, and it is
a painter's poetry. The room, the figures, the dresses,
the colour, make up a picture ; and they suggest another element in Rossetti's poetry on which I dwell for
a moment—his attempt to represent in poetry what he
had made in painting. He wrote a number of sonnets
on his own pictures. I do not think they are successful. I do not believe in the representation through a
second art-vehicle of that which has been previously
represented in another. One of the representations is
not only always weaker than the other, but also lowers

the imaginative level of the other; and where the
attempt is deliberately made to make a picture into a
poem, or a poem into a picture, the poem or the picture
is not as freshly shaped as it ought to be. The new
vehicle does not secure originality; on the contrary,
the new thing cannot help taking something of the
old, and that something, when it has been felt through
painting and realised in painting, does not fit in with
that which ought to be felt through poetry and realised
in poetry. The same may be said when the poem has
preceded the picture. Rossetti's sonnets on his pictures are mere translations of pictures into words, and
I cannot read them with patience.

But this does not prevent the interest one has when
into poetry, the subject of which has not yet been
painted, the painter intrudes, and visualises in words,
that which he sees in his mind as a picture. This is
quite different from making a poem out of a finished
picture. This is the spirit and eye of a painter giving
to the poem an additional and subordinate excellence,
which does not interfere with the distinctive poetic
conception of the subject. And Rossetti, in the poems
where he uses the powers of the painter to enhance
his poetic work, has done that which is unique in
English poetry. There has been no other poet in
England who was also a painter of genius, and who
really could use the painter's gifts to adorn therewith
the poet's work.

And now I return to my main subject. One of the

tendencies of a mystic supernaturalism in religion is, in certain moods of a poet, to enter into and represent a magic supernaturalism, such as over wide classes of men in ignorant times, ends in the belief in demons, in spirits who inhabit matter, in black magic, in witches and gramarye.   A poet like Rossetti could scarcely help feeling sympathy with this common tendency in human nature.   Moreover, his own nature had a certain pleasure in playing with these things and living in their world.   It was in the family.   Even Christina, in *Goblin Market*, shows this tendency, though the aim of the poem takes it out of the realm of superstition.   In her brother's poetry, *Sister Helen* is the finest example of this kind of work.   Helen has been betrayed by her lover, who takes to himself a wife. High on her tower she has made a pile of wood, and she melts a waxen man before its heat, and, as the wax melts, Keith of Ewern's flesh and blood melt away in fervent heat.   Her little brother watches in the moonlight from the balcony of the tower, and the two brothers of the sick man, and then his father, ride for life and death to the foot of the tower and cry to the boy to speak to Helen, "that she take away the curse, and if she will not save the body to save the soul." But she clings to her revenge, and slays her own soul with his.   Nothing can be more vivid than the realisation of this, and it is all the more vivid, through contrast, because it is carried on by the conversation of the innocent child with the guilty woman.   The tower, the burning pyre, the melting image, the moonlight on the moors and the road, the wild storm, the galloping horses, the white mane and plume and the grey hair of the great Baron, the pitiful cry of their agony, the white soul of Ewern, dead at last, that flits through the forest, lost as Helen's soul is lost, are seen with such reality that we seem to stand on the balcony and look into the room, and over the moorland road. Yet the whole thing is in an unreal world. This is the mixture of the earthly and unearthly, of the visible fact with an invisible cause, of which Rossetti was such a master. It may be said that the matter of the poem is out of human nature. But the matter of the poem was fully believed in the time of which he writes. And moreover, so enduring are these superstitions, there are those who believe it still. In my own experience I have come across it twice. I used to visit, when I was a curate in Kensington, a country girl from Devonshire who was dying of consumption. She suffered sorely from stabbing pain. She implored me to go down to Devonshire and to have arrested another girl there who had made a waxen image of her, and who every night pierced its breast with long pins again and again. This was the cause of her illness, and it was the girl's vengeance on her because she had taken her lover away. Nothing would persuade her that her belief was untrue. She died believing it. Some years afterwards two friends of mine told me the following story. They were dining alone with a woman whose husband had been seduced from her by another woman. After dinner, when they were gathered around the fire, the woman rose with a dreadful look, went to a cupboard, took out of it a wax figure of her betrayer, placed it inside the fender, and bent over it, crying fiercely— " Burn, you white Witch, burn.'' The subject is then quite modern enough to give it an additional flavour. Nor is the burning centre of the poem, the hungry passion of vengeance in it, of which all the rest is but the shell—the simple, solitary intensity of which never leaves us for a moment—less modern, less capable of being felt now than it was in the past.   Set, unrelenting revenge, the thirst of which is never slaked, exists among us now, and it would use the measures Helen uses, if it could.   A soul possessed by it needs to be almost re-made ; and it is well to have its deepset passion realised to the full here, so that, seeing it as it is, we may learn how to expel it from the soul.   That lesson is not intended by the poet, but it follows.   It is, like all the teaching of the arts, indirect, and it is the more powerful for that.

I have only one thing more to say of the poem.   It may be alleged that the subject-matter is too terrible for art.   But the dreadful in passion, or guilt, or agony is not unfit for art if the impression left at the end is one of pity or reverance for human nature, such an impression as is left by the Œdipus of Sophocles or the Othello of Shakespeare.   This saves the situation, and the soul of the audience is softened, and purified from the evil extremes of the passions represented. The play or the tale which leaves an opposite impression of human nature, which makes us mock, despise, or loathe it—*that*, no matter how clever it may be, is not a work of art, but of literary science. It is interesting as science, it is detestable as art. *Here* there is nothing left but pity : pity all round, pity for the fates of human passion, pity for the guilty, pity for the father, for the bride, pity for the souls who are lost, infinite sorrow for human nature wrenched awry from nobleness. It seems as if pity for Helen were impossible, but it is there.

We may follow this element of magic supernaturalism through the thrice-divided poem of *Rose Mary*, especially in its third part. It is full of Rossetti's suggestiveness of the lower supernatural, of his half-finished beings of evil, who, when men have forced their way by magic beyond the limits of the natural, indulge, while they seem to serve, a set purpose to betray and injure men. They live within certain cruel powers of nature as in their natural home, and direct these harmful powers against us. To be their seeming master is to be their slave. To trust them means their betrayal of our trust. It was so with Macbeth, and Rose Mary and her mother are also deceived. But, at the end, the poem maintains the lordship of the soul over these evil powers. Rose Mary dies to conquer them, and she evercomes them in death.

The poetry attains a higher imaginative range than elsewhere in this class of Rossetti's poems. It brings the spirit of the lower supernatural into the souls of the mother and the girl, makes their speech and passions unearthly, and drenches all the natural scenery with a mist of wizardry. Nay, in the very words and phrases of the poem there is such a mingling of spirit and matter, of the earth and heaven, and of the spiritual and supernatural underneath them, that one cannot tell where thought begins or ends. All things are in a whirl, yet the artistic result is clear.

At the same time in which he made these incursions into the mystic, mediæval, magic-haunted realms, he could, when he pleased, and it proves the range and power of his genius, enter, and with equal power, into the problem and sorrowful fates of our real life. I have already touched on his modernism, but I have only mentioned the poem entitled *Jenny*. No one can mistake the reality of its description, the rigid adherence to the truth of the matter, the utterly un-mystic treatment of the subject—and this from a man who shortly before was wandering in mediævalisms and in dim superstitions. That is worth our noting. Still more notable is Rossetti's imaginative sympathy and insight into the mind of the careless girl ; the finding, below her light surface, of her soul ; the thought of her fate, of the winter of her life's year ; the wonder and sorrow of it all ; the horror it is to humanity ; the contrast of her life with that of her innocent sisters

which makes a goblin of the sun ; the desperate problem of this thing having been from the beginning even
until now.   There is no poem which should make us
think more wisely, more sternly, more sincerely of
what has been, and is, and of what should be.   If Rossetti had written nothing else, he did well in writing this.
Nothing is shirked, no false veil is thrown over the
truth.   It is stern realism, and yet, as art demands, the
pity of it, the sense of sorrow for the fates of men, is
supreme.

But these modern things were parentheses in the
general story of his poetry.   So far as narrative poetry
is concerned it had chiefly to do with the past.   As a
painter, he could not paint a continuous story, for a
picture treats only a moment.   As a poet, he wished to
tell, and out of the past, long stories which seized on
his fancy.   He projected many such, but he realised
very few.   The form in which he treated these resembled the form of the ballad, a difficult form for us
moderns to use who have lost naïvete which Rossetti
never had, and simplicity which was also far away
from 'him.   Yet he had always loved the ballads ; they
were one of his earliest affections, and he resolved to
try and use their form.   He had begun with the *Staff
and Scrip*, which, save for a few verses, was not a success.   Then he wrote *Stratton Water* and afterwards
The King's Tragedy and *The White Ship*.   They are all
too long for excellence in this kind of poetry, and they
are long by the continual intrusion of unnecessary

detail—detail good in itself, but which overloads the building. These ballads are like those later churches which are so crowded all over with sculptures in the wrong places that the mind is drawn away from the plan of the whole. *Stratton Water* is nearest to the ballad, but the force and intensity of the subject is weakened by varied descriptions of the same things over and over again. *The King's Tragedy*, in itself a fine thing, is a long story, not a ballad, and the ballad metre in which it is written only makes its difference from a true ballad the more remarkable. Even in the description of the meeting of the King and the woman-seer, to write which would please his mystical temper, much detail is introduced which is not quite irrelevant, but which enfeebles the scene. Then, many verses say what the true ballad would have said in one, and left a greater weirdness on the mind. *The White Ship* has been highly praised. It is striking in parts, but I should challenge its success. On the whole, Rossetti was not good at long narrative.

Moments of passion, hours in which a fate reaches its climax, intense passages of psychological struggle, a night's thinking all in a breath, as in *Jenny*, on some problem which lies as it were incarnate before him ; the concentration into an hour's emotions of the love of years, as in *The Portrait*—these were the realms in which his imagination and his white-hot power reached their successes ; and his constant use of the sonnet in which many thoughts and aspects of a matter are fused into one amalgam, contains not only a proof of this, but also a suggestion that he would not reach excellence in the ballad or in the narrative poem. If his life had depended on it, he could not have written a single one of the stories in *The Earthly Paradise*. He and Morris were in this matter at opposite poles.

In all these different directions, and over many classes of subjects, Rossetti displayed his originating power. He was incapable of imitation; what he did arose clean and fresh out of his imagination. He made new paths for poetry as he did for painting, and along the new paths he planted trees and flowers unknown before. *The Last Confession* has, it is true, a faint odour of Browning, and Browning is the only poet whom we momentarily touch in his work. Yet, it is only with Browning's vivid realism that we can compare the realism of Rossetti. And the comparison slips away from our grasp. For Rossetti's realism is so interpenetrated with mystic elements that it is altogether severed from Browning's.

These original ways in poetry and original species of poetry are each represented by only a few examples and it is a great pity he did not give us more. But then, his creative energy was split into two directions, not concentrated on one. He made his imagination work in two arts, and he played at neither. When he wrote poetry, he gave his whole soul to it; when he painted, he did the same; and he gave an equality of energy to both. There have been other painters who wrote poetry, but it was for the amusement of idle hours; but Rossetti was as earnest a poet as he was a painter. He reached an equal originality, and it may be an equal excellence, in both arts, and I do not know of another instance of this. And this curious two-foldness in the man—which must have strangely confused the single-ness of his consciousness, doubling himself continually to himself, so that his weird picture of "How we met ourselves" may have represented an actual psycholog-ical experience—accounts for the small number of examples he gives us of the different original paths he opened out for poetry. Having to live two lives in one, having to endue another personality whenever he changed from the painter to the poet or from the poet to the painter, he had not time to make many examples of the new species he had shaped in both his arts. It is astonishing how distinct he kept these two personal-ities, and how distinct was the work of each. I have said that he used some of the painter's gifts to enhance the work of the poet, and that is true. But they were sparingly used, and were strictly subordinated to the poetic conception and its form. The poems are those of a poet, not of a painter, except those sonnets to his own pictures, of which I take no count as poems. The fact is that in all Rossetti's high poetic work, even in *The Portrait* where one might look for the painter's way, there is nothing which recalls a painter's method. He conceives the subject, composes it, ornaments it, sends his passion through it, fuses its elements together by imagination, as a poet would, not as a painter. To anyone who believes in the manifoldedness of what I may call secondary personalities under one will, this example of it in Rossetti is full of interest. To illustrate this, I may instance *The Portrait*, one of the most beautiful of his poems. It tells how in old time he painted the woman he loved, and who is now dead. But though he speaks of painting, the poet, not the painter, is supreme in the poem. There is not a line of it which is conceived or felt out of a painter's imagination. I quote a few verses of it, not only to illustrate how far apart it is from the art of painting, but also because it throws light upon those elements in his poetry of which I have already written. His mysticism is full-fledged in it, and also his psychology. That superstitious element also into which mysticism often drifts is not absent :

> In painting her I shrined her face
> 'Mid mystic trees, where light falls in
> Hardly at all ; a covert place
> Where you might think to find a din
> Of doubtful talk, and a live flame
> Wandering, and many a shape whose name
> Not itself knoweth, and old dew,
> And your own footsteps meeting you,
> And all things going as they came.

A haunted place ! Wraiths of the intruders who break into it, half souls that do not know their names, footfalls that are one's own yet not one's own, a din of doubtful voices, wandering flames, old dew—a wonderful phrase—and that incomprehensible drift of things in a world devoid of reason or of cause, all things going as they came,—are all mingled up with the bitter sorrow of love.

> O heart that never beats nor heaves,
>   In that one darkness lying still,
>   What now to thee my love's great will
> Or the fine web the sunshine weaves?

At the end steals in the ancient love of mediæval-ism—the mediæval Heaven of *The Blessed Damozel* and the Palestine of the Crusades :

> Even so, where Heaven holds breath and hears
>   The beating heart of Love's own breast,—
> Where round the secret of all spheres
>   All angels lay their wings to rest,—
> How shall my soul stand wrapt and awed,
> When, by the new birth borne abroad
> Throughout the music of the suns,
> It enters in her soul at once
> And knows the silence there for God!
>
> Here, with her face doth memory sit
>   Meanwhile, and wait the day's decline,
> Till other eyes shall look from it,
> Eyes of the spirit's Palestine,
> Even then the old gaze tenderer:
> While hopes and aims long lost with her
>   Stand round her image side by side,
>   Like tombs of pilgrims that have died
> About the Holy Sepulchre.

It remains in concluding this essay, to say a few words on Rossetti's translations, and on his relaticn to Nature-poetry.   As to the translations, he was a fine

Italian scholar, not from the outside, but the inside. Italian might be said to be his native tongue. English also might be said to be his native tongue. It is plain from his work in poetry and prose that he was a master of the intimacies of English. When we add to those two masterhoods that from his youth he had studied, under his father and in his home, Dante and the circle of poets who preceded and followed him ; and, moreover, that one-half of his mind was in close harmony with the thoughts, feelings, manners, and especially with the theology and love-theories of the end of the thirteenth and beginning of the fourteenth century, we can scarcely conceive any one better fitted to translate the *Vita Nuova* and the rest of the poetic work of that time. Moreover, Rossetti was a true poet, and it takes a poet to translate a poet ; and, through imagination impassioned by what it reads, to feel into the heart of what the poet meant whom he translates ; and then, transferring what he has felt into another tongue, to seize the phrase, the words, which rightly represent, and will awaken, a similar emotion in the English reader to that which the Italian reader, such as Giotto, felt of old. All this Rossetti has done as it was never done before in England.

As to his Nature-poetry, Rossetti felt deeply the beauty and the terror of the world of nature, but he felt, as a poet, the beautiful and terrible landscape of the soul, in its questioning, its experience, and its passions, above all, in the passion of love, a hundred-

fold more deeply;—and this, to such an extent, that
nature is, I may say, never described for her own sake,
for love of her alone. She lives in his poetry only as
illustration of the action and feeling of the heart of
man. It is curious that in all the hundred and one
sonnets of *The House of Life,* and in the other scattered
sonnets, there is scarcely one in which nature is the
main subject ; and there are very few where the natural
description extends over a third of the sonnet. Where
it does, it is to lead up to the record of some experience
of the inner life, or to enhance some phase of love. It
is much the same in the other poems. The most accurate description of nature in them is that of the birds,
especially of the starlings, coming home at evening, in
Sunset Wings, but it is only made in order to image
the hours of Hope, in flight towards farewell. There
is, however, in a single sonnet, entitled *Spring,* a full
picture of early spring in a pastoral country which
shows how well, had he chosen, he could have written
on natural scenery. It was not only spring that appealed to him. He loved the four seasons of the year,
but he loved them most as images of the course of
human love and human life. All his happy, immanent
appreciations, in one or two lines, of the weather, the
flowers, the life, the inner spirit of the seasons, drift
into humanity. The river in that pathetic poem,
Down Stream, charged with the sweet softness of June,
and again with the dark flood of winter, is yet but the
image of the love and the ruin which were wrought

beside its stream.   Sometimes a transient loveliness of
nature, felt as if it were an actual passion of the soul,
seems to lose all that is material and become a spiritual
thing.   In this intimate and vital bringing together,
without fusion, of nature and human passion, Rossetti
is able to create strange and subtle verses which seem
to be neither quite of nature or of the soul, but of some
religion between both, where nature appears to claim
the attributes of man, and man to claim the energies
of nature.   Nature and man are not united in them ;
the next moment, the next line, they change places.
They but touch and separate, but at the moment of
touching, a strange, subtly mingled, apparently mean-
ingless verse is born, which leaves a clear impression
on the imagination.   Such lines are these :

> Through dark forest-boughs in flight
> The wind swoops onwards brandishing the light.
> The empty pastures blind with rain.
> For leagues I saw the east wind blown.
> Tender as dawn's first hill-fire, and intense
>   As instantaneous penetrating sense,
> In Spring's first birth-hour, of other Springs gone by.
> The sunrise blooms and withers on the hill
> Like any hill-flower ; and the noblest truth
> Dies here to dust.

Now and then there are separate lines of vivid description of some momentary aspect or object in nature ;
states of sky in calm or storm, flowers in the woods,
insects and birds,—subjects common to all poets, but
in Rossetti's work made uncommon by words so vital,
so clutching on the spiritual heart of the thing, and so

rich in colour that one feels only a painter could have found them. Indeed nature is used by him as the great painters of Italy used her in their pictures, never as the subject of their work, but as part of its scenery. He introduces natural objects as Signorelli does the flowery meadows in his altar-piece in the National Gallery, or as Titian paints the hills and the sea in the Bacchus and Ariadne—with as deep and opulent a colour, with as careful and truthful detail, but with a more resolute symbolism. Sunlight in all its ways and moonlight he seems to have most loved ; and perhaps it is owing to the impossibility of realising moonlight in painting, that he is so fond in his poetry of moonlight. Again and again, in many various aspects the moon passes through his poems.

Finally, he is not one of the greater poets. Their work is of the sunlight, of the fresh air, of the wide landscape, of human nature. His work is of its moonlight, of perfumed air, of a precious but a confined landscape. It is poetry of a private chamber, of an isolated glade in the forest, of an island secluded in tropic seas. It is of the particular, not of the universal. Only rarely does he touch the primeval, natural foundations of man's nature, and when he does the natural passions he describes are shown in remote, involved weirds, or strange circumstances, such as appeal to the experience of only a few persons. This puts him as a poet on a much lower plane than is occupied by poets of a larger range. But then, within this enclosed garden of poetry, the flowers, the paths, the waters, the buildings, are of an exquisiteness, a finish, a colour and beauty which are rare, specialised, and of a seclusive charm. We walk in it for a time with a lonely pleasure, and then we leave it for the open country and the free air and the boundless ocean of poetry.

WILLIAM MORRIS

THE analogy I have drawn in the last essay between the histoy and the causes of the rise of a new kind of poetry in Keats and now in Rossetti and Morris is, I have said, more clearly represented in Morris than in Rossetti. I have heard of persons, anxious to free Morris's youthful life from the charge of indifference to the problems of his day, who have culled out of his letters and talk at Oxford, and shortly after he left it, phrases which seem to represent that he was vitally interested in the questions which disturbed the world of England when he was young. It is true that he spoke of these questions when they turned up, or when a friend interested in them came from the noisy world without into the quietudes of Oxford; but by the time he wrote his first book of poetry, indeed, after that journey in France when he and Burne-Jones resolved to give up going into the Church, his indifference to the theological, political, philosophic, and social questions of the day had risen into boredom. He ignored them completely, and so did his friend, Burne-Jones. And Morris cried, like Keats—"My world is disenchanted. Where shall I find loveliness? Where does Beauty sleep? *There* is the healing of humanity;

there is truth." This single faith and cry of his youth,
this identity of feeling towards the world which en-
compassed them, knits Morris and Keats together.

The analogy fits closely, yet in many points they
differed from one another. Morris was a stronger,
robuster nature than Keats, healthier in body and
therefore in soul. He knew clearly, as Keats knew
indistinctly, what he wanted to do, and to live; and
when he found it out, he put aside other objects, having
eminently the power of rejection, and went straight to
his aim; nor did he ever rest a moment till he had, as
far as he could, attained it. While his striving to any
chosen goal lasted, he saw nothing else in the world.
When he had reached his goal, fulfilled his aim, he
took up another object and marched to it with the same
absorption, with the same intensity of will. Except,
of course, in his callow youth, there was nothing tenta-
tive about Morris. In all this he differed from Keats,
and most of all in this—that in after life the social
problems of the present seized on him, and he flung
himself, with his native impetuosity, into the bettering
of the human race. The call of the present drew him
out of his beloved past.

Keats, had the world changed around him, would –
it is plain from his letters—have suffused his poems
with an atmosphere fit for such a time and in sympathy
with it. We think, with a deep regret, that had he
only lived ten years longer he would have found himself in the midst of national, political, and spiritual

emotions, and have been thrilled by them into a poetry more vital of the present. Think of Keats living in the movements of 1832 ; writing with Tennyson and Browning ; moved by their emotions ! He would not, indeed, have flung himself, as Morris did in his after life, into the hottest of the fight of humanity. He had neither the fierce intensity nor the versatility of Morris ; but he would have humanised his poetry. He would have felt in every vein the new emotions and their ideas. That fresh world would have sucked him in ; and the mythology of Greece and the stories of the fourteenth century would have yielded to the life of the England in which he lived. This Keats had begun to feel ; at this Morris arrived.

Morris had even greater reason than Keats for his rejection of the present. Beauty had wholly disappeared from life ; and the horrors of its absence had reached their height in the first half of the nineteenth century. The vituperation of a lifetime would scarcely exhaust the just abhorrence of the ugliness of the first twenty years of Victoria's reign. Art had all but perished : painting save among the landscape painters ; sculpture and architecture were mere conventions. They had neither truth to nature, nor imagination, nor originality. Restoration had raised its fiendish hands, and was tearing down what beauty was left in the old buildings, or replacing it with soulless imitation. Oxford was still fair, but its devastation had begun.

Again, I have traced in this book how the great

excitements of 1830 and the following years exhausted themselves as poetic impulse, and became first sensational, and then, met by historical and scientific criticism, were involved in a scepticism, barren of poetic passion, and in an intellectual analysis, barren of beauty. Arnold represented what the poet became in such a time ; and if poetry were again to arise, it would have to get clear of all these questions of history and science and theology. Rossetti emancipated poetry, almost altogether, from these chains. Morris altogether set it free. He fled away from the dull world around him, beset as it was with the questions of the understanding only ; and fled farther away, with horror, from the world outside Oxford, where material aims and material ugliness were wickedly despotic. He refused to live in this decay ; shut his eyes to the ugliness among which he lived, felt too much life in him to endure the exhaustion of passion and beauty which characterised society, was sick of the theological and political squabbles, felt no sympathy with the critical or the revolutionary movements—not even with 1848—flung off his shoulders, with a grim laugh, the whole atmosphere of time, and went, as if it were round the corner, to live, and move, and have his being in the thirteenth and fourteenth centuries. This was, in spirit, the very thing Keats did in his time ; and, as I have said, for similar reasons. And the poetry of Morris which came out of it was of a similar type to that of Keats—a pure romantic poetry ; a hundred miles away from the human

life of his own day ; with a touch in it of mediæval
mysticism which Keats did not possess so fully ; with
more also of humanity, but with the same supreme love
of loveliness as Keats possessed ; and especially, with
a similar, minute, intensely observant, rich and never-
wearied vision and worship of natural beauty, of birds
and wild animals, of woods and streams, and the goings
on of the earth, the weather, and the sky.

The love of the earth and all her doings and grow-
ings, and of the business, moods, and fancies of the
heavens which belonged to the earth as the great
mother's husb- id, was deep in Keats; but it was
deeper in Morris.   No tongue can tell how Morris loved
the earth ; she was his delight, his joy, his refuge, his
home; the companion of his uncompanionable thoughts ;
his mother from whose breasts he drank life, energy,
food for his work, joy for his imagination, and incessant
beauty.   No one has praised her better ; and his poetry
of nature reveals how close, how passionate he was in
his worship.   She was the only thing left here and
there in England unspoiled for him by the commercial
spirit ; unrestored by the pretenders to art ; unconven-
tionalised by the false worshippers of a false beauty.
And when he rowed up the Thames between the meadows filled with haymakers, or walked over the downs
where the yews and junipers clustered in groups along
the Pilgrim way, he could, even in the nineteenth century believe himself still in the fourteenth.   Thames
was unchanged, and the woods.   At any moment he

might see a clump of spears come along the riverway ;
or the bowman issue from the trees, or the monk come
from the grey abbey to the village green, or the farmer
bid his wife and girls farewell in the garden, or
the knight blaze the landscape into sudden colour,
as he rode under his banner to meet King Edward.
Nature, at least, in the places he loved, was not out
of harmony with the England of the fourteenth
century.

Many years afterwards, when his passionate humanity had forced him into real touch with the misery of
great cities—a misery of sordidness and ugliness and
base living, as great among the richer as among the
poorer classes, for, save for comfort, both rich and
poor lived in hideous conditions—he was not content
any longer to live only in the past. He came to live in
the faith and hope of a better future ; and, in that most
imaginative of books, *News from Nowhere*, he painted
what England might become a century or two hence
under a new régime ; the foundation of which was the
universal prevalence, among the people, of intelligent
joy in the work of their hands. Out of this joy in
work would arise, he thought, a desire for loveliness
and its expression in things made, till everything in
the whole land would be at once useful and beautiful.
But in that book, in which the whole world is different
from ours, a great deal of nature was not different from
that which he saw, and we may still behold to-day.
The vales and hills which had been destroyed are in

William Morris 211

that book rescued from smoke and dirt; the ruin of
nature by commercialism in the places where she had
been turned into hell is repaired; the towns are sweet
and clean, the architecture is noble; but there are
many places described in *News from Nowhere* which
had not in his time been ruined, and which needed no
repair. The reaches of the Thames which he dwells
on so lovingly in this book are still the same as he
pictured them in the fourteenth century; as they were
for him round Kelmscott in the nineteenth. The gardens of rustic England are the same, and the summer
woods; and the soft grey skies, or the sunshine of
June, or the fruitful rain-cloud—these, for him, were
constant. Chaucer knew them; Morris knew them;
the lovers of four generations hence will also know
them. Yes, in all his trouble and striving; in an
imaginative life which spent its days now in a world
six hundred years ago, and now in a world a hundred
years hence, and then again in the world which encom-
passed him while he lived among us—in a life, that is,
which by knowledge, and in fancy, made him partaker
of the changes of seven hundred years—Morris had
one unchanging sphere of loveliness in which to rest
and be happy—one world which never varied in its
beauty, and never deceived his love—the charmed and
charming doings of the earth and sky in winter and
spring, in summer and autumn. The most emotional
expressions, charged with the deep simplicity of passion, which occur in all his writings are those in which

he expresses his love of the earth and all its doings. Here are two :

"She led me close up to the house, and laid her shapely brown hand and arm upon that lichened wall, as if to embrace it, and cried out : ' O me, O me ; how I love the earth, and the seasons, and weather, and all things that deal with it, and all that grows out of it, as this has done.'

"She led me to the door, murmuring little above her breath as she did so : 'The earth and the growth of it, and the life of it! If I could but say or show how I love it!'"

And here is a piece of poetry which, in its poetic reticence, is not less impassioned :

JUNE.

O June, O June that we desired so,
Wilt thou not make us happy on this day?
Across the river thy soft breezes blow
Sweet with the scent of beanfields far-away,
Above our heads rustle the aspens grey,
Calm is the sky with harmless clouds beset,
No thought of storm the morning vexes yet.

See, we have left our hopes and fears behind
To give our very hearts up unto thee ;
What better place than this then could we find
By this sweet stream that knows not of the sea,
That guesses not the city's misery,
This little stream whose hamlets scarce have names,
This far-off, lonely mother of the Thames?

Here then, O June, thy kindness will we take ;
And if indeed but pensive men we seem,
What should we do ? Thou wouldst not have us wake
From out the arms of this rare happy dream
And wish to leave the murmur of the stream,
The rustling boughs, the twitter of the birds,
And all thy thousand peaceful happy words.

He who would drink deep of the milk and wine of
the earth, and honour and love the great heavens, and
know the inner life of the seasons, and what they do
for us, their guests, would do well to read the introductions to the Tales in *The Earthly Paradise*. They sing
from March to February the story of the year. They
are a fit and alluring introduction to the natural descriptions in the tales themselves, which, in their multitude
of observation and truth, will double and redouble the
love of English scenery. But of these I must write
hereafter.

This love of his kept him always ideal, always
romantic ; and in his poetry, simple, sensuous, and
passionate. In one moment, when he pleased, he
could slip out of the worries of business, the trouble
of life, the quarrels of the socialist bodies, the noise of
the battle, into peace and joy, into pure pleasure of the
senses, into the spirit and simplicity of beauty, and
that uplifted passion for it, which " after no repenting
draws." No one could detach himself more quickly,
more completely from his surroundings, and pass with
greater ease into another life and time. But it was
his love of nature which made the magic element in

which he could practise his detachments.   And if we need proof of this, it is enough to read the beginning of *John Ball* and of *News from Nowhere.*

At present, while he was young, he lived in the life, the scenery, and the feeling of the thirteenth and fourteenth centuries.   I cannot conceive a greater detachment from his own time than his was in his imaginative and musing youth.   He lived fully, it is true, in all the athleticism of the young : walking, rowing, fencing, and playing : but these were, even more fully than now, practised in his beloved centuries.   So, whatever he did, he still moved among his fellows, as if he were, by some spell, surrounded with an aura of the past ; and indeed Burne-Jones and Rossetti were, in this, not far behind him.   It was pleasant to hear Burne-Jones tell—the contrasts of the scene were so strange—how, frequently, in the long walks he and Rossetti took at night when they were young, they used to go for refreshment into the public-house nearest at hand, and, leaning over the counter, forget where they were, seeing nothing of the rough people round them, while they continued their discussion of Arthur and Guenevere and Lancelot, of Sir Percival and the Holy Grail.

The present disappeared from these men, but most of all from Morris.   Nor was the atmosphere in which he lived merely imaginary.   Ever since he was a boy he had studied the architecture, the clothing, the manners, the agriculture, the war-customs and weapons, the monastic life, the manuscripts, the ways of writing and illumination, the furniture, the dresses, the colours of armour and heraldry, the houses, huts, and castles of that ancient time. His friends at Oxford were astonished by his knowledge, and all his life long he went on increasing it. His imaginative musings had then accurate material to work upon. The world he created was true, and became so living, so actual to him, that he could, almost day by day, invent stories out of its life, with a flavour of Froissart in them, and with a strange reality. Three or four prose stories in the *Oxford and Cambridge Magazine* prove this power of his, the best of which is *The Hollow Land*. These, however, are over-fantastic; but there are poems of this imaginative world in *Guenevere*, his first book, which have all the grim reality of the wars and feuds of the thirteenth century; not tales told out of Froissart or any chronicle, but invented. Of these, *Sir Peter Harpdon's End* is one, and *The Haystack in the Floods* another.

Yet, in spite of this active life in another world, he could not altogether shake away all impressions from the world of fifty years ago. He knew what was around him, and it formed behind his imagined life a dim background of horror and hatefulness which sent into his heart waves of distress and pain. They seemed to come from far away, to knit him up with a dreadful story, to bring unreality into the happy life he lived—so that he could not tell which life was the true one, which was the dream, and which the reality. This uncertainty as to where he was, as to what world he belonged to, naturally increased when in his manhood he was brought closely into contact with the life lived by the poor and working people of this "city of dreadful night," with the vain and ugly lives of the richer classes, with all the vast blunders of society. The consciousness of this drove its pain into his far-off, imaginary life, and continually disturbed it. He rarely got completely away. What was easy for him in his youth was very difficult for him when he was forty-five. He tells at the beginning of *News from Nowhere* how one night he slipped into another world, and lived in it for many days. But always, he was haunted there with dim whispering that he was not its actual in-dweller; the people he lived with seemed to know that he must go back, till at last when the end draws near and he must return, he describes with much subtlety of feeling how this new world which had come to be very real to him wavered, closed, opened again, and again closed; how the faces and voices of his friends grew slowly dim, how they looked on him with sorrow, and talked of his going, and how at last the dearm vanished, and he found himself on the dreary road near Kelmscott House, and face to face with a miserable man.

That book with the *Dream of John Ball* reveal the double soul and life of Morris. One may read in them

what filled his spirt when he was silent. It was thus
he felt in middle age. But when he was younger, and
battered with consciousness of the present world, he
rushed into a state of fierce resentment, and spared in
his speech no one and no thing. In furies of this kind
he was like a Baresark ; and it was wonderful to hear
him. He was not eloquent in his rages, but emphatic.
And what impression he then made on his young companions—when, for example, he found himself before
a restored church—was made by furious repetition of
furious phrases. Then, having thus awakened, like
the sleeping warrior in the cavern, and drawn his sword
half from its sheath, he lapsed back again into his own
youthful world, where men were telling each other
how Arthur rode against the heathen, and Lancelot
loved the Queen, and the ladies went a-Maying, and
the hosts lay round Joyous Gard, and Tristram laid on
Isolt's lips the immortal kiss, and Guenevere sinned in
joy, repented in sadness ; and where, in real war, and
not in legend, Chandos and Manny and the Black
Prince and the Free Companions fought in France and
Spain—where the ships with banners flying returned
to England, and the Abbeys by the river received the
wounded, and welcomed the merchant and the scholar ;
and the great churches rose, day by day, into loveliness
at the hands of workmen who invented and loved their
work.

This life and its capacities were sufficiently imaginative ; a thousand miles away from the sordid psychol-

ogy of modern literature.   Out of it grew all Morris's
earliest poetry, not one line of which had to do with
any base or commonplace subject, not one line of
which was written under the belief that close and
clever description of what was ugly could, even in
madness, be called art.   But ideal as this imagined
life was, it was not more ideal than the steady temper
of his soul.   No one who met Morris for the first or
second time, or only met him as an acquaintance,
would be likely to credit him with the ideal temper,
and indeed he abhorred a great deal which is now
called ideal.   He was sometimes amazingly rude,
gruff, and let his wraths loose without restraint.   He
dressed like a rough sailor ; he liked at times to be a
bit of a boor.   He never trimmed his speech, nor his
manner when he did not like people, except when he
wanted to push forward principles he cared for.   Then
he subdued himself.   He had not a trace of luxury or
fine living.   His simplicity ran into roughness among
those who were not simple.   A being more apart from the
conception of ideality framed by the fine social folk,
or by the little gods of culture, cannot be imagined.

Yet if I were asked what especially characterised
Morris's temper of soul, all his life long, the views he
took of men and of womanhood, of life as it ought to
be lived, of his poetry and prose, of his aims for
craftmanship in all the arts of life, I should say that
they all arose out of, and were steeped in, the ideal
temper of his soul.

Sweetest nut hath sourest rind,
Such a nut is Rosalind.

He saw everything he cared to write about through
the veil of ideal beauty. What faults any subject had,
or any time or place he described, if they were natural
—that is, in the necessities of the thing—were either
unimportant to him, or were used as foils to enhance
the beauty he loved. He raised magnanimity, courage, strength, natural passion, natural good sense in
affairs, love of the commonweal as contrasted with
selfish individualism, honest labour, ardent fighting,
frank generosity, steady persistency in pursuit of a
chosen goal, to the highest point in men, and represented their ideal in the action and life of his men.
As to the women in his tales, of whom I shall say
more hereafter, I do not think in the whole of literature there is anything more ideally noble than the
women whom he has created out of his own soul in
tales such as *The Roots of the Mountains* and *The House
of the Wolfings*. Yes; the humanity Morris draws,
when he dips his pencil in the colours of his own soul,
is an idealised humanity, and for that may God be
praised.

Then he idealised the times of which he wrote, their
customs, life, and their works. He scarcely saw a
single fault in the thirteenth and fourteenth centuries,
or in the period told of in the *Northern Sagas*. Moreover, he idealised the natural scenery he loved; and
by idealising it, made it more real than it had been

before to thousands of men and women who had lived in it without seeing it. But his idealisation was balanced away from over-softness or preciosity, by his unmitigated wrath with all that was base or ugly—by his indignation with the men and the things that he hated because they crushed the soul and brains of men. It was refreshing, among the smooth and excusing folk who slur over what is mean, and exalt the commonplace, and serve the devil up in sugar, and praise the accepted, and have no individual opinions, to hear Morris launch out against the things he abominated. The lifeless maxims and conventions of society, the greed and luxury, the base competition, by any means, for wealth, the dishonesty, and bad workmanship of trade, the destruction by machinery of the workman's intelligence and his love of making something out of his own head—these, and many other revolting things, he realised, even more than Ruskin, for what they were ; and he stripped them to the bone and mocked their ugliness. The only thing in relation to them which I may say he idealised, raising it to its highest power, was his own hatred of them. It became a kind of heroic phrenzy. He felt, like Hercules, in these hours, as if the coat of Nessus wrapped him round ; and he behaved like Hercules. But his outward words of wrath were but a faint image of the vital misery his soul endured at living in a world where he often felt that his struggle to mend it was hopeless.

Dreamer of dreams, born out of my due time,
Why should I strive to set the crooked straight?

Then it was, in order to restore his soul and to relieve his pain, he flitted out of it all into communion with an imagined world—the world of the past he pictured in *John Ball*, the world of the future he pictured in *News from Nowhere.* I scarcely know anything more pathetic than the image of Morris, when — having spent a whole day in the dirty discomfort of the London streets, speaking to the poor folk in their hideous caverns in the rain and mist, attending small Socialist meetings and trying to get the quarrelling men to unite, joining processions to ask for reforms he knew would not be granted, lecturing on art to people who did not understand him, and returning utterly wearied out and depressed — when, having done all this, he rose next morning at six, and, while the air was yet fresh and pure and the Thames that flowed past his study windows at Hammersmith blue under the sky of the spring, sat down to clean his soul and pour dew upon it, to enable his powers, and make strong his hopes, by writing of the healthy, happy folk of Burgdale, of the fair valley and rivers and houses, and of the wise, strong, natural, honest, and loving people, who tilled their land and loved it so well, and who, when the hour of trial came, fought for it so joyously against the Dusky men. The hours slipped away as he wrote of his ideal, and he never thought of the torment of the day. But, when the

writing dream was over, he went out to meet the
actual he hated and helped with the courage and
strength that he had won by living in the imagined
world, which men called an impossible ideal, but
which he felt and hoped would become a reality.

So, in these later days at least, however ideal in aim,
subject, and form his literary work was, his soul, by
which he wrote, was continuously in contact with what
we ought to call real life; and it proves the fineness of
his nature that the misery, incapacity, and all the
hated things he touched to the quick, did not for a
single moment dim the beauty, brightness, clearness,
joy, peace, and possibility of his ideal. Its heaven was
always beautiful, and he rose into it in a moment.
Thus, like this earth, he went round his axis, half in
light and half in shade; night succeeded day within,
and day the night; a strange, double life, whirling
into sorrow and joy, hate and love, rage and ravish-
ment. And in either kind of life, all that was done or
thought or felt was fulfilled with such intensity that,
without any desire to be apart from his fellows, the
intensity, being heated seven times more than it was
wont to be heated in others, isolated him into a separate
and solitary life. He was a lonely man at root; and
the sentiment of this solitariness, which for the most
part was silent, and of which he never boasted, steals
forth, unconsciously to himself, through all his most
imaginative poetry and prose, and fills it with a dim,
pathetic atmosphere; which, if anyone had accused

him of creating, he would have denied with that indignation which we have when someone in conversation
attempts to lift the veil which hides the innermost
shrine of our heart.

This intensity was itself a part of his ideality, one
of its forms. Whatever he undertook—poetry, tales,
lectures, social work, designing patterns, dyeing,
carpet making, silk weaving, tapestry, glass painting,
the printing press—was lifted into the ideal world by
his impassioned desire to make it perfect, to get into
it the absolute of beauty of which it was capable ; and
in that aspiration the intensity he gave to the matter in
hand was born. Whatever was in hand, it was for the
moment the only thing in the world to do ; and he lost
in it all interest for the time in any other kind of
work, even in the work of his dearest friends. Nor
was this intense desire for perfection left in the vague,
a mere dream of aspiration. He made himself master
of all that had been previously done with regard to the
matter in hand, whether well or ill. He bought every
book likely to help him, ransacking with a kind of fury
every source of information. Then, having thrown
aside all that was merely mechanical or ill-wrought in
the practice of the past, he practised the craft with his
own hands, and, having learnt it, taught it to others.
He rejoiced in the mistakes and failures which pointed
out a better way of doing the thing ; experimented on
all the modes his predecessors had used ; and then,
disdaining and hating imitation, set his own genius to

work, invented his own ways and patterns and methods;
made afresh all the means for his work—as, for example, the paper and ink for his printing—and threw
every power he possessed into the joyous work of creation.   In this aim at perfection, in this intensity, and
in this creativeness, Morris, more than any man of
whom I know, attained joy.   If his life was sometimes
dark, sometimes overladen, it was also partaker of
rapture.   The word is not too strong ; I use it deliberately.   And it was to that becoming general over
England—to men making something to represent their
own thought with individual pleasure in the making—
it was to that he looked forward as the basis of a new
society and a new life, in which joy and not sorrow
would be the atmosphere of being and becoming.
That was one of the reasons that he liked the thirteenth
and fourteenth centuries.   He had an impression, for
which there were good grounds, that men then made
what they wanted with pleasure in the making, and,
having made the useful thing, liked to ornament it in
order to satisfy their natural desire of beauty ; and
thence became inventors, designers, carvers, illumin-
ators, builders—when they had the power.   The air of
life was artistic.   Every one made his own needs ; the
whole world was making ; and out of that general and
intelligent activity the finer artist easily and frequently
arose.   In everything that was made, even in a chair,
a platter, the personal soul of the maker was infused
and felt.   And when any personal soul among them

was inspired to more delicate and larger issues, he rose out of the lower into the higher range of makers; became the fuller artist; illuminated his book, wove his tapestries, painted his window, lifted his cathedral to the heavens—and all with joy. With all this he was not ignorant of the other side of things, of the misery and oppression the poor suffered in the bygone times. He knew his history; but he knew also that this, which is not true of the workman in our own day, was true then, that men, when they had the means to make anything, rejoiced in the work of their own hands, sent their soul into it, permeated it with what intelligence and delight they had, satisfied partly in it a hunger for beauty which their society had, and ours has not.

Ideality, then, with a clear sight of good or bad reality; intensity, with a clear knowledge and aim; joy in creation—these are qualities which appear in all the art-work of Morris from a lyric to an initial letter. In his youth they are unformed, but they grew into finer shaping every day. There was no retrogression and no exhaustion. The roots of his genius were full of sap.

I have said he had joy in creation. There are many who have this joy, but only for a few times in their life. They have no plenitude; the wells from which they draw are not deep. They have created half-a-dozen things, and then they repeat themselves. Repetition is not creation, and their joys are over. Had

Morris creativeness? Was he incessantly productive of new things? When he created, was his creation full, crowded, variously enlivened with freshly invented things to be seen, felt, and loved? That is one of the tests of genius.

I scarcely can point to more than a few who have been more productive, inventive, creative than Morris. All the arts and crafts which he practised he made afresh. His work on them was not imitative; it was new. And he poured forth from his creating hand a succession of new designs, in all branches of his work, from year to year, all his life long, without a single repetition. He restored lost arts—such as printing— but with an individual inventiveness, and minute care, which made the work not a restoration, but a fresh creation. His productiveness was like that of those untilled lands along the edge of Canada and the United States, which are so rich in material for corn, that for years they need no fertilisation. But literature, and especially poetry, are higher arts than those of the crafts. In these also Morris was as creative as in the other arts, and to the creativeness he added an aston- ishing rapidity of execution. Of him the old phrase was really true—"To begin is to have done half." He often wrote five hundred lines of verse a day, or rather in half a day. When he determined to re-cast what he had written, as was the case with his long in- troduction—*The Wanderers*—to *The Earthly Paradise*, he did not tinker at the old work, or keep it lest he should lose some of its good things. He flung the whole of it aside, and re-wrote the thing quite freshly, so confident was he that his invention and productiveness would not fail him, nor his ardour lessen. That is not common with literary men. Great fecundity is not their failing. Good measure, pressed down, and shaken together and brimming over, we do not often receive into our bosom.

It is pleasant to think of all Morris has created for us. There is his re-cast of the Arthurian elements ; it is not very good, but it is original. There are the lyrics in his first book which, with all their weaknesses, seem to come out of a world unknown to us before, and haunted with the things and people we have not imagined. There is the story of Jason, with added inventions, all the natural description re-imagined, full of unwearied and minute detail, and re-conceived as a mediæval Greek—had he lived—might have conceived it. There are the many stories of *The Earthly Paradise*, each of them also re-conceived, re-dressed, and localised in a multitude of varied landscapes. There is the Morality of *Love is Enough : The Norse Sagas* re-animated for us in prose and poetry, and the greatest of them re-poetised from end to end ; the Æneid, the Odyssey and Beowulf translated for English reading, with Morris's soul flitting through the translations like a dim scent of forgotten leaves ; the time of *John Ball* made real to us with a modern application ; the years of the coming time when society may be re-made into

peace, happiness, and beauty, with all their possible
changes, told for us, in lovely scenery and with gracious
people—so imagined that the book is the refreshment
of sick and wearied men and women in this weary and
sick time, who as they read seem to live in the happier
world.   There are two great stories, the first of which
builds for us the German life when Rome was pushing
at it in the second or third century, and the second the
life of those who lived in his invented town of Burgdale, when the roving Huns came down upon it, a
story which I think the most beautiful prose thing that
he ever wrote ; not of the witching beauty of the later
dream-stories wholly outside of history and this world
where everything is frankly and freshly created, but of
a grave, steady, solemnised beauty, lovely as much by
its strength as by its grace.   But I need not dwell on
the rest.   Creativeness is at full richness in Morris.
Whether the creations ever rose into the higher excellences of the greater men is another question.   It would
not seem so, so far as his poetry is concerned.   For,
first, his range was limited, though' inside the range
the poetry was of a high excellence ; and secondly, he
ceased to write poetry, ceased indeed to care to write
it.   And none of the greater poets have ever been able
to do that.   Morris exhausted his fountain ; they could
not.   They cared, to the end, for their special art as
the most loved, the most precious thing, in the world,
and they wrought at it till they died.

There are many more things that were made by

this genius, whom so many wiseacres looked on only
as a decorator of houses, but I have said enough to
prove his creative power—the power which evokes from
the soul things unknown, unseen before, for the pleasure
and good of men ; which shapes and executes into fine
form what is conceived within, and which sends a spirit
through the new forms into the heart of humanity ; but
I have said enough on this point, and I turn now to
the poetry itself. What rank it takes ; where lies its
weakness or its power ; what are the special elements
which make it precious ; its range and its limitations ;
the originality of its impulse, and the continuity of its
pleasure-giving ; how far it realises beauty, and its
feeling for beauty ; how close it is to human nature,
and how far from it ; its matter of thought, its manner
and melody ; its description of nature and its love of
nature, and its development—these are matters all of
which one cannot discuss in a short essay, from which
one has to choose a few only, or which one can only
briefly touch. I hope I shall not say too much or too
little on them.

When in 1854 Morris was twenty-two years old, the
sorrows of the Crimean War and the sacrifices it had
demanded from England, had awakened the country,
which had too much settled on its lees, from a kind of
lethargy. War is an unhappy and extravagant cure
for this evil sleep in which the diseases of the common
weal are neglected, but in the present state of the social

organism it seems to be the only thing which arouses the comfortable classes out of a selfish into a self-sacrificing life, which brings classes together, or which knits the nation into a sense of its unity and the duties of that unity. It is a miserable thing that the social state should be so organised that only by blood-letting and by the death or sorrow of thousands can any wide-reaching remedy be applied to the evils of greed, indifference to public diseases, and the isolation of class from class—and no indictment of our existing state of society can be stronger than this. Yet so it is. War does awaken a country from covetousness; does reveal mismanagement and degrade dishonesty, does unite a people under the banner of ideas not of self-interest; does preach to a whole nation that pain and death are better than dishonour; and that, not only to those who go to battle, but even more to those who send their loved ones to the battle. The spiritual result is greatest when the war is just and needful, but it follows even when the war is neither one nor the other. It is independent of the cause of the war.

The Crimean War, though a mistaken war, did kindle the country into some enthusiasm for ideals, did stir and strengthen the sense of duty, did awaken the sense of honour, of courage for an unpersonal cause, of sacrifice for the State and our fellow-men; and that so strongly that the devotion to base and selfish ends was for a time lessened in England. The nation was excited into unwonted and unselfish emotion. Public life gained some spiritual aims. That was the net result of a dreadful folly.

A certain national excitement of this kind, with some ideal aims connected with it, not necessarily a war-excitement, puts all men, and especially the young, into a state of thrill, into such a condition that the powers they possess, whatever they may be, desire to exercise themselves, to shape themselves into some creation. The powers of the mind and the imagination are then like young people who wake on a summer morning and cannot rest till they are moving with the morning. The national excitement flows into the hearts of men. And if the men whom it touches have the gift of writing poetry they will suddenly begin to exercise it. They break into creation.

It by no means follows that they will write poetry on the subject of the national excitement. No, they will write it on their own subjects, on the things for which they care, and these may be quite apart and away from the national excitement. But, nevertheless, that national excitement awakened their powers. In the case of Morris, he had been driven, in disgust with the lifeless years before the war, to find his interests wholly in the past, and the emotion he now gained from the national excitement—even if it was only fury with the idiotic mismanagement which slew our soldiers like sheep—was employed not on the causes of that excitement, or on the excitement itself, but on his own subjects. The excitement supplied the soil in which

a new poetry could grow.   But the plant which came
up had nothing to do with any excitement in the
present.   It was a new thing, and it seemed a stranger.

No one at Oxford or elsewhere thought it likely that
a new spring of poetry would arise in the fifties of the
last century.   The general opinion was that poetry
had culminated in Tennyson, and that nothing of another kind would be produced.   Nevertheless, Morris,
quite unconsciously and with a strange imagination
working intensely on uncommon matter, did begin
something which was quite distinct in poetry.   He
thought as highly as the rest of his friends of Tennyson,
but he was not so wholly carried away as they appeared
to be.   He ventured to criticise.   Then, too, he had
read and derived some impulse from Mrs. Browning,
and through her from Browning, to whom he gave an
unstinted admiration when he came to know him better.
So, when the desire to write verse came upon him, he
was not, like most young men, checked into silence or
imitation by the pre-eminence of Tennyson.   And one
morning, moved by his own mediæval enthusiasms and
thrilled unconsciously by the national emotion which
streamed in on him from England, he could resist the
inner impulse no more, and the fountain of verse broke
forth in his soul.   He found his first poem, *The Willow
and the Red Cliff*, finished before he was aware of it.
He read it to his friends and they proclaimed him a
poet.   "If that is poetry," he said, "it is easy to make
it," and for some time he produced some verse every

day. I do not know whether this first conviction of
his friends was always as sure as Canon Dixon thinks.
I know that Burne-Jones said that he did not feel at
first certain that Morris's poetical power was of that
quality that would endure, but that afterwards he felt
assured of it. "How," I said. "Well," he answered,
"he brought me a poem one day—*A Good Knight in
Prison*—and when he had read the lines—

> Now tell me you that are in love
> From the King's son to the wood-dove—

I was sure it was all right." It is not difficult to see
what he meant.

Any kind of true art-passion fills every nook and
corner of the soul; its flood drowns all interests but
its own, until it has given birth to some creation.
Then it ebbs, and another form of art becomes the
ideal, and in its turn swells over the soul—a fresh in-
coming tide. But whatever it be, nothing else, for the
time, seems worth doing. It is life itself, and all
future life seems filled with the ideals it aspires to
approach. This came now on Burne-Jones and Morris.
Their Catholic ideals—they had actually projected a
monastery—no longer limited their thoughts or hopes.
And they, and the whole small brotherhood of men
who were gathered round them, now began, brimming
over with the waters of immortal joy, to pursue art and
literature into the new paths they had discovered.
They gave up everything else to live and work in this

charmed world. They felt, like Wordsworth, that they were dedicated spirits. All day long Burne-Jones worked at painting, and Morris at literature and drawing. Each gave to, and received from, the other impulse and criticism, and knit together a friendship which lasted unbroken all their lives.

It was now 1855, and the brotherhood projected a magazine to advocate their principles. This was the *Oxford and Cambridge Magazine*, which was first published in January, 1856, and lasted a year. In it Morris inserted five poems previously written. " Previously," for he had now ceased to write verses for a time. In the summer of 1855 he had begun to write prose tales instead of verse, and eight of these tales appear in the magazine. Meanwhile, still in 1855, he had made acquaintance with the work of the Pre-Raphaelites and read *The Germ*. To Burne-Jones and Morris *Hand and Soul* became an inspiration. They had not yet met Rossetti, but in that tale the profound personal influence which he had on all the men he touched had already begun. The prose tales now continued for a year or so ; but about 1856 a new poetic impulse fell on Morris. One day Burne-Jones read a few pages of *The Morte d' Arthur* at a bookstall, and spoke of it to Morris, who bought it instantly. They read it together, and that great book did its spiritual and impelling work upon them. Along with it came the first reading of Chaucer, whom these two friends went through night after night in 1856. That poetry fell like fertilising dew on them, and for thirty years, after this rapture with Chaucer, Morris scarcely touched prose. Only in verse did he speak in literature, and he spoke under the mighty leading of him whose poetry he loved so well ; whom he called his master, under whose influence he wrote *The Earthly Paradise*, and the noble printing of whose greatest book was the last work he did on earth.

This is a sketch, briefly touched, of how he grew into a poet. As to the poetry itself, it is best to take it as it was published. *The Defence of Guenevere*, which is the title of the first book he sent forth, was published in 1858. It consisted of poems written in the two previous years, and of a few of the poems written in 1854 and 1855. Many poems, previously written, were not included in it, and it is a pity that some of them perished. He made a holocaust of them after the publication of *Guenevere*. A few, published in the *Oxford and Cambridge Magazine*, remain, and are enough to show his early hand. All of these, with the exception of one—*Pray but one prayer for me*—belong to romance, but are somewhat tinged with the manner and sentiment of the Border Ballads of which he was so fond. *Winter Weather* may serve as an example of these. A knight rides out to meet his enemy who has insulted his lady. They tilt together under the walls of the town, and the slanderer is slain. His body is borne through the night and laid beneath his own castle walls. The poem, with its strong individual quality, is written straight out of the youthful soul of Morris, and that gives it its charm. The pictures of the horses and banners and weapons of war ringing and flapping in the midnight stillness; of the castle walls and towers, of the chiming cities, of the wintry landscape, of sudden fate and fierce revenge, are drenched in the spirit of the adventurous feuds of the fourteenth century. Moreover, the poem realises the same remarkable combination of an ideal subject, imaginatively conceived in complete apartness from the life of his own century, with that close realism which we have already observed in Rossetti's work. And, it was quite new poetry, of a clear original turn and opening out a fresh region in the past for imaginative work. The Arthurian legend had, of course, been used by modern poets before this, but the fierce passions and deeds of the French and English war-captains and adventurers, with their historical and legendary romance, such as we find enshrined in the Chronicle of Froissart, these had not, with all their change and colour, been touched as yet.

Morris found out this untrodden land, and ran into it with a daily joy—every day he made a new poem— and he saw a multitude of events, and battles and adventures therein, of which no chronicle told him, but which he witnessed with the intellectual eye. He created their passions, their loves, their landscape; nor did he fail to create in them the spirit and life, the beauty and the pity, as well as the ruthlessness and cruelty, of the centuries in which he dwelt. What difference there is between such old stories, and Morris's invented representations of them, is not made by the distance of his time from them—he was borne backward into the period and was a part of its life—but by his individuality working within his own image of the time. They were old by imaginative transference of himself into another age, but in themselves they were underived from any previous poet; as original as a new island in the seas. This gives him even in this early work, his specialised place as a poet. There are two little fragments of verse in *The Hollow Land*, the first of which is like Melchisedek—without beginning of descent or end of days—so uncaused and original it is; and the second, though a piece of a Christmas carol, especially in the gorgeous colouring of it, unlike even the earliest carols.

This is the first, and we cannot miss its curious charm, its remoteness, its mystery of feeling and of landscape.

> Christ keep the Hollow Land
>   All the summer tide;
> Still we cannot understand
>   Where the waters glide.
>
> Only dimly seeing them
>   Coldly slipping through
> Many green-lipped cavern mouths
>   Where the hills are blue.

And this, which is better, is the fragment of a carol

sung in the snow by a sentinel under Queen Swanhilda's castle—

> Queen Mary's crown was gold,
>   King Joseph's crown was red,
> But Jesus' crown was diamond,
>   That lit up all the bed
>   Mariæ Virginis.
>
> Ships sail through the Heaven
>   With red banners dress'd,
> Carrying the planets seven
>   To see the white breast
>   Mariæ Virginis.

A haunting note is in that little thing. It comes from the world beyond the weariness of this earth ; half of mediæval mysticism, half of fairyland.

Of course, being written by a youth of twenty-two years, these early poems, and those of the *Defence of Guenevere*, are thin, not well-knit together. They begin things which are not ended; they run away from the subject—Morris was never concise—they have the faults of over-swift production. There is scarcely any true composition, sustained thought, or arrangement. They flow like a quick torrent over broken rocks. But they are alive with a new man from end to end ; they break into a novel world ; in them imagination kindles itself by its own breath into livelier flame ; their humanity is that of one man—particular, not universal—but it is deep. The passions are strong in them, natural, vivid ; they are those of Morris, their web drawn out of and coloured by his youth—imagined, not experienced—but they want neither vitality nor intensity.

What I have said is to be applied to the larger number of poems in the *Defence of Guenevere.* That book may be divided into three parts—the poems which concern the Arthurian legend; those which belong to a thirteenth or fourteenth century cycle of events; and those lyrics and lyrical pieces which belong to no century of earth, but are sent down to us out of the woods and lands beyond the world.

They are also a series of experiments, made by a young eagle flushing his wings. Many different metres are chosen and worked. A rude dramatic form, imitative of the miracle plays, is used. One piece is almost a short drama. Narrative poetry is tried, but fails to realise itself. It 'is strange that he did not now approach success in that form of poetry of which he made so great a success. There is a little fairy-folk-piece which stands alone. Ballad poetry also laid its hand upon him, and he tries his prentice hand upon it in this book. Moreover, he recreated here certain lyric forms with a refrain to them which English poetry had not seen for a long time. The book may be called a book of experiments. Like a young man who has many lighter loves before he settles down into the love of his life, as Romeo had before he met Juliet, so Morris tried many forms of poetry before he settled down into narrative poetry.

Of the poems suggested by Malory, the finest is said to be *King Arthur's Tomb*. It suffers greatly, and the others suffer more, from ill-composition, but the unwearied succession of pictures and passions fitted to each other, kindles, and deepens the kindling of our pleasurable pain, as we read of the riding of Lancelot to his last tryst with Guenevere, and of all the memories of his past love with which he fills his ride; and then of Guenevere dreaming into repentance and prayer, and of her last speech to him in which she saves his soul. A few modern touches in the descriptions are not enough to dull the strong impression we receive of a similar temper of mind in Morris to that which Malory had when he wrote his book—and which Tennyson had not. The remoteness of Tennyson's temper from Malory's is almost wonderful; and at every point of life it clashes with Malory. But the chief difference between Morris and Malory is not in the temper of their mind, but that Malory tells this last story of Lancelot and Guenevere with a great simplicity of feeling and description; and Morris, like a young man, and like one who loved—as he always loved—full ornament and minute detail, fills his story with an opulence of description, and with a complexity of feelings, which, as they are richly coloured with imagery let loose to wander where it will, we pardon with pleasure. Copiousness, when it is imaginative, is too precious a thing to be blamed.

Of the Arthurian poems this made the most impression, but for my part, *Galahad, a Christmas Mystery*, pleases me more. It has a wilder, a more mystic charm; the conception of Galahad is original, not so finished as Tennyson's, but less frigid, more human; and when the Sangreal comes, and the supernatural world of angels and saints crowds round Galahad to console him, the conception, the sentiment, the landscape, and the celestial spirituality, are not only in full harmony with romantic mediævalism but with something of that far-off Celtic spirit out of which the first form of the Greal legend grew.

It is original and human, but not mediæval, to make Galahad regret that when he rides alone he had no woman (like Lancelot or Palomydes) to think of, and thereby to fill the lonely forest paths with memories and hopes; no sweet meetings or partings like other men. Nor is it less original to bring, in this fashion, the vision of Christ to console him:

> In this way I,
> With sleepy face bent to the chapel floor,
>   Kept musing half asleep, till suddenly
> A sharp bell rang from close beside the door,
>   And I leapt up when something pass'd me by,
> Shrill ringing going with it; still half blind
>   I stagger'd after; a great sense of awe
> At every step kept gathering on my mind,
>   Thereat I have no marvel, for I saw
> One sitting on the altar as a throne,
>   Whose face no man could say he did not know,
> And though the bell still rang, he sat alone,
>   With raiment half blood red, and half white as snow,

who tells him that he is not alone, for He will be with
him always, and those lovers whose happiness he regrets, time and passion will weary them, but he shall
never be weary. " You are mine forever." When the
voice ceases the women of heaven come to arm him—
the virgin martyrs, full of joy for him ; Margaret of
Antioch, Cecily, Lucy, and Katherine. Henceforth,
his riding will be graced with lovelier visions of womanhood than ever fled before the eyes of Lancelot. The
piece breaks off abruptly, but its beauty of the other
world, the world within this world of ours where the
mystic visions rise and fall, is great ; nor is the human
pleasure or sorrow in that dream-fed region less fair
and true than in this world of ours, which we are so
amusing as to call real. As to the landscape of this
piece—the lonely chapel, the snow on the ground, the
wet fern and weeds of the wood, the winter wind, the
bell shrilling through the " forest deep," and the light
of the angels streaming over the snow—it fits the conception, the mysticism, the mediæval and spiritual
romance of the time, as a glove fits the hand.

A Good Knight in Prison is a piece of true romance,
done in a romantic manner of his own, full of pictures
in fine colour, of tender humanity, and in a charming
melody. At the end of it, midst of the tender com-
plaint of the knight and his memories—for the introducing of pictorial memories into the soliloquies of his
warriors is one of the methods Morris uses to enliven

his poems—Lancelot, with a fine stirring and clamour
of the verse, breaks into the castle and delivers him.
No English poet had ever done this kind of thing before, and none have done it since.

In such a world was Morris at home when he was
twenty-five—a soul born and bred in the fourteenth
century, but forced to eat and drink and sleep in the
nineteenth. These poems, while we think of their
want of finish, their abruptness of thought, their huddled imagery and disconnected trains of feeling, may
not appear to be worth dwelling on so long; but their
matter is new in poetry, so is their manner, and in both
the imagination is glowing with fresh fire. That is
the great quality, and where that is, it overtops all
elaborate skill in the technic of poetry and lifts its
maker into a far loftier chair than all these excellent
masters of words and rhyme and metrical arrange-
ments occupy, who pour over us floods of artistic verse
without orignality, with fancy, with science, but not
with imagination.

Of the second group of poems, originating from his
love of Froissart, *Sir Peter Harpdon's End* is the most
powerful—a kind of dramatic romance well but boy-
ishly realised; but also so full of a crude mannerism,
neither mediæval nor modern, of strange and strained
phrases, that on the whole it is disagreeable. The
blank verse is also as mannered and abrupt as the
phraseology. The characters speak, even to the Lady
Alice, on stilts; and we long for them to descend to

that ordinary English speech Morris uses afterwards so
well. *The Little Tower*, with its desperate ride through
the flooded lands ; the *Riding Together*, banners and
spears afloat in the air in the swiftness of the ride ; its
noise and clash of war when the Christian band meet
the Pagan host, and the tragic misery of the end ;
Geffray Teste Noire, with the wayside episode of the
slain knight and his lady unburied in the wood ; *The
Haystack in the Floods* with its passionate realism, its
close touch on the brutality of the times, even to their
savage ruthlessness to women, and yet the ineffable
pity of the tale ; *Shameful Death*, better told and composed than the others, a record of cruel, then of just,
vengeance—these are living records, poignantly keen,
of the miseries of the mercenary wars, that other side
of the shield of chivalry. I only mention *The Judgment of God*, because it smacks of Browning—the only
Morris poem which clearly comes near to Browning's
banner. And I mention this because Morris himself
was accustomed to say that if his poems owed a debt
to any one, they owed it to Browning.

All these are of his youth, and share in the over-
quaintness, the ill-conception, and the long-windedness
of youth, but they are true to his own impassioned
temper, alive with colour and the tumult of war, savage
in their realism, clear-eyed in their imagination. The
most charming, however, of the poems, is *Rapunzel*,
which cannot be said to belong to any of these three
groups. It stands alone, drawn out from the Arthurian

or mediæval story, and, as Morris has conceived it, not wholly outside of the actual world. The subject was given him in the old folk-talk of the Solitary Tower, the Princess who dwells alone in it, and who lets down her golden hair for the witch to climb up by, and the Prince who delivers her. Morris has mediæval-ised the old tale. Its Greek connexion he has entirely ignored, and its mythical elements. It is remade according to Morris; and nowhere, not even in *The Earthly Paradise*, has he remade a story more delight-fully. He has added enough reality to it to take it out of fairyland, and yet left round it the fairy atmosphere. The Prince and the Princess are quite human, and their love passages full of delicate charm. The form of the poem is quaint and fanciful, but clear, connected, and well concluded. And the incidents, the conversation, the landscape are invented and varied with grace and change, and so is the verse. All fit together, and over it youthful love, like a sunny atmosphere in early spring, breathes unity and enchantment. The soul of Morris, in his dreaming youth, is there.

The third type of poems in this volume is quite dis-tinct from the rest. They are not of this world at all, but, even in their immaturity, prophetic of the air and light and landscape of *The Wood Beyond the World*, out of whose star-begotten creatures he made a prose romance. In this far other-world, full of magic and fairy, he lived in the last years of his life, when the fourteenth century, and the Greek life in its mediæval dress, and the early Teutonic communities such as he painted in *The House of the Wolfings* and *The Roots of the Mountains*, and even the Norse Saga-land and life, and the future world of a regenerated humanity—having been long dwelt in, were finally left behind by this spiritual wanderer through many times and nations; the Ulysses of the soul, who, working and walking among us, yet never truly lived save far away from us, in a hundred rovings of imagination. This last country he lived in was described in many tales—in *The Glittering Plain*, *The Wood Beyond the World*, *The Well at the World's End*—and last of all, just before he died, in that most delightful book, *The Sundering Flood*, a very flower of imagination, yet so real that we believe, as we read, in every word of it. This is a country of great rivers, hewing their way from the mountains through deep gorges to the plains, of deep woods, and silver lakes, and green sea waves, and many-visaged weather, and cities by the sea, and tall castles, and chaffering towns where knights and mechants meet, of farms, and of forest land where robber bands are slain and fair women wander and love, and love is long and full; where in the woods are green-clad women whose life is not human but whose affections are, and wizards and witches, good and bad, and magic and immortal warriors, and all the wonders of fairy—a lovely land to live in, far away from our sordid ugliness; far away even from the earth itself, even in its social regeneration—a life such as may, for

all we know, be lived in some happier planet than ours,
hidden in some galaxy in space, but human to the core.
Most men, when they write tales of fairy, of a world
imagined, make their men and women unlike ourselves,
not quite human. But Morris, in all these tales, rests
his story on the universal passions and ways of natural
humanity—humanity, it is true, freed from the conventions of either society or morality, but all the more
natural and real for that freedom. The world in which
we live, while we read, is not our world, but the men
and women are ourselves as we are in the secret life
within where we ignore or despise the rules and
maxims of society.

I know nothing more refreshing, in this overladen
world, and when life, with its relentless goad, drives
us on to so many vain labours and to so many duties
which are not duties but conventions—to take out one
of these books, and slip out of it all, like some released
and happy spirit, into a natural world. This releasing
power is one of Morris's best contributions to the good
and consolation of man. And the power to create such
a world, under the terrible pressure of our unnatural
commonplace, is perhaps the finest capacity of his
genius.

It is in the air of this world of dream, such as Keats
lived in when he saw the

> magic casements opening on the foam
> Of perilous seas in fairy lands forlorn,

that certain poems in this early book were composed ; and it is characteristic of the consistency and continuity of the elements of the soul of Morris that he should recur at the end of his life, in romantic prose, to the regions of which he had written, when he was young, in romantic poetry. The very titles of these poems take us into the atmosphere of dreaming phantasy in which they were conceived—*The Sailing of the Sword*, *The Blue Closet*, *The Tune of Seven Towers*, *Two Red Roses Across the Moon*—nor is the fine, half-languid, half-fiery loving of *The Praise of my Lady*, with its Latin refrain, outside of the fairy world of the later romances, where true and natural passion, in admiration of the outward and inward beauty love spiritualises, plays so great a part.

Only one poem in the book, in its tragic passion, its dreadful remorse and horror, as well as in the unexplained mystery of its crime of love or jealousy, belongs not only to mediæval times, but to all times. *The Wind* is its title. It might be invented by a modern poet, and it is touched here and there by modern thoughts. Its melody and rhythm are different from all the rest, better managed, and of a singular charm. And the telling of the tale and the scenery of it were done in an artist hour.

Only one poem in the whole book has quite a modern air, and moves in a lovely and wildering melody, with an involved overlapping of thought, and of changing feelings echoed by the metrical changes,

—most like a fugue, and penetrated throughout with a tremulous passion of music. It is written, in spite of its two curious faults, with the grace of a matured artist, and yet was one of his earliest pieces, being published in the *Oxford and Cambridge Magazine*. *Summer Dawn* is its name, and I quote it—

> Pray but one prayer for me 'twixt thy closed lips,
>   Think but one thought of me up in the stars.
> The summer night waneth, the morning light slips,
>   Faint and grey 'twixt the leaves of the aspen, betwixt
>   the cloud-bars,
> That are patiently waiting there for the dawn :
>   Patient and colourless, though Heaven's gold
> Waits to float through them along with the Sun.
> Far out in the meadows, above the young corn,
>   The heavy elms wait, and restless and cold
> The uneasy wind rises ; the roses are dun ;
> Through the long twilight they pray for the dawn,
> Round the lone house in the midst of the corn,
>   Speak but one word to me over the corn,
>   Over the tender, bow'd locks of the corn.

That concludes what I have to say about this first book. I have dwelt on it at perhaps too great length. But it is not so well known as the poems which followed it, and a great interest gathers round the youthful work of one who proved so well that he had that enduring power which ripens and matures into noble fruitage. There is a delicate exquisiteness of feeling, as of that which may quickly perish ; an apartness of joy such as is never felt again ; an appealing hope and promise ; all the sweetness and courage of bold attempt, in the first flowers and leaves of early spring, which may well image the first poems of genius. Their very incompleteness suggests completeness, prophesies the fulness of summer, and ᵢirresistibly attacks the imagination.

When we next meet Morris in print, he has ceased to be immature and unfinished. He has found out clearly what he can best do. Spring is over; summer has come, and indeed he brought the summer into narrative poetry; for since Chaucer no one, not Dryden, not Keats, had re-attained in England the Chaucerian charm, the gliding sentiment, the fluidity of narrative and of verse, in narrative poetry, till Morris came. Scott may be instanced, but Scott's narrative work in verse diminished in excellence and in quantity as he went on. Morris increased his productiveness, and its excellence was fully supported, till he, like Scott, gave up narrative poetry and turned to prose. Indeed, no poet is likely to go on writing narrative poetry all his life. For poetry seeks naturally for concentration, intensity, conciseness of thought, action, and emotion brought to a burning centre—elements which, introduced continually into narrative poetry, would undo the very essence of that kind of poetry. When people complain of the flowing looseness of Morris's tales, of their minute and lingering detail, of their expansiveness, they are complaining of things which actually make the essence of narrative poetry. What do they want? Can they not understand that they must not

have the excellences of the lyric in a narrative poem,
and that to introduce them would be wholly out of
place—would, indeed, destroy the elements of poetic
narrative ? Each form of poetry has its own customs,
laws, and necessities, its own times, places, and moods
of mind in which it ought to be read. Narrative
poetry is not to be read in the great crises of life and
thought, but as Omar wished to read—

> A book of Verses underneath the Bough,
> A Jug of Wine, a Loaf of Bread, and Thou
> Beside me singing in the wilderness—
> Oh, Wilderness were Paradise enow.

Chaucer was in this the master of Morris, and when
Morris sent forth *The Earthly Paradise* completed, he
enshrined in an epilogue the honour he gave to his
master in a set of verses full of tenderness ; and revealing, with that strange unreserve which many poets
have in verse while they are reserved in life, the verit-
able temper of his soul while he was yet quite young,
while poetry was dear to him, and life a dream of love
and joy, with the darkness of death beyond to make
love and joy too dear for happiness ; while he was yet
only the idle singer of an empty day :

> "Children we twain are, saith he, late made wise
> In love, but in all else most childish still,
> And seeking still the pleasure of our eyes,
> And what our ears with sweetest sound may fill ;
> Not fearing Love, lest these things he should kill ;
> Howe'er his pain by pleasure doth he lay,
> Making a strange tale of an empty day.

" Death have we hated, knowing not what it meant ;
Life have we loved, through green leaf and through sere,
Though still the less we knew of its intent :
The Earth and Heaven through countless year on year,
Slow changing, were to us but curtains fair,
Hung round about a little room, where play
Weeping and laughter of man's empty day.

" Then let the others go ! and if indeed
In some old garden thou and I have wrought,
And made fresh flowers spring up from hoarded seed,
And fragrance of old days and deeds have brought
Back to folk weary ; all was not for nought.
No little part it was for me to play—
The idle singer of an empty day."

He began this narrative poetry while he was still at
the University, and he began it with his usual impetuosity and plenitude. He projected and did a great
part of a poem on the tale of Troy—on that part of the
tale which, after the events of the *Iliad*, was recorded
in the lost Greek epics, and which stirred the mediæval
and romantic poets into making the many poems that
constitute the Cycle of Troy. In that cycle the Greek
tales are told in the mediæval and romantic manner
and with mediæval surroundings and beliefs ; the
landscapes, buildings, towns, furniture, armour, warriors, and women, are all mediæval. That was just
what Morris wanted, and he, of set purpose, mediæval-
ised (with the inevitable modernism in natural description, and in sentiment) his Greek stories both in *Jason*
and in *The Earthly Paradise*. The objection then,
that his Greek stories are not Greek in character, falls

to the ground. He did not, any more than Keats, in-
tend them to be classical, but romantic ; and he took
pains in the story of *The Wanderers* to invent for this
purpose a Greek colony in some far seas, the dwellers
in which, though descended from the Greeks, had lived
on into the fourteenth century, and, like the late Greeks
of Byzantium, held their old traditions in very different
forms from those they had received in ancient Greece.
They are supposed to tell their tales in mediæval fashion. This view is excellently laboured by Mr. Mackail
in his *Life of Morris*, and Morris himself maintained it.

Jason is written in that fashion. *The Story of the
Golden Fleece* was to have been one of the stories of *The
Earthly Paradise*, but it enlarged under his hand till it
became a separate book. Published in 1867, it made
him at once famous, and established him as a poet.
That the English people, who hate long things ; that
the lovers of poetry, who were then enamoured of the
idyll and brief dramatic lyrics, should read it all, was
a triumph of good story-telling. It was something
that the story was well known. It was something
more that into the known outlines of the story many
freshly-invented episodes were introduced, so that the
reader, in surprise and pleasure, was lured on by rapid
incident. But these things do not fully account for the
favour with which it was read from end to end. It
was, first of all, excellent narrative, eminently clear,
flowing, well knit together, naturally wrought. It
never left its own level, and it preserved its own

atmosphere from the beginning to the close. Jason is foremost in it; we never leave his side. The unity of the narrative is therefore unbroken. Boy, youth, man, adventurer, warrior, lover, wanderer, king, we follow him till weariness comes on his maturity and success, and he is faithless to love and honour. He had no pity, no shame; he felt no Nemesis press upon him. Vengeance, not only of Medea, descends on him; the house of life falls in ruins, and the great warrior, in his exhausted sorrow, in grey apathy, dies ignobly in his sleep, half-dead before he dies. This irony of life, this image of the victory of decay, of vanity, broods over the whole book. The futility of human endeavour at the last was always more deep than it should have been in the mind of Morris. It lies beneath many other stories; it has sunk deep into *The Earthly Paradise;* it is the dominant note in *Jason.* It is human enough; and it deepens all the other human elements in the story. The Greeks, no doubt, felt it profoundly in the tale, but they could not have felt it more profoundly than Morris.

Naturally, as it paints the whole of a man's career the poem is close to humanity. Morris never wanted humanity, even in his dream-romances. But here he has got out of the vagueness and inexperience of his earlier work into the real stuff of mankind; out of particular forms of feeling at moments of event, into the universal business and passion of the world of men. And weight and dignity now enter into his work, nor did they ever leave it. In passion, in thought, he rarely went deep in the tales, but when he did, he wrote with a reality to which enough credit has not been given. The most real piece of human nature under the power of the passions—a true piece of fine tragedy, where many passions mingle threads of beauty and terror, "dyed with the hues of earthquake and eclipse" —is contained in the last book of *Jason* after the story of *The Golden Fleece* is ended. It paints the desire of change in a mature man; that crisis when the worn pilgrim of life, weary of good and evil, desires innocence and freshness and the dew of youth in a woman to renew his heart upon, and seems, in such a love, to taste again the sweetness of youth. It paints the passion of love in a young girl for the man who embodies for her the heroic. It paints the passions, in an experienced woman, of jealousy, hatred, fierce sorrow, untameable revenge, wrath at betrayal of love—deepened by passionate memories, intensified by conscious power, contempt of weakness, and unmitigated will. It paints, when Medea has had her vengeance, and left Jason, stripped of everything, as naked as a wintry tree, his loneliness, his days and nights of misery, till misery devoured itself in lapse of time. It tells then how, a broken man, he thought of active life again, of new adventure, war, and kingship; how as he thought of it, the stem of Argo, under which he dreamed and slept, fell, charged with the irony of fate, on him; and he died, not in the ringing ranks of battle, but on the unfamed edges of the shore and sea, by a fameless accident.

That Morris felt that this episode was most tragic and needed his finest work, most human and needed his most imaginative insight, is proved by his invocation at its beginning to his master, Chaucer, for his help. The verses are full of himself, of his love of nature, of his love of the old times, of his ideality and his delight in reality, of the closeness of his work to things and men, of his clear vision of what he saw, and of his power to shape it into form.

> So ends the winning of the Golden Fleece,
> So ends the tale of that sweet rest and peace
> That unto Jason and his love befell ;
> Another story now my tongue must tell,
> And tremble in the telling.   Would that I
> Had but some portion of that mastery
> That from the rose-hung lanes of woody Kent
> Through these five hundred years such songs have sent
> To us, who, meshed within this smoky net
> Of unrejoicing labour, love them yet,
> And thou, O Master !—Yea, my Master still,
> Whatever feet have scaled Parnassus' hill,
> Since, like thy measures, clear, and sweet, and strong,
> Thames' stream scarce fettered bore the bream along
> Unto the bastioned bridge, his only chain.
> O Master, pardon me, if yet in vain
> Thou art my Master, and I fail to bring
> Before men's eyes the image of the thing
> My heart is filled with : thou, whose dreamy eyes
> Beheld the flush to Cressid's cheeks arise,
> When Troilus rode up the praising street,
> As clearly as they saw thy townsmen meet
> Those who in vineyards of Poictou withstood
> The glittering horror of the steel-topped wood.

Jason was followed in 1868–70 by the volumes of *The Earthly Paradise*, and this publication confirmed and increased the reputation of Morris. *The Apology* with which he prefaced the book expresses the temper of mind which, while he wrote, lay underneath the stories, and the same temper appears more fully in the endings and introductions to the tales.

The first lines of the Prologue to the whole book, the story of *The Wanderers*, tell where the tales were supposed to be written and by whom. They were delivered in an island dwelt in by Ionian Greeks who had been driven there centuries before, and who retained their ancient worship, language, manners, and traditions. To this island, after many wanderings, seafaring men from Norway, Swabia, Brittany, France, and England came in the fourteenth century, were welcomed by the Greeks, and lived in the peace of their old age. And the time was in the latter half of the century when Chaucer was alive. Morris dwells on the date.

> Forget six counties overhung with smoke,
> Forget the snorting steam and piston-stroke,
> Forget the spreading of the hideous town ;
> Think rather of the pack-horse on the down,
> And dream of London, small, and white, and clean,
> The clear Thames bordered by its gardens green ;
> Think, that below bridge the green lapping waves
> Smite some few keels that bear Levantine staves,
> Cut from the yew-wood on the burnt-up hill,
> And painted jars that Greek hands toiled to fill,
> And treasured scanty spice from some far sea,

Florence gold cloth, and Ypres napery,
And cloth of Bruges, and hogsheads of Guienne ;
While nigh the thronged wharf Geoffrey Chaucer's pen
Moves over bills of lading—mid such times
Shall dwell the hollow puppets of my rhymes.

Having thus brought together, in an admirable frame-work, the old Greek world and the fourteenth century, the Greeks tell their ancient tales and the Wanderers theirs, meeting twice a month in the great Hall of the Island State, for a year, twenty-four tales in all ; and a marvellous piece of opulent inventiveness is the book.

Yes, the first thing to say of the narrative poetry of Morris is that it is characterised by unfailing invention. The main events were marked down for him in the original tales, but he filled up the outlines of each with a wealth of incidents, descriptions, and characterisation, to the inventiveness of which I know no parallel in modern story-telling poetry. Take the first book of *Jason*. The boy is entrusted to Cheiron, the Centaur, to be educated. He meets Juno when he is grown up, and is sent back to take up his duty and his fate. That is the slight outline, but it is filled up with such a host of small events, all bearing on his future, and with so delightful a sketch of the Centaur's life with Jason, seen so clearly and told so connectedly that the book, which runs to several hundred lines, is a self-rounded tale which would enchant a summer night. Then, again, the great adventures of the story were easy to make interesting, but it was a bold thing

to take Argo and his crew right across from the Black
Sea, through the wastes of Russia, to the northern
ocean ; and yet this dreary voyage is made interesting
enough for reading by an invented series of strange
adventures with strange folk, and by vivid descriptions
of the forests, the rivers, and the winter. Even the
crew itself have no weariness of life. The buoyancy of
Morris supports them with his own vitality. And the
greater adventures of the tale, in themselves so exiting,
are embroidered, illuminated, like the background of a
tapestry, or the pages of a missal, with hundreds of
small and delicate inventions. There is not an inch of
the surface of the story which is not filled with ornament as a summer meadow is with flowers, and none
of it is apart from the tale. It is kept down to its due
proportions. It enriches, it does not minimise the interest. All this is true of the various poems of *The
Earthly Paradise*, some of which leave the original outlines for a fresh creation, as in *East of the Sun, West of
the Moon*. The incessant invention of the Prologue is
another good example of this quality. It is worth
while to recall, as an example, the meeting of the
Wanderers' ship with King Edward's fleet off the coast
of France, and the admirable sketch of the person and
character of the King, of the figures of the young
Prince and Chandos, of the Royal ship, its gorgeous
sails and heraldic glories. But there are a host of such
inventions in every tale. This great inventiveness
saves the long narratives from the monotony which is

the greatest danger of narrative poetry, a point on which it is not worth while to enlarge.

Then, secondly, there is a remarkable equality of excellence, an equality which ought to belong to narrative verse. The level at which Morris begins any story is supported throughout ; the atmosphere is not changed. The level rises where it ought to rise, but it does not rise too high for this kind of poetry, or for the rest of the story. Then, though it rises, it never falls. I cannot recall in that vast production any sinking into plainly inferior work. Certain stories are not as well told as the rest ; those he loved best are best told ; but even the least good ones do not fall below the level at which he began them. This continuity of imaginative emotion, always and equally present, without haste and without rest, is excessively uncommon, especially in poetry, which depends so much on the unstable rise and fall of emotion. Abounding vitality was a marked characteristic of his whole life and character, of what he thought, invented, worked at, and proclaimed. " 'T is life whereof our nerves are scant " could not be said of Morris.

Another quality of the poetry is the great clearness with which the things described are seen. Everything is seen as if in full sunlight, and his clear sight of what he saw was accompanied by an equal lucidity in its description. The execution is equal to the vision, the form to the image on the mind. So defined, for example, are the landscapes, so too like pictures sometimes, that some of that suggestiveness is lost which, in stimulating the reader's imagination to create for himself worlds beyond the world described, is so high and fine an element in the arts of poetry and music. However, owing to the clearness of sight and execution, all the detail is exquisite. I know no other poetry so rich, so accurate, in portraiture of flowers and trees, of sweet meadows, of the waves of the sea, of the flowing of rivers, of the play and work of the weather, of the village houses, of the towers and walls of cities, of dress of men and women, of armour, and furniture, of tapestries and architecture, of a hundred things that we ought to see, but do not. In comparison with Morris, most of the other poets are blind. Sharp, receptive, and retaining were his eyes.

This brings me directly, through his clear-seeing, and his power of shaping in words what he saw, to Morris as a poet of nature. Nature is described by him exactly as he saw her. No mystic veil is thrown over her. No philosophy of her appears in Morris. I have said this with regard to Arnold's nature-poetry, but Arnold wavered from the position. Morris never changed it. That kind of thing was repugnant to him, nor indeed did his favourite, Keats, indulge in it. Morris was content to see things as they were. A cloud was only a cloud, a stream only a stream. It was enough for him that the cloud was lovely, and the stream. Nor did he make out of nature texts for teaching lessons of any kind. He did not use her as

the prophet or the moralist has done ; nor did he make
analogies between her doings and the doings of men in
the fashion those poets and preachers do, who conceive
that she and man proceed from the same creative
thought, and therefore touch and answer one another.
He places man in the midst of nature's solemn, constant, and lovely movement, but she has no relation of
her own to him.   Indifferent to us, she passes on her
way,—the beautiful and changing background only of
our sorrow and joy.

What he does describe, with regard to her and us,
is the contrast, which Arnold also felt, between her
constancy, continuity, strength, her stately, quiet
movement, her beauty and apparent joy, and our in-
constancy, fleetingness, weakness, hurried and broken
life, our enduring sorrows and our momentary joys.
She has no pause, and seemingly no end.   But we are
creatures of a day, and old age is with us in a moment,
and death divides us from love and pleasure.   Therefore
let us snatch our day, and take what we can, and
quickly, and be brave and thankful.   This is a sad
temper, face to face with nature ; yet it was the temper
of Morris, up to the close, at least, of *The Earthly
Paradise*.   The lyric which some say is one of the
most beautiful he ever wrote—I do not agree with
them—and which occurs in the story of Ogier the
Dane, enshrines this ; but it is also enshrined in almost
every one of the lovely introductions to the different
months in *The Earthly Paradise*, short poems in which,

were it not for their want of joy and their trembling
melancholy, more dramatic than actual, he reached his
highest level in lyric poetry.

These descriptions, unlike most of the natural descriptions in the tales themselves, are mixed, in contrast, with human feeling, and chiefly with the varied
phases of love. They are not only nature-poems, but
love-poems. Their main character is that of sorrow.
At this time of his life love seemed to Morris so over-
shadowed with transiency and the inevitableness of
death, that he could get but little joy out of it. However, as time went on, and the interests of the present
entered into his soul, as well as those of the past, this
element of sadness disappears from his treatment of
love. The lovers in his prose romances are sensible;
honestly and passionately happy. Their present joy
makes them careless of the future; quite thoughtless,
save at moments, of death. As to old age, the imagination of it does not cloud their youth. Sufficient to
the day is the good thereof.

It is worth while to linger a little round these poems.
They are twofold. One portion of them is dedicated
to a description of the natural scenery of the year.
The twelve months are so painted, with their weather,
their work, their landscape, that each of them seems
to grow before us into a personage, with a separate
character. Morris does not himself impersonate them,
but we do under his impulse. We breathe the air of

their separate natures. In addition to this impression—
as in the symbolism of the months round cathedral
doorways,—the special human work of each month is
represented by Morris, and imaginatively inwoven with
the landscape. And moreover, the distinct spirit of
each month (proceeding from nature's doings and
man's doings in each of them) enters into the soul of
the reader, and wakens there its distinct thought and
feeling,—the soul transmuting the natural impression
into its own imaginative passion. This is a vital element in the work of Morris. Nor are the landscapes
left unanimated. The sky is full of flying birds, and
so are the woods and moors and pools. The kine feed
in the pastures, the bees sing from flower to flower,
the dragon-flies dart by, the sheep wander to their folds
in the evening. The blue-clad horseman rides from
vale to vale, the traveller hails the ferryman across the
swirling river. The reapers, the shepherd, the plough-
man, the girls in the orchard, the labourer in the farm-
yard, the vintagers ruddy with the juice of the vine, a
host of human creatures at work and play, fill the
landscape. This natural description is one side of these
poems, and it is supported and enhanced by a hundred
descriptions of a similar kind in the conduct of the
stories.

The other side of these poems is personal, and has
to do with the affairs of love. Whether they represent
any real experiences of Morris, one cannot of course
tell. They seem to be passionate. I wonder if they

are. They were most probably invented. But the spirit of the man at this time of his life is in them. Their temper is his own, and it is uniformly sorrowful with regret, with the hatred of old age and death. He sees in *May* a vision of the Lord of Love go by, in bright procession, but behind them he sees Eld and Death. The rest of the world did not; May had so filled them that they forgot they must die. *June* is so beautiful that hopes and fears are gone. We take her beauty—but we are pensive men. Then phase after phase of love is touched; not the simple, constant phases, but subtle, transient, involved feelings, such as pass through a lover who fears what will become of love because he has known love decay in the past, because he is sure of inevitable decay in the future, and because of dreadful weariness, so dreadful that no world there seems

Beyond these four walls hung with pain and dreams.

Again, he has seen the death of all things, which, living, once were fair—image of dread eternity.

In whose void patience, how can these have part,
These outstretched feverish hands, this restless heart?

Then the faint hopes of love are touched. Cast nothing away you have once loved ; perchance love's day may come. There may yet be a rest for me, and for the world.

These are some of the motives, most minutely varied,

of these poems. One would not dwell on them, if the temper in which they were written did not change into a healthier temper, as his life and work opened out before him. This mood was transient. It sometimes recurred in after days, but he had conquered it. But now it pervades, not only these poems, but some of the most important tales in *The Earthly Paradise*. It fills the Prologue. *The Wanderers* have left the affairs of love behind, for old age is on them and death near, but while they remembered how futile was all its striving, they are sorry it is past. They see the young men and the maidens, and bid them take their joy, while they can. It is true they are themselves at peace, but it is peace with sorrow. With them, however, personal love was never the first thing, but insatiable desire of the perfect land. Nothing was good but pursuit, until they could pursue no more. This is the temper of the Prologue, but in the stories which follow it, love runs, for the most part, on well-known lines, natural, simple, clear, personal, unmixed with subtle, complex, or obscure feeling, quite unlike the love-poems on which I dwell at present.

There are, however, two tales in *The Earthly Paradise* where the confused wanderings of love-thinking, the obscure involutions of love-emotion described in these short love-poems, occur again—*The Death of Paris* and *The Hill of Venus*. It is difficult to find one's way among the by-ways of incessantly changing feeling in the passionate converse of Paris and Ænone,

each feeling before it is half expressed being tript up
by another; but that is probably the impression the
poet desired to make. It is still more difficult to discover the real reason why Tannhaüser left Venus, but
the impression, imposed on us, as we read, of a human
soul in a forbidden, unhuman land and hopelessly lost
therein, of a mortal linked in passion to an immortal
who has had a hundred mortals' loves and will have a
hundred more when he is dead, of an immortal shadow
in a shadow land, who knows neither sorrow nor aspiration, whose high godhead is dead while her lonely
sensual joy survives—remains most vividly, and drives
our curious thinking into incursions over undiscovered
realms within the soul.

Leaving these personal poems, of so remote an interest, I return to his nature-poetry. The descriptions, so
opulent in colour, of so great a clearness, so enlivened
with animal life and figures and done with so careful
a love of beauty, have a general adaptation to the story
and the time it belongs to, but they have no other relation to humanity. In this he is quite modern and of
his age. We may choose, as an example, those in the
tale—*The Man Born to be King*, and in *The Story of
Rhodope*. The journey of Michael to the Castle of the
Rose takes two or three days, and the successive landscapes of the countryside are described with so much
charm and accuracy that we see them with the rider's
eyes and heart. Rhodope leaves the house in the

morning and walks through the fields and woods to the seashore. The landscape changes as she moves, and every change is described, till we reach with her the sandy bay between the rocky capes and hear the river meet the sea. All the countryside is full of the works of men, but everywhere also is the soul of Rhodope.

Such creative vision does not belong only to a few poems. It is present in every story of the book. It is only, however, the modern landscapist who would have seen and chosen them. When I think of all Morris did in this way, of the vast number of scenes he saw, recorded, and invented, I am astonished by his memory—which must almost have equalled Turner's— of what he saw ; and as grateful for the power by which, like Ruskin, he has opened our eyes to see, ob- serve, and keep the beauty of the world. I have already said that his love of the earth, its life and all the life of animals and man upon it, was one of the strongest passions of his character. But that which he loved the most—and wrote of with unwearied pleasure both in poem and romance—was the quiet river life of England, its cornfield and meadow, the granges and villages on its banks and on the hills that looked upon it ; the woods that lived by its waters and saw their image in its pools, the flowers it nurtured, the birds that haunted its shallows, the full or rippling streams that from the bases of the swelling downs flowed into it. Mountain scenery, with its savagery and splendour, did not move his heart deeply, not even the Icelandic scenery which was loved, so far as he loved it, not so much for itself, as for the sake of those brave and honourable freemen who strove for life therein from tragedy to tragedy. It is remarkable that in the story of Gudrun, in *The Earthly Paradise*, the description of nature, so varied and constant in the other tales, scarcely exists at all. The wide firth, black beneath the morning star, and all the waste of snow, did not please him half so much as the reaches of the Thames, or the hamlets hidden in the downs, or the Danish barrow on the hill top, or the grey frontage of Peterborough Cathedral looking over the wide fen. The island to which the Wanderers came, and where the Greek folk live, is really England in its natural scenery; the doings and weather of the months therein are taken from the England of the fourteenth century—even to the vintaging ; and half the descriptions at least in the stories of the whole book are transferred direct from places he had seen in England, or in Northern France. Nor is this deep affection for this still scenery absent from the prose romances. *The Dream of John Ball*, and especially *News from Nowhere*, are thrilling with it,

Celt by descent, he was not Celtic in his natural description. He loved rather a Teutonic scenery, when he left in poetry his beloved England. If he painted only a sketch here and there of Icelandic landscape—desolate plain, savage mountain gorge, and fierce seas, matters which did not lie close to his heart—he painted, with a vital touch, with a wealth of luminous description, and with pleasure that breathes in every line, the scenery of the Teutonic lands in a more temperate clime than Iceland, in *The Roots of the Mountains.* The valley of Burgdale lives in its readers; I see its tillage, corn land, sweet meadows, clear streams and the beautiful people who live in it day by day; and the dark woods above it and the wild moorland, and beyond, the mountain range. How Morris loved to get his descriptions definite! The valley, the town, the hall, the farmhouses of Burgdale, each in their relation to the scenery and the waters, might be mapped out in every detail from his description of them in words. In the beginning of *The Sundering Flood* he has made a lucid map of the whole country of which the story tells, and the country is none we know. It existed only in his imagination, but when we have read of it, we know it to its remotest nook and smallest stream. This is enough, perhaps, to say of his poetry of nature. Each reader can say for himself more than I can say. It is for us, who dwell in cities over much, a blessing to possess it. Even in London, we may live in the country while we read.

The finest charm in the stories of *The Earthly Paradise* is their romance. The Greek stories are told in the same romantic temper as the mediæval tales; that is, Morris added to the classic outlines the ideals, the longings, the passionate thoughts concerning life and death and love and beauty which a modern romantic

would naturally feel. And this is done quite frankly.
There is no imitation of the classic forms, or of the
classic way of thought. Nor are the stories Palladian,
if I may use that metaphor, but Gothic; remade by
fresh, individual emotion out of the old material. *The
Love of Alcestis*—to take an example—can anything
be less Greek and more romantic than the way the tale
is told by Morris? It is curious to imagine Euripides
reading it. The Perseus story is told with a great delight in the story itself, but the telling of it is trans-
formed by the multitude of details, and by delicate
windings of emotion, out of all harmony with the
Greek Spirit, and into harmony with the romantic.
The story of Cupid and Psyche, which Morris wrought
with the utmost care, is not so far separated from the
classic temper as the others, because his original was
exquisitely done at a time when the Greek Spirit had
itself become partly romantic. It was bold of him to
rival the beauty of his original, but he has, while
losing its brevity and a certain stately and steady
loveliness in the brevity, lengthened it with so much
delightful scenery and ornament that we enjoy its
romantic furniture from end to end. The two Bellerophon stories are almost entirely invented by Morris.
The whole countryside in both poems, at Argos, and in
Lycia, with the towns and their buildings, is so clearly,
so pictorially painted, that we might map out the
landscape. The streets and temples and palaces of the
cities; their gardens, halls, pleasure-chambers; their

crowds, processions, music—details which the Greeks would scarcely have touched—would have been dear to the Romance-writers.

These two poems are, however, more modern than classic or romantic by a closer and more careful elaboration of human character than usual; and this is due, I think, to the strong influence which the strong and deep humanity of the story of Gudrun had exercised upon him. Bellerophon, who is quite uninteresting at the beginning, is wrought into a higher ideal of manhood than any other in the book. Sthenobæa, in the invention and delineation of whose character and fate, Morris has reached a high tragic level, and reached it, not with the Greek reticence, but with so fluent and opulent an invention that romantic richness can go no further, is contrasted with Philonoë's pure, delicate, natural, passionate girlhood—a lovely picture—nor are the other characters less carefully drawn. As to the Chimœra story it is a masterpiece of suggestion.

The lighter Greek tales, of Acontius, Atalanta, Pygmalion, the Golden Apples and others are delightful narrative, at intervals quaintly mediæval in feeling, modern in their love of natural scenery, romantic in their love emotion, and Greek only in their story. Of the death of Paris, which stands apart, I have already said something. Of the story of Rhodope, which also stands apart, it may be said that it is neither Greek nor romantic, but of Morris alone. It is a curious study of the soul of a woman, born into a world which is not hers and in which she can love no one and nothing ; unawakened to life till she attain the world which fits her nature—one of Morris's vague, subtle, elusive imaginations. How he has done it is much more interesting than the thing done.

A still more interesting matter in these Greek tales is the way Morris conceives the Greek gods, Athena, Apollo, Diana, and Venus. His images of them and of their thoughts are naturally according to tradition, but only in part. His own imagination played around them and made them new ; and that which is new in them is half romantic, half of modern thought ; such thought as collects around the conception of beings who know not age or death, or the useless quarrels, aspirations, moralities, or hungers of the life of man. I give one instance in the strange song Apollo sings at the beginning of *The Love of Alcestis*. It is pure Morris speaking through the god. But it not only in their classic realm that the Greek gods are treated by Morris. In the imagination of the Middle Ages, the Greek gods, banished from the Christian world, lived on, as distant allies of Satan, who did not understand them, in secret places of the earth, whence sometimes they came forth to meet in ritual procession to ancient sacred places ; retaining still their characters, their splendour though fallen, and their beauty. Their nobleness had perished ; their evil remains. In two stories— *The Ring Given to Venus* and *The Hill of Venus*—Morris has embodied this mediæval imagina-

tion with a fine intelligence and invention.   His
Venus of the Hill is no longer the goddess he has
made in the Greek tales, but the fallen power, who
can give the enjoyment of sensuous love and no more,
but who retains the exquisite beauty of the past ; who
loves beauty, but has no knowledge of moral or
spiritual beauty ; who has power to bring around
her in phantom imagery the great lovers, even of
Christendom if love was all in all to them, but who is
totally unable to understand the human longings and
questionings of Tannhaüser.   In this conception, there
is little of mediæval thinking on the matter, and a
great deal of Morris's imagination, curiously roving
through his knowledge of mediæval legend, through
his own soul, and through the modern subtleties which
have gathered round the old simplicities of love.   The
Venus of the Hill is still the same to-day, but the
Tannhaüser of Morris is not the Knight of the Legend.
He is one of ourselves.

The Ring Given to Venus also brings into mediæval
life the Greek gods.   The story is told delightfully,
but in the midst of its delightfulness is the terrible
pageant of the ancient deities, shown now in their
cruelty, passing by Laurence into the dawn, in procession from the lonely glen where their glorious
temple once stood among its groves.   The tale of this
watching by the sea, of the strange company passing
by, of the dark Lord of them on his marvellous beast ;
the charactering of Iris and Mercury, of Mars and

Venus, are done with intense imagination. I am all
the more sorry that Morris did not paint Apollo,
Athena, Artemis, and Poseidôn, as he thought the
mediæval phantasy would have conceived them. In
his tales, however, the gods are still romantic, but
since then, they have fallen even lower than their
mediæval place. In that little half-mocking, half-
pathetic record of Heine's, they are out in domestic
service in Germany.

We are in full romance in the tale of *Ogier the Dane*.
It is mixed up with the cycle of Charlemagne, with
Morgan le Fay, and with the land of the Ever Young,
where the great heroes still live and love ; and a
happy mingling it is. One of the Oriental tales enters
also into the series ; and is not so good as the rest.
Out of folk-stories, worked from various variants, *The
Man Born to be King*, and *East of the Sun and West of
the Moon* are borrowed. The first of these is told with
extraordinary charm and invention. The second is full
of romantic additions and incidents, and is rendered
more interesting by the transference of the well-known
beginning to a northern land with its scenery, and with
the home life of the North such as Morris loved to
paint. The hero, too, possesses the character, the
sentiment, the sub-mysticism, the truth, and tenderness of the North ; and the mystic atmosphere is
enhanced by the sketch made of the narrator of the
tale. Gregory dreams the first part, dreams that he

hears it told by a stranger in the hall of King Magnus. In the next part of the dream, he himself tells the tale ; is himself the stranger in the hall. In the next part, he dreams that he has become the actual hero of the story, that the previous adventures which the stranger and he have told were in truth his own. He it is who wins at last to happiness and love in a perfect land. And then he wakes to the rude, common life of the world, and cannot bear it ; but walks apart trying to remember that other life and all its beauty. This is that subtle mysticism of Morris, pushing itself into the romantic tale, and the invention is of great interest, and all the more because the motive of it is repeated in some of the prose tales, notably in *John Ball* and in *News from Nowhere.* Lastly, the northern drift of his genius, at this time, appears in the beautiful and romantic rendering of the story of Aslaug, and in the noble strength with which he has told the tale of Gudrun.

We are then, always, even in the northern tales, still more in the Greek tales, in the land of romance ; and with a perfection of story-telling which has not even been approached since Chaucer, and of which, if we could get it as good, I wish we had a hundred volumes more. For, as I have said, these tales have a releasing power. We breathe a clean, clear atmosphere, even in the tragic tales. The men are free, and the women. What oppresses them is Fate and Death, not their fellow-men. Also, they are individuals, not mere numbers in the social prison, forced into a few common grooves in order to live ; who, if they break loose into individuality, are punished or sacrificed. Morris abhorred as the curse of society—and indeed it was part of his socialism—the withering of individual thought, feeling, and act ; and even in his lightest story-telling we may trace the dominance of that opinion.

While he was still doing this romantic work, he came more closely into touch with the Icelandic sagas and their severity ; with the courage against fate which is one of their most ennobling elements ; the silent endurance of their heroes and women in sorrow and death and passion ; their belief in dreams and a supernatural world, their pleasure in fighting and in law ; their fateful love ; their deep humanity, the quietude and justice and honour of it ; their tragic note, in that tragic scenery which called on all the fighting manliness of those that lived in it and in the life it shaped ; their grave view of human life, even of their gods whose decrees they sternly endured, but against whose will they often set their own in fearless even moral, opposition ; their stately and tragedy-making women—and he rejoiced. These qualities in the Northern Muse and the Northern characters seized on his imagination and fitted the maturer man in whom had already grown up the desire to be no longer only "the idle singer of an empty day." This new element appears in his noble rendering in *The Earthly Paradise* of the *Laxdœla Saga*, the *Story of Gudrun*. The

very character of the poetry has altered ; also its style
and its melody.   It cannot any longer be classed as
merely narrative poetry.   It is not indeed epic, but it
is epical.   Its style ceases to be romantic ; and its
melody is Dorian, fit for that dignified and tragic tale.
This change, which many persons have remarked—it
could scarcely be passed by—enters into his rendering
of the story of *Bellerophon*, and I wish it were more
clearly and plainly to be felt in the last story in the
book, the tale of *The Hill of Venus*.

When, then, *The Earthly Paradise* was closed and
published, he gave all his energy to the translation of
the Norse Tales, only interpolating a poem, *Love is
Enough*.   It is a modern reanimation or remaking of a
morality play—we might even call it a miracle play,
one of those that represented secular subjects,—it has
touches of both.   It is a short piece such as might be
acted at a wedding feast before bride and bridegroom.
But, save in its form, it gives no idea of what such a
play would have been in the fourteenth, fifteenth, or
sixteenth century.   Its poetry is excessively modern,
and full of modern motives.   But I dare say Morris—
just as he mediævalised the Greek stories—chose
deliberately to modernise this ancient form of drama.
Hating direct imitation as he did, and loving to bring
the new out of the old form, he had a perfect right to
do this ; but the form did not suit his special narrative
power.   He was precluded by it from invention of incident and scenery such as animates his long stories ;

and the poetry, both lyric and dramatic, drags, yet is
too much diluted. There are some lovely descriptions
of nature in it, but they are sparsely scattered. The
fairy-story meeting of the King and his sweetheart of
whom he has dreamed for years, and whom he has left
his throne to seek, is told with idyllic beauty. It
shines, both in feeling and in truth, among the rest of
Love is Enough, like Venus among the lesser stars.
The pastoral life and loves of Joan and Giles, who are
spectators of the play, are done with Morris's dreaming
grace. Not so the love-passages of the Emperor and
Empress at whose wedding the play is represented.
These want nature and fire. Moreover, there has been
a great deal of researching pains spent on the verse
and its various metres, so much so that the poem for
those who read this kind of criticism is injured by
over-explanation. The introduction of science into a
work of art always troubles it. Natural passion is
taken out of the verse. Even Morris himself seems to
have somewhat lost it in endeavour after various forms
of verse. Therefore, in spite of the great technical
interest of this poem, and perhaps on account of that,
reality seems to be for the first and last time lost in a
poem by Morris. It made no impression on the world.
Critics may hereafter choose it as a kind of Exercier
Platz for their skill. We touch it and pass it by. It
is an interlude in his work.

It was now that the Muse of the North laid her
alluring hand upon him, and claimed his love. Her

nature, her teaching, her eyes, now grave, now wild, her feeling, deep but austere, her view of life, suited his autumn character, and he fell in love with her.   He had gone through his romantic period, and, coming out of the other side of it, found himself alone, somewhat desolate of heart, and needing a new impulse. What he felt, and how he felt, when into him poured the flood of these new stories of human life, is told in a poem—*To the Muse of the North*, which, for its insight into the northern nature and his own, ought to be read throughout, but of which I can only quote the beginning and the end.   It describes a landmark in the development of Morris, and is to be found in *Poems by the Way*.

> O Muse that swayest the sad Northern Song,
> Thy right hand full of smiting and of wrong,
> Thy left hand holding pity ; and thy breast
> Heaving with hope of that so certain rest :
> Thou, with the grey eyes kind and unafraid,
> Thy soft lips trembling not, though they have said
> The doom of the World and those that dwell therein.
>
>   .   .   .   .   .   .
>
> O Mother, and Love and Sister all in one
> Come thou ; for sure I am enough alone,
> That thou thine arms about my heart should'st throw,
> And wrap me in the grief of long ago.   .

These were the passionate elements in this new love of his, but there were other elements in it which also suited that part of his nature which was not romantic. There was a roughness, grimness, and fighting passion in him, combined, or rather existing side by side with his love of beauty, love of nature, and love of love, which found themselves at home in the northern world ; and were more fully developed by his journey to Iceland, in the scenery and life of which, at least in memory, he revelled like a Troll on a holiday. If Iceland was once started in conversation, Morris clung to it like ivy to the oak. Nothing else, for hours together, was allowed into the conversation. It was sometimes terrible, and he looked like Snorri Sturluson himself.

I partly regretted this development, but it gave to us his splendid epic rendering, in original verse, of the mighty story of Sigurd, Brynhild, and Gudrun—the finest story perhaps in the modern world.* But I only gave it this partial regret because it seemed to do away with his poetry. We had afterwards, it is true, the translations of Virgil's *Æneid* and of the *Odyssey*—interesting and effective, but neither of them Virgilian or Homeric ; but now, with the sole exception of this new

---

* NOTE.—It is interesting to compare the accurate translation he made of the Icelandic form of the *Volsunga Saga* with his poetical rendering of it. I do not mean in the lavish ornamentation he added to the story, but in the way he added his own thoughts to these portions of the tale in which the Northern thoughts on human life and the gods are expressed. In those additions the soul of Morris is opened to us ; and I instance especially the way in which he has expanded the long, sententious speech of Brynhild to Sigurd after he had wakened her on the Hill of Fire. He has even inserted in it thoughts which would never have occurred to a Northern hero, much less to a daughter of Odinn.

rendering of the *Volsunga Saga*, a little volume of lyrical poems and the verses in the prose romances, the poetry of Morris closes. He is absorbed in the north and the northern spirit. But after all, it is best for an artist to do that which impassionates him, and to take with thanks what he offers us. And it is good for the English people to be brought closely into contact, otherwise than by scientific scholarship, with the high, courageous and human stories of our northern ancestors ; to realise their free and noble temper at a time when we are commercialised, and have forgotten too much the manly virtues of a great state ; it is good for us to hark back, in an age of luxury, to a time when men lived in continual strife for their lives with the cruel forces of nature, and fought to the death in desperate straits for honour and for fame ; when women were honoured and played their part ; and when the best religion for men, was to live, without fear and with justice, in fellowship with one another, and then to let the gods, if they were able, do their part also without favour. That is no bad thing to infiltrate into the weakened blood of England.

I think that living in these stories nursed the modern revolutionist in Morris, and added imagination to the energy with which he took up, in his Socialism, the cause of the enslaved in England. The wild poetry, the steady temper of the tales, idealised and strengthened the grim realism of his four years' work from street to street, from one small lecture room to another ;

and enabled him for a long time to resist the despair
which crept upon him in contact with the blind and
useless quarrels of which he knew too many. Like
Sigurd, he fought with the Dragon of Capitalism,
lying like Fafnir round its gold; like Sigurd, fate and
the time were against him, and ancient feuds; and like
Sigurd, his battle has won for him an immortal name,
and handed down an impulse full of power and use to
the future; when, not in the Communism he pictured
in *News from Nowhere*, but in a higher organisation of
universal Labour—justly and quietly established by
law, and performed by all men—his hopes and faith
may yet be realised. It is the divine and human faith
by which we endure, and live. He came to that view
in the end, but at first he felt that there would be a
desperate, even a sanguinary, struggle between the Old
and the New; and I dare say this fighting expectation
was born in him out of the temper induced by the
northern stories. Could he but have set, at this time,
oppressive wealth and enslaved labour to fight the
quarrel out on Holmgang, how much he would have
loved it.

Moreover he found in these stories natural, even
primæval, passions, seeking their natural ends in a
natural society; and they appealed for treatment to the
second half of his nature which was not satisfied with
romantic food. In them he found a grimmer realism, a
closer truth to human strife and sorrow than he could
isolate from the beauty of the Greek or the mediæval

stories. This suited him now, for the problem, as they call it, of life lay hard upon him. He could not put it aside, and live with Cupid and Psyche, even with Ragnar and Aslaug. And his love of beauty was for a space in abeyance ; and his pity for the sorrow and the unrelenting fates of men uttermost. His Socialism and its propaganda were simmering in his heart. No more were his four walls hung with his own pain and dreams, but with the pain and the dreams of the world.

I have said that poetry concerned only with the past, like that of *The Earthly Paradise*, and receiving no emotion from the living present, is in itself often of great beauty, but has no element of continuity. The poet cannot go on producing it. It was so with Morris. Actual human emotion flowing in upon him from all sides mastered him, and he found some outlet for this in the record of the austere loves, bitter revenges, fateful sorrows, undying honour, heavy fighting, and transient joys of the Icelandic Sagas ; and in their iron scenery. This culminated in his rendering of the *Volsunga Saga*. His recreation of the tale gallops along with sufficient rapidity to excuse its length. It is pleasant to read long poems when we are lazy with enjoyment of the world, and have not time to hurry, and when they are ornamented enough with inventive incident and detail. Those who are not capable of this temper can read Morris's translation of the Icelandic version of the tale. That is short enough not to give the poor folk who love to live in a hurry too much trouble. But one or other ought to be read. It is a shame not to know the great story. English people, whose blood is Teutonic by three several strains, have little acquaintance with the most ancient records of the thoughts and lives, the passions and manners, of their ancestors. *Beowulf* has only lately been well put in their power, but the *Volsunga Saga*, in its German form, was open to the public sixty years ago in many versions of the *Niebelungen Lied*. One would have thought that when Morris translated and then with a splendid joy and force poetised its northern form, English people, who knew the stories of the origin of the Jews, of Rome and Greece, would have been anxious to read of their own origins. Not at all! They were interested in *Jason*, not in *Sigurd*. This book of Morris's was but little read when it was published. It has, and no wonder, steadily increased in favour among the general public, but even now it has not come home to England.

And if the beginning be too terrible, too primæval, we may read alone the Sigurd story. It is objected to Morris's poem that it would have had a greater epic unity had it used the story of Sigurd only, and left out the barbaric prologue of Sigmund, Signy, and Sinfiotli; and there is much force in the objection. The art of the poem, that is, of its shaping, might have then been better. But Morris, who I dare say agreed with this objection when he had finished the poem, liked, I conjecture, the primæval savagery of the Sigmund story ;

and did what he liked, even when he did not quite
approve of what he did. For my part, I am glad he
wrote it.   I have no wish to whip the story of the
Volsungs into an artistic epic.   It never was a piece of
fine art, and I hope it never will be subjected to its
canons.   It is rudely built up out of many sagas, as a
cathedral which ten generations have worked upon,
each with its own design ; and the best principles to
apply to its treatment, as to the cathedral, are the
principles of the Anti–Scrape Society.   And, moreover,
it ought to please us, overdone with our cultivated surroundings, to step, at least in imagination, and with
Morris growling with pleasure at our side, into that
very ancient country, where savagery and honour, and
faithfulness to love and vengeance, went together;
where Odinn came to the feast, and drove the sword into
the Branstock ; where, one-eyed, in his blue cloak, he
looked from under his slouched hat, amidst the din and
swording of the battle, into the face of the fated hero,
and bore him, when dead, to Valhalla ; a land where
men might still become wolves ; and Signy could lie
with her own brother to beget a son who shall slay
her husband and his children for the sake of avenging
her father and her brothers, and yet die with the
husband she hated, rather than live with those she
loved and with the memory of what she had done.
This is a world, into which, out of this world, it is
not unuseful to step at times. We are too forgetful
of the roots of savagery in humanity, and think too

carelessly that they are altogether worked out ; and when we meet them, to our vast surprise, in our civilisation, we find them worse than they were in Sigmund's time, because there is not with them the truth, the promise-keeping, the courage, and the honour which the Volsungs had. I had rather live with the men and women of the Sigmund story than with the wolfish men and women who ruined the French Revolution by their savage bestiality, or with the financial dogs who to-day plunder and destroy the innocent and the fools who trust them.

Then, having done that piece of work, he was borne away on the stream of Socialism, and looked forward, through a violent revolution, to a changed society. To dwell on this socialist struggle is not in my subject. It does not take much trouble to be a Socialist now, and it does not bring with it now any sacrifice. But Morris did take trouble, and suffered trouble. He sacrificed money, health, peace, his darling work, his passion for beauty in literature and art, to his convictions, and for nearly four years of unremitting exertion. Were it not for the noble moral effort he made to regenerate society, were it not for the incalculable good, which, for the cause of a better world, emerged out of his work, and will continue to breathe its helpful spirit into men, there would be something more pathetic than usual in the fate which drove this artist into this sad and weary work. But we cannot mourn for that. The seeds were sown ; and Morris would have said, with sad content—The harvest is yet to be.

When this active propaganda of his was over, he was able to give a fuller attention, while he continued his quiet work for Socialism at Hammersmith, to his literary work. He published his translation of the *Odyssey* and got back, through it, to his darling story-telling. Then he recurred to his beloved centuries in *The Dream of John Ball*, in which he expressed not only his social views, but also his inner life. It paints English society as it was when the feudal system was breaking up, and contrasts it with what English society is now. And a noble book it is. It closes with a vague hope of what society might come to be. What that society was to be he painted in *News from Nowhere*, and in it also Morris opens his soul to those who can comprehend it. The communism of the book is not likely ever to arise, but, as we read, we may put that by. What remains is a lovely vision of a world of beauty, peace, and joy, where men are as happy in work as in play; where humanity and nature are loved, and all men are brothers, save when jealousy intervenes; where, above all, for that was his first principle, all work was done with personal pleasure.

And in that is the charm, the use, and the refreshing of the book. It falls like dew upon our hearts. I declare that in the emotions these two books awaken more impulse is given to the cause of a great fellowship of men banded together to establish a righteous,

just, free, and happy state, than will be given by all
the scientific economists of Socialism. These books
nourish that inward spirit, without which all their
science, needful as it is, is blown like chaff from the
threshing-floor of the earth. Morris did more useful
work for his cause by them than by his four years'
propaganda in streets and lecture rooms. Then it
struck him that he would picture, not a half-mediæval
society such as he paints in *John Ball*,—in whose moral
and imaginative life he could not find the qualities of
character he wished to display, and in whose society
there was decay rather than vigorous life—but another
kind of social state, which should have the noble and
masculine qualities of the northern character, without
its grimness and fierceness and with the love of beauty
and of nature which it did not possess ; which should
be youthful and full of the future, with the hopes and
faith of youth, and with an intense love of life ; joyous
and free ; grave in counsel for the state ; brave in war
for defence of home ; inured to war, yet eager for peace ;
rejoicing in the tillage of the earth, in hunting, in
keeping of cattle ; devoted to home ; honouring its
women, and having in it women worthy of all honour
for intellect, for the work of daily life, for counsel and
for war, for love and motherhood. This he thought,
as I believe, would realise an ideal life before our sad
and spoiled society. And he wrote *The House of the
Wolfings*, but especially *The Roots of the Mountains*.
The first, though stronger in note, is not so imagina-

tive nor so actual a representation as the second. There is more possible history in it. Moreover, it contains in it a supernatural element, which takes away from the naturalness of the story. The second has nothing of this. It is realistic enough, and the supernatural does not intrude. Nor do I think there is a more beautiful, more enchanting story in the world, nor, with all its realism, a more ideal thing. "This" —Morris is saying through all his tale—"this is the true temper of the world as it ought to be; this is the noble society, and this its spirit."

We cannot go back to that kind of life, but we can re-establish its spirit, and love its beauty. And, indeed, the love of beauty, lost to Morris in its fulness in those northern tales, returns to him in these stories, and never leaves him again. The love of nature has come back, and flows like a stream through *The Roots of the Mountains*. The descriptions of valley and meadow and clear waters and mountain woods and fells are as lovely, even lovelier, than any in *The Earthly Paradise*. and they are filled with a nobler, happier, and more hopeful humanity. Fate and Sorrow do not brood over them, and Death is not the woeful wonder it is in *The Earthly Paradise*. The undertone of life is happiness; the undertone of happiness is fulness of life. Morbid regret does not exist among the people, full of pleasure in their daily work when they are at peace, and going to war with a high heart which takes them singing into the battle.

Above all, there is in these stories, and indeed in the stories which follow, but not so fully as in these, a representation of womanhood which is more perfect than any that I know in literature. It might be called ideal, but I prefer to call it real, for it is that which womanhood would easily be, according to her nature, in a nobly organised society. And it is not a representation which makes her an object of worship to man, or exalts her by depreciating man. She and he are naturally equal and necessary to one another. It is the real, the true thing ; but it will seem unreal to our society for a long time. Some way or other, one had not been led to expect this from Morris. The women in the early poems, in *Jason* and *The Earthly Paradise*, have charm and naturalness, are never debased ; but they are the women of the stories, acting and thinking in harmony with the stories ; only with a grace, especially when they are young, which arises from Morris, not from the story. But here, in these two stories, there are three women who are not goddesses, for they know and rejoice in mortal love and life, but who have the moral qualities of Athena in their thought and act — high intelligence, physical beauty, imaginative love — the woman called the Sun in *The House of the Wolfings*, the Bride and the Friend in *The Roots of the Mountains*. Naturalness — pure natural womanhood with its sensible passion nobly felt, openly acknowledged, are given to " The Bride " and " The Friend," great personal beauty and dignity, gentle manners, lovely dress, swiftness, strength, and grace. "The Sun" is of the same nobility, but being a prophetess, is more removed from natural humanity. All of them —even the less important women in these tales, while living close to the realities of life, are of a natural sweetness and greatness. They are never apart from domestic life and motherhood, but they are also never apart from the interests of the community. They stand in intelligence, and for advice, and wisdom, on a natural level with the men. They are always consulted in matters which involve the safety or progress of the commonweal. They even go to war, and join in the battle. In matters of love, they are natural, frank, chaste, and passionate. No one could imagine from anything Morris says in these stories that there was ever such a question as the equality of the sexes. The men are men and the women, women, and each are absolutely necessary to one another, and to the State, and equally necessary. The question of man versus woman has never occurred to the dwellers in Burgdale. When we see the relations of men and women in this happy place, we say—this is the natural thing—this is what was intended, this is civilisation ; and when, in a better society, womanhood reaches the heights it is capable of gaining, and man steps along with her into worthiness, Morris's women in these stories will be remembered. They came out of his soul, and were built of his imagination ; and this conception of her was one of the hidden things which, unsuspected,

lay like pearls in the deep and solitary sea within him.
Womanhood should be grateful to him, but no attention, as far as I know, has been bestowed by women
on this noble representation.

And now, like a child, who, having wandered far
over wild moorland and stony places, finds at last the
path to home, and knows that weariness will end,
Morris came back to the full-coloured dreamland of
his youth, where the Sword goes out to sea, and the
knights ride through the Hollow Land, and the red
roses are seen across the moon, and Gwendelen lets
down her golden hair to the Prince, and the Seven Stars
ride through Heaven. All the later romances are in
this world beyond the world. They have no historical
element like *The House of the Wolfings* or *The Roots of
the Mountains*. They began with *The Glittering
Plain*, and the passage Mr. Mackail quotes from that
book describes their world and its temper so accur-
ately, that no better image can be given of it. "She
had in her hand a book covered outside with gold and
gems, even as he saw it in the orchard-close aforetime;
and he beheld her face that it was no longer the face of
one sick with sorrow, but glad and clear and most
beauteous. Now she opened the book and held it before Hallblithe and turned the leaves so that he might
see them clearly; and therein were woods and castles
painted, and burning mountains, and the walls of the
world, and kings upon their thrones, and fair women

and warriors, all most lovely to behold, even as he had
seen it aforetime in the orchard where he lay lurking
amidst the leaves of the bay tree.   So at last she came
to the place in the book wherein was painted Hallblithe's own image over against the image of the Hostage ; and he looked thereon and longed.   But she
turned the leaf, and lo ! on one side the Hostage again,
standing in a fair garden of the spring with the lilies
all about her feet, and behind her the walls of a house,
grey, ancient, and lovely ; and on the other leaf over
against her was painted a sea rippled by a little wind
and a boat thereon sailing swiftly, and one man alone
in the boat sitting and steering with a cheerful coun-
tenance ; and he, who but Hallblithe himself.   Hallblithe looked thereon for a while and then the king's
daughter shut the book, and the dream flowed into
other imaginings of no import.''

It is strange to think that, while he was living continually in this far-off country of creative imagination,
where the supernatural still lingered and companied
with men, where the personages and manners were for
the most part of that thirteenth or fourteenth century
which, having loved from the beginning, he loved to the
end ; where the women were not so lofty in character as
in *The Roots of the Mountains*, but were fresh, loving,
true, and charming ; where his love of nature and of mediæval colour and architecture recurred again in a flood
of pleasure—it is strange to think that in another and
an outward life, he was doing steadily all the practical

work he had begun of old, and inventing new labours. He carried on his business, and added to its interests. He started the Kelmscott printing press, made new founts of type, new paper, new ink, and wrought the initial letters and the ornaments. This was his latest passion. " I wish I had been a printer from my mother's womb," he said, with almost a fierce intensity. At the same time he was publishing and translating the *Icelandic Sagas* and *The Heimskringla*. Then he gave a good deal of time to the Society for the Preservation of Ancient Buildings ; he lectured on Art, its aims, its relation to work, and he published the lectures ; and he steadily supported and attended the Hammersmith Socialist Society, which met in his own house. Meanwhile he translated some old French romances and published them. Then he took up *Beowulf* and put that English Genesis into verse. The only poetry he published in book form were the lyrical verses in the romances, and some of the *Poems by the Way*, and inscriptions for tapestry and pictures. But though his work as a poet was done, it is a poetical world in which we live in the romances. At this period of life he found more freedom for imagination in writing prose than he found in the strictness, restrictions, and difficulty of the higher art of poetry. Moreover, he could not have written verse now with the ease, rapidity, and beauty with which he wrote *Jason* and *The Earthly Paradise*. He had passed through too much work, weariness, and trouble.

If he did not, however, write much poetry, he now, as we draw near to the close of his literary life, collected and published some occasional poems, chiefly lyrical, under the title of *Poems by the Way*. The publication of them belongs to this later time, after he had become a Socialist. They appeared in 1896. Some of them were written in earlier years for magazines, and other prints, and such of these as he thought worth living, he now assembled in this book. Taken together, they illustrate the changes in his interests during a number of years. Some belong to mediæval life, others to the Norse and Danish influence ; some to his Socialist prophesy. Some link together mediæval and northern subjects, invented or borrowed, with the modern hopes, aspirations, and angers of his Socialism. Others live in the world of the later stories of pure invention, like *Goldilocks and Goldilocks*, which closes the book ; and a certain number are personal lyrics of a sweet, natural, and subtle tenderness. The little book, by this biographical interest, by its poetic charm, by its revelation of the heart of Morris, and by its wide range over many various subjects, is a delightful companion in holiday time, and ought to be published in a companionable form. It is too romantic for a wide circulation in this country whose fault is not romance, but there must be a large remnant of silent persons who hunger for a healthy romance with which to adorn their lives. It is too socialistic for a privileged society, clinging with all their fierce suckers to their money

and their comfort, but the increasing legions of Socialism ought to gladly buy it for their inspiration. Nor
will its romance do them any harm. Socialism needs,
not only strict economics, but, with them, the romantic
spirit.

The Socialist Lays in this book were intended to be
sung as chants. They are not quite successful. They
are too literary to be popular. The poems to which a
socialistic turn is given, but whose subjects, like *The
Folk-mote by the River*, are taken from mediæval times,
are far more successful, and often beautiful. But the
best of these socialist poems are those taken out of a
poem—*The Pilgrims of Hope*, which made its sole public
appearance in *The Commonweal*. Three of them are
called *The Message of the March Wind, Mother and Son,
The Half of Life Gone*. They are redolent of a tender
humanity ; they are full of the sad, quiet, and lonely
secrets of his nature, and they enshrine again his impassioned love of the earth and sky and the sweet
waters of England. They tell of his unshaken hopes
for the future when the cause shall triumph, but also of
the deep despondences which fell upon him when he
knew that he could never see them realised in the
present ; they tell also of the sadness which sometimes
looked back to the days before the strife, when he was
happier. To read *The Half of Life Gone* is to read his
very heart. It begins

> The days have slain the days,
> And the seasons have gone by,

> And brought me the summer again ;
> And here on the grass I lie
> As erst I lay and was glad
> *Eve I meddled with right and with wrong.*

Yet the despondence was only for a time ; he never
ceased to be a pilgrim of hope.   Nor did the sorrow,
the bitterness, or the solitude of the battle dismay or
lessen the courage, the grim resolve with which, like
his beloved Northmen, he fought the battle to the end.
When the world is awakened at last, men shall remember

> Of thy love and thy deeds and thy valour,
> And thy hope that nought could quell.

I have not spoken of his limitations as a poet.   They
are plain, and it were an easy task to speak of them.
What I have tried to do, and it is the useful thing, is
to speak of his excellent things, and to bind them up
with the man himself.   When we have learnt to see
the excellent in him, we shall see, if we shall then care
to do so, where his faults were, and where his limitations as a poet.   Whatever they were, he has his own
place in the great roll of English poets, and it is a place
select ; and those who love him love him well.   And
here to close this essay, and to bring us back to the
man himself, to a true, pathetic image of him, full of
tenderness and sad courage—is a little poem written a
few years before he died.   To read it is to love him :

> The Wind's on the wold
> And the night is a-cold,

And Thames runs chill
'Twixt mead and hill.
But kind and dear
Is the old house here,
And my heart is warm
'Midst winter's harm.
Rest then a rest,
And think of the best
'Twixt summer and spring,
When all birds sing
In the town of the tree,
And ye lie in me
And scarce dare move,
Lest Earth and its love
Should fade away
Ere the full of the day.
I am old and have seen
Many things that have been ;
Both grief and peace
And wane and increase.
No tale I tell
Of ill or well,
But this I say,
Night treadeth on day,
And for worst and best
Right good is rest.